METHOD AND MEANING IN JONSON'S MASQUES

METHOD
AND
MEANING
IN
JONSON'S
MASQUES

John C. Meagher

COSTUME SKETCHES BY INIGO JONES

UNIVERSITY OF NOTRE DAME PRESS

PR
2638
.M4

University of Notre Dame Press
Notre Dame—London

Copyright © 1966 by
University of Notre Dame Press
Notre Dame, Indiana
Library of Congress Catalog Number: 66–14625
Manufactured in the United States of America

The line drawings that appear on the cover
and throughout the book are typical costume
sketches done by Inigo Jones for masques by
Ben Jonson and other writers of the genre.

PREFACE

The worst possible way to approach the Jonsonian masque is precisely the way it usually happens. One reads *Comus* first, and accordingly forms a fairly well-delimited notion of what a masque is capable of accomplishing. After this, a glance at one of Jonson's masques (usually the *Haddington Masque,* under the misleading and further distorting title, "The Hue and Cry After Cupid") reveals a surprising jumble of machinery and dances and confusing stage-directions, among which the poetry seems to be reduced to a few scattered songs which are graceful but apparently empty. In consequence, one normally first sees the Jonsonian masques as extravagant and very rudimentary anticipations of the authentic—i.e., Miltonic—masque, to which they relate as the early tilts to the *Faerie Queene.* It is understandable that few students of the English Renaissance have seen fit to take them seriously, even understandable that a capable commentator on the Jacobean literary scene could misunderstand them enough to dismiss them thus:

The famous combined works of Ben Jonson and Inigo Jones were spectacles with no didactic content, well suited to the rather pompous frivolity of the queen and her ladies.[1]

Yet this is no longer the dominant view. Over the last twenty years, scholars have begun to accept Jonson's claim that his masques were serious poetic undertakings, dedicated to the provision of "nourishing and sound meats" for their courtly audiences.[2] And if the massive spectacle in which they were presented still often distracts the modern reader from their essential seriousness, Jonson faced the same problem in his original audiences, who were too often inclined to prefer the "bodily part" of the masques (the spectacle) to the immortal and edifying "poetic soul." Indeed, this caused the death of the Jonsonian masque early in the reign of Charles: Jonson's insistence upon the subordination of spectacle to poetry in the masque came a cropper over the court's preference for spectacle, and consequently Jonson was eased out of his near monopoly of court masques in favor of poets who were more cooperative with Inigo Jones' insubordinate and spectacular imagination.

The decline of the Jonsonian kind of masque thus reveals in its own way something about Jonson's principles for masque-writing. But it also reveals another important truth: even when Jonson had his way, his masques were susceptible to being appreciated for what he considered wrong reasons. They were from the beginning more extravagant spectacles than the masque had ever been before, and this must undoubtedly account in part for their immediate and long-lived success. For some of Jonson's contemporaries, and for some of ours as well, this was also the explanation of their excellence. But Jonson would have us be more careful about being distracted by mere show. If his masques are, as it has generally been conceded, the finest flower of the (pre-Miltonic, if you will) English masque tradition, their proper understanding must begin in discovering from what roots and in what air they grew.

This book is an attempt at placing the Jonsonian masques in their rather complicated context in order to elucidate their meaning and explicate their design, but it is far from being a comprehensive study. In aiming at an exposition of the "classical" Jonsonian masque, I have neglected almost entirely those masques which depart very far from the methods and preoccupations of his main body of masques. In pursuing those central methods and preoccupations, I have omitted numerous other

angles of interest; in concentrating on certain consistent direc-
tions and techniques of Jonson's masques, I have underplayed the
differences between masque and masque and paid little attention
to chronology. In focusing on Jonson, I have deemphasized the
contributions of his collaborators and neglected most of the
other Stuart masque-writers. Anyone familiar with Jonson's
masques will readily observe these limitations; I ask those who
are not to remember that I am attempting only to isolate a few
important patterns in a vast and fascinating design.

And, finally, I would like to point out a few of the patterns in
the great design of my indebtedness, by extending my deep
thanks to the Danforth Foundation, under whose benevolent
tutelage this work was begun; to the University of Notre Dame,
for grants which sustained it; to Dr. Louis B. Wright and the staff
of the Folger Shakespeare Library, whose books and generous
hospitality I had the good fortune to enjoy during the final
revision of the manuscript on a Folger Fellowship; to the editors of the *Journal of the Warburg and Courtauld Institutes* in
whose pages Chapter 4 of this book appeared in 1963 (Vol. XXV,
pp. 258-77) as "The Dance and the Masques of Ben Jonson";
to Miss Frances Yates, Dr. D. P. Walker, Mr. Joseph Trapp,
Professor G. E. Bentley, and Professor Alan Downer, who read
the manuscript in various stages and made helpful and encouraging suggestions; and to my charming wife, whose utter indifference to this project has been a constant source of perspective.

TO JOHN F. AND ELEANOR MEAGHER,
MOST GRATEFULLY

CONTENTS

ix

Chapter I • Backgrounds

In 1604 Queen Anne, in a moment of temporary good sense, com-missioned Ben Jonson to invent a masque in which she and her ladies might present themselves to the admiring court during the Christmas festivities. Her own contribution to the planning of the show consisted of one awkward proviso: "It was her Maiesties will, to haue them *Black-mores* at first."[1] Her Majesty's will was done, and the result was the *Masque of Blackness.*

This was Jonson's first court masque, and his first collaboration with the great Inigo Jones. For more than twenty-five years thereafter, Jonson was the principal composer of masques for the courts of two Stuart kings. With the assistance of the scenic designs and costumes of Inigo Jones, the musical compositions of Alfonso Ferrabosco, and the choreography of Thomas Giles (to name only three of his most prominent collaborators), Jonson continued for nearly a generation to supply the English court with the most spectacular entertainments it had ever seen. Under his direction, the masque adapted old fashions and adopted new ones, controlling them within the purposes of a poetic design— until finally a growing taste for novelty and spectacle resulted in the ascendency of the designer over the poet, a development putting an end to the remarkable masques of Ben Jonson. By that time, there were probably few persons in court with memories long enough to appreciate what Jonson had done in the *Masque of Blackness*.

Not every poet in 1604 would have responded to a request for a masque of female blackamoors in the way Jonson did, and the splendid appropriateness of his masque should not be permitted to make us forget that he created that appropriateness. When Jonson wrote his masques, he was confronted with a wide range of possibilities. He was obliged to fit kings and courtiers into shows which would entertain the court, but the precedents were various and the specific obligations few. Jonson worked with the precedents, accepting and turning to good advantage those which would probably be expected in his masques, and making use of a great variety of optional devices according to their ability to serve the purposes of his poetic designs. There are few elements of Jonson's masques, in fact, which are altogether without precedent in earlier English masques and entertainments. However, the choice of which to use and how to use them was largely his own, depending only on what he wanted his masques to be; and they themselves are unprecedented. To see this, one has only to turn to the history of the masque; and that is, of course, where

Jonson too had to turn in order to decide what would constitute a satisfactory fulfillment of the Queen's request for a masque of blackamoors and to discover what materials he could exploit toward achieving something even more than satisfactory.

Queen Elizabeth was not fond of undertaking elaborate entertainments at her own expense, and the standard kind of masque to be found in the festivities of her court was consequently rather simple in form. It consisted of a group of costumed figures performing a formal dance, after which it was customary for the masquers to take members of the audience to dance conventional dances such as galliards and corantos. There was considerable emphasis upon the costumes, which were usually rather elegant—Spenser uses the verb "masque" as an equivalent for "dress in gorgeous clothes"[2]—and the thrifty Revels Office occasionally altered them in order to permit them to be reused in other masques. They were also sometimes bizarre; there are records of masques involving Turks, fishermen, clowns, moors, Patriarchs, satyrs, Amazons, barbarians, hunters, astronomers.[3] The masquers were usually, and perhaps always, accompanied by torchbearers who provided the additional illumination necessary to show off the masquers' costumes. The torchbearers were often costumed as well, though not necessarily in a manner relevant to the masquers; in a masque of barbarians in 1560, the torchbearers were costumed as Venetians. Although the masque was frequently marched into the hall, it was occasionally presented in a scene, such as a mountain or a bower or a device built on a pageant-car. In such cases the scene would be revealed or wheeled into the hall, and the masquers would descend from it to perform their dances and return to it in the conclusion. In the reign of Elizabeth's more extravagant father, Henry VIII, scenic devices of a mountain, a bower, a castle, and a forest were used within a single year for presenting similar shows, but during Elizabeth's time such props were apparently not the rule. The costumes and dances were usually considered to be entertainment enough.

There were several ways of elaborating or varying this basic form of the masque. The most frequent elaboration was the addition of speeches or songs, as explanations of the presence of the masquers or as occasional pieces of praise, congratulation, or advice. An example is preserved in Anthony Mundy's *The Pain of Pleasure* in 1580, in the form of two brief compositions: one is a letter to be read in a wedding masque by a man costumed as Mercury, in which Jove announces that he is sending a troop of knights to entertain the guests "by fayre demeanour, and seemely showes" in honor of marriage and of the newly married couple; the other is a six-line poem (beginning "First honor God . . .") by which the bride was instructed later in the same masque.[4] The Revels Accounts occasionally mention speeches and even fair copies of speeches presented to the Queen in court masques, and one brief description of an Elizabethan masque suggests that fair copies may on occasion have substituted for the speeches themselves.[5] But although such literary additions provided pleasant ornamentation, they were apparently not considered standard equipment. When the friends of Viscount Montague devised a masque for the celebration of the double wedding between Montague's children and those of Sir William Dormer in 1572, it was not until their Venetian costumes were prepared that they decided it might be a good idea to commission an introductory speech to justify their Venetian attire—and the resulting 300 lines of poulter's measure by George Gascoigne may well have retarded the association of poetry with the masque.[6]

Occasionally the Elizabethan masques were of a decidedly serious nature. A masque of wise and foolish virgins was danced at court in 1561, apparently for the same didactic purpose for which the parable was originally told; and in 1595 Arthur Throgmorton, who was at that time out of favor with the Queen, prepared a "sorrowful and solemn" masque of Muses to "modify the easy softened mind of her Majesty as both I and mine may find mercy."[7] But despite Mundy's didactic poem, the wedding masques for which he and George Gascoigne wrote verses were in general considerably less weighty, and the court records' frequent citations of droll and outlandish costumes suggest that the Elizabethan masques were usually rather frivolous entertainments, designed only for the amusement and diversion of the spectators. One does not expect the activities of fishwives or swartrutters to be edifying, even if one of them speaks a few lines to the Queen.

There were, however, other varieties of masque which were perhaps more serious though less frequent. Spenser inserts in the *Faerie Queene* a masque which is not a dance but a procession in which emblematic figures, allegorically representing the realities of love which lie behind the conventional terms of romantic poetry, "marcht in masking wise" thrice about the chamber.[8] Although records of this kind of masque, processional and mute, are few, Spenser is clearly taking it for granted that his readers will find its general form familiar. Verses were joined to processional masques too. One of the best examples is Henry Goldingham's "excellent princely maske" with which Elizabeth was entertained on her visit to Norwich in 1578.[9] This masque was composed of gods and goddesses marching in couples with their attendant torchbearers, led by Mercury and accompanied by musicians. The performance consisted of alternate grand marches around the room and speeches by the pairs of deities (and a song by Apollo), with the addition of emblematic gifts presented by the gods to the Queen after their addresses. The marches were probably designed to provide a chance for Her Majesty to admire the costumes, for the masquers were "strangely and richly apparelled," while in Spenser's "Masque of Cupid" the marches provide an additional advantage in giving time for the spectator to interpret the emblematic attire through which the figures were defined.

The Norwich "Masque of Gods" required some interpretation to be intelligible; and if the identification of the gods was undoubtedly infinitely easier than the decoding of Spenser's symbolic masquers, there were other masques which taxed the understanding of the audience somewhat more—though it must be remembered that the courtly spectator could support a fairly high rate of taxation, being well trained through the Renaissance flourishing of emblem books, literary allegory, pageants, and the ubiquitous tapestries and painted cloths which spread symbolic figures across the walls of English mansions and palaces. One such masque, founded on emblematic tableaux and symbolic action, was designed for the projected meeting between Elizabeth and Mary Queen of Scots in 1562. And although this "Masque of Peace" was never presented, its composition is an important landmark in the history of the masque, and the detailed description preserved in Lansdowne MS. 5 under the title "Devices to be shewed before the quenes Matie by waye of maskinge" is worth a careful look.[10]

The three parts which compose the "Masque of Peace" were to be performed on three successive nights, but they are coordinated with each other as three stages of the same symbolic action. The first night's entertainment begins with a prison, Extreme Oblivion, kept by Argus (alias Circumspection). The "maske of Ladyes" enters, led by Pallas on a unicorn, Prudence and Temperance on crowned lions, and the "Ladyes maskers" with their captives Discord and False Report. After they march around the hall, Pallas delivers a speech in verse explaining that Jupiter has, after long suit, yielded Discord and False Report to Prudence and Temperance for punishment: the prisoners are now to be installed in Extreme Oblivion with a lock called "in eternum," whose key is named "nunquam." The trumpets blow, and the masquers take the Scottish lords to dance. The second night follows the same pattern: this time the scene is a castle called Court of Plenty, and the procession is led by Peace and Friendship in a chariot—Friendship delivers the speeches explaining the tableau—and the entertainment is again concluded with a dance, this time of Scottish ladies with English lords. The third night introduces a bit of dramatic conflict. Disdain, mounted on a boar, and the serpent Prepensed Malice enter pulling an orchard in which the masquers are sitting—a curious entry which is probably not intended to be meaningful. Disdain announces that Pluto has sent Prepensed Malice in defiance of Jupiter, to secure the release of the prisoners or to capture Peace. But now Discretion leads in Hercules as Valiant Courage, mounted on the horse Boldness, followed by a masque of lords. Discretion announces that if Prudence and Temperance merely signify to Jupiter their proper reception of Peace, Jupiter's warrior will easily vanquish the enemy. Prudence and Temperance accordingly present Discretion with the sword Never and the armor Ever; Discretion lays them before the Queens and delivers a speech, then presents them to Hercules, who slays the serpent and drives away Disdain. The lady masquers come forth from the garden with a song. With this, the masque is apparently concluded.

The "Masque of Peace," with its unabashed discontinuity between the activities of symbolic figures and masquers, is not yet a unified masque, but it is an orderly one. It is clearly more ambitious than the other masques I have cited, preserving a didactic design in its emblematic presentation and executing that design with clear and interesting action. The additional ornamentation of the song and the dances provides an element of grace, even if it is not successfully integrated with the main design. It is, for its time, a relatively complex entertainment; and indeed one of its most interesting features is that it is composed of an amalgamation of elements which can be found separately in later entertainments as well as earlier ones. The description gives no hint of the most common Elizabethan form of masque, a formal dance by the masquers alone, but the procession, the emblems, the symbolic action, the speeches, the song are all detachable elements which reappear throughout the sixteenth century in various combinations. The "Masque of Peace" is, in fact, a solid reminder that Renaissance entertainments comprised a large family of closely related devices and that although one can find rules of thumb for distinguishing masques, tableaux, pageants, disguisings, mummeries, tilts, barriers, arches and triumphs, it is perilous to take the rule strictly. An imaginative poet could easily take hints from specimens of four or five of these categories for the composition of a Lord Mayor's Show; a masque might lift an appropriate device from a Royal Entry entertainment only to be plagiarized in turn by an Accession Day Tilt. All the major European courts enjoyed a continual trade in these varied and varying forms of diversion, and the untraceable exchanges among all the parades, charades, and masquerades of Europe were probably staggering.

As this brief survey[11] suggests, by the late sixteenth century, the composer of a masque had a wide range of possibilities to choose from, and almost no requirements to which he would be strictly bound. His masque might be a dance or a procession, droll or solemn, silent or musical, static or dramatic; he might use scenic devices or tableaux or emblematic costumes if he chose, and his masquers could be presented as anything from gods to fishwives. He could include speeches, songs, or dumb-shows to introduce, gloss, welcome, compliment, advise, or amuse; his overall aim might be diverting or didactic. He was, in short, dealing with an extremely flexible tradition in which he could largely choose his way as he wished, governed only by his own ideas of decorum. His audience was ready for almost anything.

It was with such a range of possibilities that the Gentlemen of Gray's Inn were confronted in 1594 when they decided to entertain the Queen with a masque during the Gesta Grayorum, their festival of Christmas revelry. The result was the "Masque of the Adamantine Rock," the only genuinely literary masque extant from the reign of Elizabeth.[12] We do not know to what extent its authors were indebted to antecedent masques, since not enough evidence has survived; and we do not know whether Ben Jonson knew the "Masque of the Adamantine Rock." But since its form is closer than any other extant Elizabethan masque to the basic organization used by Jonson in the majority of his masques, it is an important document for the ancestry of Jonson's masques whether it be an exemplar of a common late-Elizabethan form or a revolutionary achievement whose success influenced the character of subsequent masques.

The "Masque of the Adamantine Rock" takes its central cue from the mainstream of Elizabethan masques and builds upon a dancing masque which issues from a rock and returns to it at the conclusion. There was nothing novel in that particular formula,[13] but there are other features of this masque which point the way to the standard Stuart form: the introductory and concluding songs, the framing of the revels between formal dances, the celebration of the Queen toward which the whole device moves, and especially the careful unification of the whole show by the literary component.

The masque begins with a hymn to Neptune, sung by tritons and nymphs, after which the dramatic exposition takes place through a conversation between Proteus, the tritons, and a Squire from the company of the Prince of Purpool (the Leader of the Gray's Inn festivities). The Prince, it transpires, had encountered and captured Proteus while on a quest for brave adventures. Undaunted by the wily metamorphoses of Proteus, the Prince had finally defeated him and demanded ransom. Scorning, for the sake of virtue, the sea-god's offers of foreknowledge and easy successes, the Prince had held out until Proteus finally had offered to place the Adamantine Rock wherever the Prince should demand, assuring his captor that "the wide Empire of the Ocean" (xvi) would follow the Rock. But Proteus had set one condition: the Prince must produce a power superior to the Rock in attractive virtue. The Rock was moved to the Prince's chosen place, pending final settlement; the Prince, confident of success, gave himself and seven knights as hostages, to be kept within the Rock until the matter should be resolved; the hour has now come. Proteus therefore speaks in praise of the power of the Adamantine Rock and claims the Prince's defeat;

but the Squire replies with a lengthy tribute to Elizabeth, the "trew adamant of Hartes" (xviii), and Proteus admits that he has been bested. The Prince and his knights are released, march to the stage accompanied by pygmy torchbearers,[14] dance "a new devised Measure, &c." and then perform galliards and corantos with ladies chosen from the audience. After a final "new Measure" (66), the masquers' escutcheons, with their devices thereon, are brought by the torchbearers to the Squire, who presents them to Elizabeth; the masquers return to the rock, while another hymn praises the "true majesty" of the Queen, before which the "cullors of false Principallity"—i.e., of the Prince of Purpool—must fade (xxi).

It is altogether a charming piece, and Elizabeth was quite taken with it—when courtiers began dancing after the masque, her comment was, "What! Shall we have Bread and Cheese after a Banquet?" (67).

The banquet is deliciously prepared. The plot developed in the speeches not only gives the masque-dance occasion and meaning but also creates a dramatic need for the graceful eulogy of Elizabeth as Cynthia, the true adamant of hearts, a great advance over earlier masques in which the compliment to the sovereign was often frankly disjunct from the masque itself. The scenic rock may have been foisted on the authors or may have been their own choice; at any rate, although it was a thoroughly conventional element, their verses build the action cleverly around it and endow it with more conventional significance: it is the fulcrum of the dramatic conflict between the Prince and Proteus and is made emblematic of England's mastery of the sea (which the Squire assures us has already taken place, making the rock an "Impresa apt thereof, but sure no cause" [xx]) and of Elizabeth's mastery of hearts—and as the temporary prison of the masquers it is even a token of their confident loyalty and admiration for their sovereign. Given the fiction of the Prince of Purpool, the authors exploit it skillfully, especially in the final song which makes the return of the "Prince" to common life an allegory of Elizabeth's majesty. Even the presentation of the symbolic escutcheons, a device probably borrowed from the tilts, is made to fit within the graceful execution of the literary frame, leaving the whole masque a cleverly contrived eulogy of Elizabeth and an allegory of what the entertainment is in fact: an act of loyal devotion by the excellent gentlemen of Gray's Inn to their more excellent Queen.

The "Masque of the Adamantine Rock" probably stands near the beginning of the masque's emergence as a unified literary form. As Gascoigne's experience with the Venetian masque for Lord Montague testifies, the earlier masques incorporated a literary text as an additional grace rather than as anything essential; seven speeches "framed correspondent to the day" were written for a masque scheduled for Twelfth Night 1576/7, but when the masque was postponed until Shrovetide, it was simply presented "without anie speeche,"[15] the literary ornament being dispensable. The compiler of the manuscript from which the "Masque of the Adamantine Rock" was eventually printed (in 1698) probably reflects a general assumption when he makes a division between the dance and the speeches, observing that the entertainment "consisted of a Mask, and some Speeches, that were as Introductions to it."[16] To present that masque without speeches, however, would have been unthinkable: whatever Elizabethan masques had been, they were now emerging as a species of poetry. By the time of the Stuarts they were apparently established literary forms, for the task of preparing the Queen's first Christmastide masque in the court of King James was given to the noted poet Samuel Daniel.

Daniel's *The Vision of the Twelve Goddesses*[17] is, for a number of reasons, one of the most important landmarks in the background to Jonson's masques. It is, in the first place, more adequately preserved than any English masque before Jonson's, and is one of only two pre-Jonsonian examples of that form of entertainment which Jonson certainly knew. It is one of the first of the Stuart masques—the most spectacular event in King

James' first season of Christmas revelry and therefore the most pertinent paradigm and standard for judgment of Ben Jonson's *Masque of Blackness,* which appeared the following year. It is also interesting and informative because of the reflection, in Daniel's preface to the published masque, of a critical controversy stimulated by *The Vision of the Twelve Goddesses* and extending to basic questions about the nature and purpose of masques in general—a controversy in which Jonson joined. Daniel's masque is worth a careful look as an examplar of what the court masque had become when Jonson took it over.

Like the "Masque of the Adamantine Rock," *The Vision of the Twelve Goddesses* borrows liberally from the rich tradition of entertainments which had gone before it, unifying the various devices in a single organized movement which anticipates the masquers, presents them, and ushers them into the dance. And although Daniel thought of his masque as a series of linked spectacles, "entertainments that were to depend one of another, during the whole Shewe,"[18] his term "maske" refers to the complete production; the standard Elizabethan form was now firmly embedded in a poetic matrix.

Daniel's design is fairly simple: "the intent and scope of the proiect," he writes, ". . . was openly to present the figure of those blessings, with the wish of their encrease and continuance, which this mightie kingdome now enioies by the benefit of his most gracious Maiestie, by whom we haue this glory of peace, with the accession of so great state & power."[19] This is a conventional formula; Daniel's description of his purpose would serve equally well as a gloss on the Norwich "Masque of Gods"—and like the Norwich masque, Daniel's presents the figure of these blessings as goddesses, "vunder whose Images former times haue represented the seuerall gifts of heauen,"[20] giving tokens of their powers to England, figured as the Temple of Peace.

The Vision of the Twelve Goddesses begins with the appearance of the figure of Night, who awakens her son Sleep and charges him to charm the audience, and to conjure up the "Strange visions" of the masque.

> Make this to seeme a Temple in their sight,
> Whose mayne support, holy Religion frame:
> And 1 *Wisdome*, 2 *Courage*, 3 *Temperance*, & 4 *Right*,
> Make seeme the Pillars that sustaine the same.
> Shadow some *Sybill* to attend the Rytes,
> And to describe the Powers that shall resort,
> With th'interpretation of the benefits
> They bring in Clowdes, & what they do import.
> Yet make them to portend the true desire
> Of those that wish them waking reall things.[21]

The Temple is, of course, England, and is situated in the middle of the hall while at the lower end of the hall rises the conventional mountain. Iris descends the mountain to announce the arrival of the goddesses and to present the Sibyl with a "prospective" (telescope) by means of which she can see and describe the goddesses at a distance, for the practical reason that "well mayest thou there obserue their shadowes, but their presence wil bereaue thee of all, saue admiration and amazement, for who can looke vpon such Powers and speake?"[22] The Sibyl accordingly describes each goddess in a quatrain; when she has finished, the procession begins down the mountain—first the three graces, and then the goddesses in ranks of three, descending to a march played by cornets. When they reach the foot of the mountain, the music changes to a consort, and the graces sing of the three graces of society (desert, reward, and gratitude) while the goddesses walk to the Temple of Peace, present tokens of their power to the Sibyl, and march twice around the hall.[23] The Sibyl places their gifts on her altar and prays that the blessings figured in the emblems presented by the goddesses might glorify England in substance as well as shadow. After Sibyl's prayer the masquers perform their formal "measures," and then, after another song, the galliards and corantos with men from the audience. Iris delivers a final speech, to the effect that since the invisible goddesses chose to present themselves in the forms of ladies of the court (in order to "be in the best-built-Temples of Beautie and Honour"), they would therefore be swift to answer the prayers of these ladies themselves with "the Reall effects of these blessings represented."[24] The goddesses perform a final dance and ascend the mountain to the music of cornets.

Daniel successfully links together the several members of his masque, and the result is a graceful expression of patriotic piety, a charming compliment to the ladies, and a splendid display. The various pieces of the text provide adequate transitions from part to part of the show: Night and Sleep give a pretext for the whole masque in general and for the Sibyl and the Temple in particular; Iris and the Sibyl provide a strong anticipation for the entry of the masquers in their procession; and the Sibyl's prayer of thanks and hope glosses the significance of the emblematic action for anyone who was too dazzled by the spectacle to catch it.

Daniel's masque was successful enough to have been honored with the compliment of piracy. An unauthorized edition of the speeches and songs was printed by Edward Allde soon after the performance—Lord Worcester had paid 6d. for a copy by February second.[25] Daniel responded shortly by bringing out his own edition of the masque with a description of the performance and a preface; thus there were two editions of *The Vision,* whereas there are no known masques before it which went to press at all. The implication of success is inescapable. But it was not, for all that, a total success: one need only read between the lines of the preface to Daniel's authorized version, addressed to Lucy, Countess of Bedford, who apparently was responsible for the Queen's selection of Daniel to write her masque. The purpose of this second edition, Daniel claims at the beginning of his preface, is twofold: to prevent the pirated version from discrediting the true excellence of the entertainment by its having been "verie disorderly set forth," and to supply a description (absent from Allde's pirated edition) of "the whole forme thereof in all points as it was then performed."

The first reason is a ludicrous pretense. Allde's edition is in fact a very good one, probably printed from a souvenir copy made by Daniel for one of the participants or for an interested courtier; Carleton enclosed such a copy along with his letter to Chamberlain on January fifteenth, just a week after the performance.[26] Another of Daniel's excuses, that he wished to supply the text for the benefit of those distracted by the splendor of the original performance, must be disallowed accordingly— Allde had taken care of supplying the text. Daniel is probably being more honest in his expressed concern to provide a description of the performance (which is absent in the Allde edition), but the description is not ample enough to suggest that this was an important consideration. But toward the end of the preface Daniel introduces one final motive which rings more true than all the others; he wished to relieve Lucy "of any imputation that might be layd vpon your iudgement, for preferring such a one, to her *Maiestie* in this imployment, as could giue no reason for what was done." This is, I think, the whole reason for Daniel's edition, since all the others are quite unconvincing: Daniel wished to defend himself publicly against criticisms of carelessness and inaccuracy in *The Vision of the Twelve Goddesses.*

The concluding paragraph of the preface makes it clear that Daniel had come under some sort of critical fire. "And for the captious Censurers," he writes, "I regard not what they can say." He challenges them to produce a better masque, contemns their attempt to show off by striving to show wit over such trifles, assures them that in these "Dreams and showes" there is no necessity of accuracy or scholarly care, and admits that no matter how many pains a man may take some errors will still remain. The tone of embarrassed and angry self-defense is heightened by Daniel's having placed this final barrage in the preface just after his insistence that he could give reasons for whatever he did in the masque.

The body of the preface bears the same marks of disorganized self-defense. When Daniel introduces the descriptions of the goddesses' costumes, he pauses to observe that he has not faithfully followed the contemporary authorities on classical mythology, since authenticity is not dependent upon them and since they are so confused and inconsistent. Shortly thereafter, he uses three quotations to defend his representation of Sleep as a gesturing speaker, and cites two Latin authorities concerning the wands with which Sleep was provided. Yet in the midst of this documentation, he makes the point that Sleep is an appropriate figure to employ for the summoning of the masque, because these shows are like dreams in substance—and because, since no one demands accuracy of a dream, a dream-vision form should cover and excuse "whatsoever error might bee herein presented."

In fine, Daniel's preface appears to be a response to charges of careless inaccuracy and superficiality, arguing that: (a) he couldn't be accurate, because of human frailty and conflicting mythographical authorities; (b) he didn't have to be accurate or profound, because these shows are too puny and spectacular; and (c) he was both accurate and profound.

To whom was Daniel replying? The answer is unknown. But some important bits of information can be inferred from the fact and manner of his reply. In the first place, although the earlier masques which have survived were clearly not produced with pained concern over scholarly accuracy, a much more rigorous standard was apparently being applied to Daniel, and being applied by persons who mattered enough to force Daniel into print, probably hastily, in his own defense. The kind of extreme to which their demands were reaching can perhaps be measured by Daniel's observation—undoubtedly ex post facto—that after the Graces descended the mountain, the goddesses "followed three and three, as in a number dedicated vnto Sanctitie and an incorporeall nature, whereas the *Dual, Hierogliphicè pro immundis accipitur.*"[27] This sort of mystery-hunting is a long way from the straightforward emblems of the "Masque of Peace" and the unerudite cleverness of the "Masque of the Adamantine Rock"—and probably far also from Daniel's original intention, which is perhaps honestly and accurately mirrored in his assertion that

> though these Images [the goddesses] haue oftentimes diuers significations, yet it being not our purpose to represent them, with all those curious and superfluous obseruations, we tooke them only to serue as Hieroglipicqs for our present intention, according to some one property that fitted our occasion, without obseruing other their misticall interpretations, wherein the Authors themselues are so irrigular & confused, as the best Mytheologers, who wil make somewhat to seem any thing, are so vnfaithful to themselues, as they haue left vs no certain way at all, but a tract of confusion to take our course at aduenture. And therfore owing no homage to their intricate obseruations, we were left at libertie to take no other knowledge of them, then fitted our present purpose.[28]

There can be no question about the main problem: Daniel was pilloried by critics for his disregard of the "misticall interpretations" which had been given by mythographers to the goddesses in his masque, and for certain other unscholarly slips of classical fact. As I shall suggest shortly, this critical attack has significant implications for Jonson's masques.

Daniel's huffy insistence that a masque is not to be taken seriously probably indicates a similar critical attack directed against the lack of depth in the message of *The Vision of the Twelve Goddesses,* which led Daniel to state his position with respect to the purpose and nature of masques. This too is an important part of the background to Jonson's masques, since Daniel's general position is one against which Jonson battled throughout his masque-writing career—and to which he finally lost.

In Daniel's opinion, audiences viewed masques as extravagant spectacles, not as poems. "Pompe and splendor of the sight," he remarks, "takes vp all the intention without regard what is spoken," which is agreeable to him, since "the present pompe and splendor" is "that which is most regardfull in these Shewes."[29] To the critics who objected to his lack of serious care in the composition of the masque, Daniel replies with a contemptuous sneer that "whosoeuer striues to shewe most wit about these Puntillos of Dreames and showes," for "in these matters of shewes (though they bee that which most entertaine the world) there needs no such exact sufficiency in this kind. For, *Ludit istis animus, non proficit.*"[30] This stand was not merely an ad hoc defensiveness about *The Vision of the Twelve Goddesses,* for six years later, Daniel was still hewing to the same line, writing in the preface to *Tethys' Festival* that "in these things wherein the onely life consists in shew: the arte and inuention of the Architect giues the greatest grace and is of most importance: ours, the least part and of least note in the time of the performance thereof."[31]

From the evidence that survives, it appears that Daniel's position on the nature of masques was a reasonable one to take: the history of the Elizabethan masque is foggy, but the discernible outlines do not suggest that Daniel's notions would be unrepresentative. Many years later no less a figure than Francis Bacon expressed a similar opinion, beginning his essay "On Masques and Triumphs" with the scornful and patronizing dictum: "These Things are but Toyes, to come amongst such Serious Obseruations."[32] The most important thing signified by a masque, as far as Daniel was concerned, is the magnificence of its sponsor, for masques help "the decking & furnishing of glorie, and Maiestie, as the necessary complements requisit for State and Greatnes."[33]

It was not, however, universally agreed that magnificence was adequately served by spectacle alone, and it was not long before a counterposition was printed. "It behoues then vs, that are trusted with a part of their honor, in these *celebrations,*" writes Ben Jonson in the preface to the *Haddington Masque,* "to doe nothing in them, beneath the dignitie of either."[34] Nothing beneath their dignity—for Jonson, as he reminded his readers a year later, that meant that "it was my first, and speciall reguard, to see that the Nobilyty of the Invention should be answerable to the dignity of they^r persons."[35]

The dignity of persons and nobility of invention were not utterly indifferent for Daniel, but for him they are problems of simple decorum. There should be a splendid spectacle, and the masquers' parts should permit them to conduct themselves in a manner befitting their ranks—as Bacon put it, "it is better, they should be Graced with Elegancy, than Daubed with Cost."[36] But for Jonson, the decorum demanded in a masque was considerably more complex. It was not simply a matter of providing an extravagant display and avoiding inappropriateness, for that would be to neglect the important superiority which the intellectual elements of the invention have over the spectacular parts: the latter are merely bodies while the former are souls and therefore much more consonant with the dignity of princes and nobles. In one of his most important statements on the masque, Jonson wrote what almost seems a direct reply to Daniel:

It is a noble and iust aduantage, that the things subiected to *vnderstanding* haue of those which are obiected to *sense,* that the one sort are but momentarie, and meerely taking; the other impressing, and lasting: Else the glorie of all these *solemnities* had perish'd like a blaze, and gone out, in the *beholders* eyes. So short-liu'd are the *bodies* of all things, in comparison of their *soules.* And, though *bodies* oft-times haue the ill luck to be sensually preferr'd, they find afterwards, the good fortune (when *soules* liue) to be vtterly forgotten. This it is hath made the most royall *Princes,* and greatest *persons* (who are commonly the *personaters* of these *actions*) not onely studious of riches, and magnificence in the outward celebration, or shew; (which rightly becomes them) but curious after the most high, and heartie *inuentions,* to furnish the inward parts: (and those grounded vpon *antiquitie,* and solide *learnings*) which, though their *voyce* be taught to sound to present occasions, their *sense,* or doth, or should alwayes lay hold on more remou'd *mysteries.*[37]

Having thus stated his position, Jonson deals summarily with

those critics who protest that such an approach is too ponderous
for a little masque:

And, howsoeuer some may squemishly crie out, that all endeuour of
learning, and *sharpnesse* in these transitorie *deuices* especially, where
it steps beyond their little, or (let me not wrong 'hem) no braine at
all, is superfluous; I am contented, these fastidious *stomachs* should
leaue my full tables, and enioy at home, their cleane emptie trenchers,
fittest for such ayrie tasts."[38]

If we place Jonson's remarks with Daniel's, some important
points can be inferred. The most obvious conclusion is that
Daniel and Jonson were in radical disagreement on the question
of the nature of a masque, Daniel insisting that it was a group of
shows gracefully linked with a text that doesn't get in the way,
and Jonson maintaining that it was a unified production whose
body is spectacle and whose soul is poetry. Each man had a point.
If one's aesthetic (or pedantic) sympathies lie with Jonson, both
Bacon and the previous history of the English masque seem to
side with Daniel.

But that is only part of the matter. Another and at least equally
important implication of the remarks made by Jonson and
Daniel is that there were critics on both sides of the question as
well as poets. If Daniel's stand in this controversy was somewhat
unpopular, Jonson's was by no means altogether safe, and critical
voices continued to be raised against Jonson's scholarship and
seriousness as they had against Daniel's lack of them. It was
Jonson who eventually lost the argument: and, prophetically,
the architect to whom Daniel refers in his statement of policy
prefixed to *Tethys' Festival* is Inigo Jones, who finally succeeded
in imposing the primacy of spectacle in the English masque so
successfully that he forced Jonson's retirement.

That process, however, took over twenty years. For the beginning of Jonson's masque-writing career there is one further
implication in Daniel's preface to *The Vision of the Twelve
Goddesses*. Daniel's defensiveness and his annoyance with those

who strive "to shewe most wit about these Puntillos of Dreames and showes" clearly suggest that there was a market for a more pedantic and serious variety of masque than Daniel himself offered. It is not clear from Daniel's remarks that these captious critics were also insisting on "more removed mysteries," but his strategies in self-defense indicate that they were, and Jonson's later remarks claim that he was not alone in holding out for them—that his point of view was shared by the highest members of the court as well: "the most royall *Princes,* and greatest *persons*" are, like Jonson, "curious after the most high, and heartie *inuentions* . . . grounded vpon *antiquitie,* and solide learnings" through which a masque may "lay hold on more remou'd *mysteries.*"

Where did this taste come from? There is certainly no sign in the extant Elizabethan masques of the kind of curiosity after mysteries which drove Daniel's *apologia* to the Roman poets and Pythagorean numerology. In the next chapter I shall sketch a possible route by which this taste could impose itself upon the Jacobean masque, in the development of Renaissance mythography and its relatively late entrance into England. But now I would like to pursue another possible source, perhaps hinted at in the curious wording of Jonson's manifesto: "the most royall *Princes,* and greatest *persons* (who are commonly the *personaters* of these *actions*)." If he is referring to James and Anne, he is being unnecessarily oblique; the vagueness of "most royall *Princes*" seems to me to make most sense if we assume that Jonson is speaking not parochially of the English masque, but of the general European family of stately court shows of which the English masque is a member. If this is the case, then the wording is intelligible: the greatest princes of Europe demand high and hearty inventions, grounded on antiquity and solid learnings. If the masques of Elizabeth's reign do not support this asseveration, then perhaps the Stuart court was turning toward the more humanistic continental tradition of courtly entertainment rather suddenly—this too would help to explain

Daniel's plight, if his reliance on earlier English masques reflected a misunderstanding of the extent to which a new vogue was upstaging the less ambitious Elizabethan variety of masque. It is perhaps significant that in his response to the critics of his masque, Daniel extends the boundaries of pertinent comparison in its defense: "by the vnpartiall opinion of all the beholders Strangers and others," he writes, unconvincingly, "it was not inferiour to the best that euer was presented in Christendome."[39]

I mentioned a few pages ago that *The Vision of the Twelve Goddesses* was one of two earlier masques which Jonson certainly must have known. The other was a French entertainment, the *Balet Comique de la Royne* by Baltasar Beaujoyeulx, performed in 1581 and published the following year.[40] Jonson owned a copy of the published version, which contains the text, the music, an ample description of the performance, and extensive comments by Beaujoyeulx and others. In this book Jonson possessed an example of a masque which thoroughly satisfies his principles of what masques "eyther haue bene, or ought to be,"[41] and the *Balet Comique* must certainly have helped to shape Jonson's own ideas of what constituted the best that ever was presented in Christendom.

The *Balet Comique* was, like Jonson's masques, a formal court spectacle designed for a particular occasion. In 1581, during what turned out to be only a lull in the Wars of Religion, one of the favorites of King Henry III of France, the Duc de Joyeuse, married Mlle. de Vaudemont, sister of Queen Louise de Vaudemont, and the marriage was seized as the occasion for some of the most extravagant festivities ever seen. The King employed Pierre Ronsard, Antoine de Baïf, and the noted musician Claudin LeJeune to provide entertainment; the Queen, not wishing to come short, picked from her train an ingenious Italian named Baldessare Belgiojoso or Baltasar Beaujoyeulx and instructed him to prepare a show which would not be inferior to the other entertainments, either in beauty of subject or in the conduct and execution of the work (in which she wished to perform, according to the custom: the greatest persons are commonly the personators of these actions).[42]

The *Balet Comique* owes more to the Italian forms of court-show than any of the masques we have dealt with so far, reflecting the Italian practice of inserting spectacular *intermezzi* between acts of a play. As the name implies, the *Balet Comique* is a combination of drama and ballet, in which the dancing *intermedes* mark pauses in the overall dramatic action. The scene is a garden, a conventional scene for masques; but this is the garden of Circe, and the action begins when a man comes running from it to explain how he had foolishly allowed Circe's seductive ways to interrupt his duty of bearing the message that the Golden Age is returning to earth, in France. After recounting his enchantment and subsequent escape, he begs the King to win immortality by aiding him against Circe's charms. He escapes to safety, and Circe enters to lament her folly in allowing a man to escape and spread the truth about her. Resolving to cast aside all pity and be herself, she leaves in anger, giving way to the first *intermede*.

Now three sirens and a triton enter, singing the praises of the King; the Queen and eleven ladies, dressed as naiads, are drawn into the scene on an elaborate fountain. As the songs celebrate the Queen, the naiads descend and prepare for their first dance. They dance toward the King, executing several geometrical figures, only to be interrupted by Circe who comes in enraged and touches the naiads and musicians with her golden wand, leaving them frozen in their places as she goes triumphantly to her garden.

With a thunderclap, a cloud descends bearing Mercury, who describes his power over Circe's enchantments and frees the naiads with his magical moly. Circe comes forth in rage, turns the naiads to stone again, moralizes briefly on her powers over the human will when it flirts with pleasure, and (observing that Mercury is powerless unless aided by Minerva) touches even Mercury with her wand. Mercury's caduceus falls from his hand,

and the whole group follows Circe to the garden. The act ends with Mercury seated at the feet of Circe while the beasts parade through the garden.

The second *intermede* now enters, eight satyrs, singing of Diana's nymphs, who are celebrating Jove's victory over the Titans and "the virtue of a king [i.e., Henri III] who has fought vice not with force but with his example."[43] Four dryads perform a dance, after which one of them moralizes the enchantment of Mercury and the naiads, proposing to rescue them with the help of Pan. Pan is now discovered in a brightly illuminated scene, the dryad begs his intercession, and he consents. All exit, giving way to the third *intermede* of the four virtues, "representing the perfection of those who follow virtue,"[44] who sing of their intention to remain in France, and beg Minerva to intercede on behalf of the virtuous and victorious King Henry. Minerva accordingly enters in a chariot drawn by a huge serpent, moralizes the action so far, pledges her aid to King Henry in his battle against Circe in France, and invokes her father Jupiter.

While a song celebrates heaven and vice-banishing France, Jupiter descends to proclaim in song that men deformed by following their baser inclinations can take from him a better life when they have regained reason. He goes with Minerva to Pan's wood, where the dialogue reveals that Pan, though sustainer of all things, is powerless to stop Circe; only Minerva can. Minerva, Jupiter, the four virtues, the satyrs, and the dryads then march on Circe's garden. Circe defies them (claiming that only the King of France can defeat her), but under Minerva's influence her golden wand gradually loses its effectiveness; when she attempts to flee, Jupiter stuns her with a thunderbolt. Minerva snatches away her golden wand and leads her in triumph around the hall, followed by the four virtues and by Jupiter leading the disenchanted Mercury. With Pan, the satyrs, and the dryads, the procession approaches the King, to whom Minerva presents Circe and her wand, while Jupiter gives him

Minerva and Mercury. They throw themselves at the feet of King Henry "signifying that they come short of this great King in power to command, in wisdom to govern, and in eloquence to draw the hearts of even those most distracted from their duties."[45] The music plays again, and after the disenchanted naiads have danced the Grand Ballet, they go to the royal stand and present medals to men of the court; with that, the *Balet Comique* is concluded.

Beaujoyeulx, like Jonson and Daniel, saw his Ballet as an expression of the King's magnificence. "There is," he writes, "no more need to declare the reasons and necessities for dedicating this book to your majesty than there would be for crediting these beautiful harmonies of the world around us to the praise of the author of all things."[46] The publication of the *Balet Comique,* he continues, can only serve to reveal "to all neighboring kings, and to all the more distant peoples, the king's grandeur, what obedience he commands, the fertility and abundance of his kingdom—not only in valiant men but in great and subtle minds."[47]

The *Balet Comique* is therefore an expression to foreigners of the excellence of the kingdom and of the King. It is also expressive to the people of France, for such a show will serve "to breathe sweetness, delectation, and the sweet scent of peace upon [the King's] people."[48] In a country just recovering from civil war, such a symbol has particular point. Beaujoyeulx goes on to elaborate, observing that in a body recovered from a grievous malady there may be left an unusually healthy disposition; and likewise after political turmoil there now is in France such an affluence of good dispositions and good will that "this will serve as a true and infallible mark of the good and solid foundations of your Kingdom."[49] Proper credit for this political well-being is given in passing to the contributions of the counsels of "that Pallas, the Queen your mother"[50] and of Queen Louise (whose ballet this is). But the real purpose of introducing this train of thought is quickly made clear in an important statement:

The argument of all this, Sire, is here represented to you in a lively and pleasant manner under the fabulous story of the enchantress Circe, whom you have vanquished by your virtue even more laudably than Ulysses—whom Alexander the Great envied for having been so worthily celebrated by Homer. In short, this will be your poetical—or, if you will, comical—history, which will make you renowned among all manner of men, even among those who do not concern themselves with serious matters. You shall be found with Jupiter among the greater part of the Gods and Goddesses (by which I understand the divine aids) exterminating the enchantment of vice. Thus your name, Sire, will live for ever, perfumed with the gracious odor not only of virtuous reputation, but of agreeable delectation.[51]

Regarded from one angle, then, the *Balet Comique* is a political allegory describing the restoration of order after the civil wars and the establishment of peace and deeper unity in France. It is also incidentally expressive of Henry's magnificence in the pleasantness and splendor of the entertainment which reveal his bounty and the ingenuity of his kingdom. To this extent it is a symbolic representation of truths and aspirations.

But neither political allegory nor the expression of the King's glory is central to the *Balet Comique*. At the heart of Beaujoyeulx's show lies an ethical design. As Miss Frances Yates has observed, "the plot of the *Balet Comique* is concerned with that constant theme of the Palace Academy debates, the establishment of the rule of reason, harmony, and order in the soul, and the taming of the beasts of the passions."[52] Or, as Volusian summarizes it in a prefatory poem of commendation, "In fine, you have revealed, under this pleasant shell, that vice has no power being confronted by virtue."[53] The ethical lines are made quite clear during the performance by the moralizations to which I have referred in the summary: Circe describes herself as the principal responsible for the vacillation of the human will in the face of pleasure and her victims are "under the cruel chain of pleasure which enchants the reasonless spirit."[54] Mercury's enchantment revals that "eloquence serves for very little without reason." Circe herself admits that Mercury is at her mercy only when he is unaccompanied by Minerva: "Of all the gods, I fear only that Minerva, who alone protects men from my arts."[55] And Minerva reminds us of this when she comes on the scene: "Those who achieve virtue by many a labor safely dwell with me, always in my protection."[56] Even the *intermedes* retain the ethical focus, celebrating the King for the improvement wrought in France through his virtuous example; the third intermede, it will be recalled, is performed by the Four Virtues. In short, there is very little that takes place in the *Balet Comique* that does not have implications in ethical allegory.

But the mysteries touched by the *Balet Comique* are not exhausted in moral readings. After the conclusion of his description of the performance, Beaujoyeulx inserts in the printed text of the *Balet Comique* an interesting appendix: three allegorical interpretations of the fable of Circe, forming part of the background to his use of her story in the composition of his ballet. The first is by the noted Renaissance mythographer Natalis Comes, who gives to Circe an interpretation in natural philosophy in which she signifies "the mixture of the elements, which can take place only through the movement of the Sun which is father and form, and Perseis, mother and matter."[57] Circe's four serving-men are the elements; her transmutation of men to beasts signifies the production of new forms from the corruption of old ones; the unchanged Ulysses denotes the imperishability of the soul. The second allegorical reading is by the composer of the verses for the *Balet Comique,* the Sieur de la Chesnaye, and is in two parts: a metaphysical reading, in which Ulysses is time, his companions Past and Present, and Circe the turning of the year; and a moral reading, with Ulysses as the reasonable part of the soul, his companions as the soul's faculties and powers, and Circe as concupiscence (born of heat and moisture, and deforming the soul if allowed to achieve mastery over it).

The final allegorical reading is a long article by "Sieur Gordon, Escoçois, Gentilhomme de la Chambre du Roy," and is more interesting than the others for the purposes at hand. In the first place, it not merely glosses the Circe of the Odyssey but attends specifically to the meaning of the *Balet Comique* itself; in the second place, it provides still another link between the *Balet Comique* and the English court. Sieur Gordon is without question to be identified with John Gordon, D.D., a man of notable learning whose kinsman James Stuart, upon his accession to the English throne, summoned him from France to the deanery of Salisbury and to a firm place in the royal favor.[58] Gordon preached frequently before King James and was singled out by him for commendation at the Hampton Court Conference for the learning he there displayed; it may be noted that if Gordon arrived a few days early for the conference, he could have seen at Hampton Court the performance of *The Vision of the Twelve Goddesses*. He was in a position to make invidious comparisons.

Whether or not Gordon ever commented on Daniel's masque, we do know what he said about Circe. He sees in her that generalized and ambivalent desire from which all movement springs, capable of being directed toward either good or evil—the nymphs of the fable are virtues, the beasts vices. The beauty of Circe and that of her palace signify that beauty which is required to move desire: "Desire cannot be moved without the appearance of beauty, be it true or false."[59] One can avoid being deceived into vice only by becoming imbued with the precepts of virtue through the divine aid; Ulysses signifies to Gordon just such an achievement. And after these considerations of the Circe of the *Odyssey,* Gordon concludes by applying his method also to the work at hand, the *Balet Comique:*

From this little discourse on the allegory of the fable of Circe, one can see the idea and the example of virtue which the Queen, together with the princesses and ladies of the Court, have represented under the character of Naiads, who signify the immortal pleasures and delights which attract desire, when led by virtue, to use and exercise itself in generous and valorous acts; and to admonish everyone that one must not desire that which is merely beautiful and splendid externally, but rather that interior and less obvious beauty. On the other hand, the animals imprisoned in the palace of Circe are an attempt to portray the miserable servitude of those who are led by the bestial desire of sensual pleasure, which seduces men by an appearance of exterior beauty—which is, in effect, an eternal ruin and perdition.[60]

One could not fault Beaujoyeulx as Daniel was faulted, for his ballet is steeped in the mysteries which Daniel took too lightly—and in addition, his figures are portrayed with a sensitivity to the "Puntillos" of authentic classical representation, faithful to "antiquities, and solid learnings." The self-descriptions given in the *Balet Comique* by Mercury and Minerva reveal that Beaujoyeulx carefully costumed them according to the descriptions of the classical poets and employed them not merely in terms of "some one property that fitted our occasion" but with an eye to "other their misticall interpretations."[61]

The Queen had told Beaujoyeulx that she wished to take part in a ballet "which would not be inferior to the other entertainments either in beauty of subject or in the conduct and execution of the work." The *Balet Comique* fulfills this charge with a splendid show which not only responds topically to the political situation but achieves as well a further dimension of ethical allegory and echoes of other mysteries beyond that. It is in view of this, I think, that we can best understand Jonson's assertion that "the most royall *Princes,* and greatest *persons* (who are commonly the *personaters* of these *actions*) [are] not onely studious of riches, and magnificence in the outward celebration, or shew; (which rightly becomes them) but curious after the most high, and heartie *inuentions,* to furnish the inward parts: (and those grounded vpon *antiquitie,* and solide *learnings*) which, though their *voyce* be taught to sound the present occasions, their *sense,* or doth, or should alwayes lay hold on more remou'd *mysteries*."[62] In the *Balet Comique,* this prescription is fulfilled, and I suggest that it was from the *Balet Comique* above all that Jonson derived it. For Jonson's statements and his practice show him to be in sympathy with the principles by which Beaujoyeulx composed his ballet; and Beaujoyeulx's use of the classical gods, of music and dance, of allegory, of the king, can all be found paralleled in Jonson's work in a way that apparently never occurred in earlier English masques. It is not impossible to read Jonson without Beaujoyeulx, but because the *Balet Comique* so closely resembles in its most significant features the kind of masque Jonson ultimately chose to write, it is illuminating to look at Jonson's masques with the *Balet Comique* in mind; it is perhaps more pertinent to the background of Jonson's masques than any of his English predecessors.

Had Daniel's *The Vision of the Twelve Goddesses* been judged exclusively according to the background formed by the eclectic metaphorphoses of the Elizabethan masque, it would probably have been a resounding success. But the evidence clearly implies that this was no longer a sufficient standard by 1604, that some powerful voices, probably tuned to the achievements of such continental entertainments as the *Balet Comique,* demanded of a court masque something considerably more than extravagant spectacle. They asked for a more weighty and profound production, meaningful in detail and ambitious in scope, faithful to classical sources and sensitive to the theories of mythographers—worthy of being compared with the best court-shows of Europe. It was on that cue that Ben Jonson entered the scene.

Chapter II · Nourishing and Sound Meats

Before turning to Jonson's masques, it is instructive to take a look at one of his first attempts at entertaining King James, the arches devised for his procession through London to his coronation. These entertainments are interesting with respect to the masques in several ways. In the first place, they are distant kin of the masques, being members of that vast family of Renaissance fêtes which never departed very far from each other. Like the masques, they involve a mise-en-scène and a poetic text, the former being an elaborate structure of symbolic visual elements which required not only care in their presentation but an ample capacity in the beholder. Interestingly, a disagreement arose with respect to the coronation arches, with Thomas Dekker insisting that they should be designed for the multitude, and Jonson characteristically denying this position.[1] Jonson's arches were not accessible to every Londoner: he designed them to "declare themselues to the sharpe and learned: And for the multitude, no doubt but their grounded iudgements did gaze, said it was fine, and were satisfied."[2]

Well might the vulgar gaze, and even some of the moderately learned occasionally be perplexed. The arch at Fenchurch bore an effigy of London at the top, with an inscription adapted from Martial; on other parts of the arch were, among others, Theosophia, whose garments "figur'd truth, innocence, and cleerenesse," Genius Urbis with a goblet and a branch to signify increase and indulgence, Prothymia ("or *Promptitude*"), who was "crowned with a chaplet of *trifoly,* to expresse readinesse," and Agape, who, like all the others, had a Latin motto, hers being "*non sic excubiae,*" adapted from Claudian and "Inferring, that though her sister before had protested watchfulnesse, and circumspection, yet no watch or guard could be so safe to the estate, or person of a Prince, as the loue and naturall affection of his subiects."[3] This is, be it noted, only a partial description of fewer than half of the symbolic figures on the Fenchurch arch; that at Temple Bar was no less demanding of the spectator. The verses make good sense of the whole, if the parts are first grasped—if one can trust the spectator's learning to be worthy of Jonson's simple formula: "the garments and ensignes deliuer the nature of the person, and the word the present office."[4] The arches were intended to be compositions of great dignity, presenting "the expression of state and magnificence (as proper to a triumphall Arch)" as well as the essence of the subject depicted—in the Fenchurch arch, for instance, "the very site, fabricke, strength, policie, dignitie, and affections of the Citie."[5]

In addition to his concern for a monument worthy of its royal object and expressive, if only to the sharp and learned, of an essential meaning, Jonson was concerned with the artistic unity of the arch,

> The nature and propertie of these Deuices being, to present alwaies some one entire bodie, or figure, consisting of distinct members, and each of those expressing it selfe, in the owne actiue sphaere, yet all, with that generall harmonie so connexed, and disposed, as no one little part can be missing to the illustration of the whole.[6]

The same principle obtained in the case of the device in the Strand, a simpler affair which Jonson apparently had no hand in designing but "To which bodie (being fram'd before) we were to apt our soule"[7]—by which he means simply that the speech which he was hired to contrive for this portion of the King's entertainment was intended to embrace, illumine, and unify the parts of the device in an expressive whole.

If Jonson had never written a court masque, one might still have speculated about what his masques might have been like on the basis of the coronation entertainments. The most evident conclusions are these: since a masque, like the arches, is a species of royal entertainment, it must be an expression of state and magnificence, elegant and dignified; it must be expressive of some worthy meaning and may to that end employ learned symbolism or intricacy beyond the capacities of the vulgar; its soul must be poetic and unified, and therefore nothing should be introduced which does not contribute to the harmony of the whole and anything which the poet is obliged to accept into the bodily part must be exploited and given a meaning through the operation of the poetry. I think that these principles might be arrived at even in the absence of the masques, and I advance them with all the more confidence because this is precisely what Jonson did when he became a masque-writer.

As I suggested in the previous chapter, Jonson's main divergence from the position held by Daniel and Bacon lies in his insistence on the dignity of the masque as a form of literature. Daniel to be sure saw a certain kind of dignity in masques, since although their "pompe and splendor" is more for the eye than for the mind, they are nevertheless symbolic expressions of the magnificence of the King, "concurring to the decking & furnishing of glorie, and Maiestie, as the necessary complements requisit for State and Greatnes."[8] Daniel is not merely rationalizing. The association of expense with virtue was a firm Renaissance tradition, especially with respect to entertainments. Laneham, in his report of the enormously extravagant Kenilworth entertainment in 1575, exclaimed "what may this express, what may this set oout vntoo vs, but only a magnifyk minde, a singuler wizdoom, a prinsly purs, and an heroicall hart? . . . hiz Lordships great honor & magnificens,"[9] and although we might be inclined to concentrate our attention on the "prinsly purs," Laneham sees an expression of virtue—a virtue so distinguished that a writer at the turn of the century places it as high above mere Liberality as a temple above a sepulcher, or God above man.[10] This was, indeed, an argument to which King James was responsive. In speaking to the Parliament in 1609 he referred to criticism of his expenditures for pomp and festivities, saying "it is trew I haue spent much: but yet if I had spared any of those things, which caused a great part of my expense, I should haue dishonored the kingdome, my selfe, and the late Queene."[11] Aristotle's remarks on magnificence insist on taste, decorum, and appropriateness in the expenditures of the magnificent man,[12] but this was not always remembered—the virtue was appropriated to rich displays without particular concern for the qualifying values. But the logical conclusion of equating mere expensive display with the expression of greatness is the potlatch; and although the custom of permitting courtiers to destroy the decor of a masque after the performance may bring us uncomfortably close to this, it is easy to understand that a man of the Renaissance might think of a more dignified way of expressing Majesty. Jonson found it in a conception of the masque which, with greater decorum, aligns the glory of the monarch not with the physical part of the masque but with the intellectual, and to the very end he insisted that a masque ought to be serious literature, and that the dignity of the King and of the court demand that a masque be edifying as well as spectacular:

all Repræsentations, especially those of this nature in court, publique Spectacles, eyther haue bene, or ought to be the mirrors of mans life, whose ends, for the excellence of their exhibiters (as being the donatiues, of great Princes, to their people) ought alwayes to carry a mixture of profit, with them, no lesse then delight.[13]

Proficit istis animus ludendo. To Jonson, a masque was essentially a poem, and it was therefore obliged to serve up "nourishing, and sound meates" in the banquet of its spectacle, "obseruing that rule of the best *Artist,* to suffer no obiect of delight to passe w^thout his mixture of profit, & example."[14]

Poetry had been measured by that Horatian rule for a large part of the sixteenth century, but a dissociation began to take place in England toward the end of Elizabeth's reign, and the *dulce* of poetry began to outstrip the *utile;* delight began to be considered an independent poetic value, capable of legitimate existence even without the protective presence of an instructive element. This is a revolution which is in fact implicit in the sugared-pill conception of poetry, for if pills are unattractive without sugar, sugar is nevertheless quite palatable without pills. Daniel was right in suggesting that a masque can be a confection rather than a medicine.

But the sugared-pill theory does not represent English criticism adequately. Taken by itself, the Horatian formula for mixing profit with pleasure seems to imply that the two elements are indeed separate (or at least separable) and independent, and there were some who held this position in late Elizabethan England. But the Horatian formula was not always taken by itself. The sixteenth century produced a vast amalgamation of critical ideas, in which the Horatian components were not only mingled with others of a different hue but even took on their colors. In describing this process as it occurred in Italy, Professor Bernard Weinberg outlines three separate traditions descending from Horace, Aristotle, and Plato, but adds that

since little attention was paid to strict definition and sharp distinction, it was possible to find in all three roughly equivalent concepts and statements and to build in this way a roughly unified theory of poetry. According to that theory, poetry was by its nature an imitation or representation of reality in order to produce moral effects desirable both for the individual and for the state.[15]

This is precisely what took place in England, although the even less intellectually rigorous temper of the English Renaissance may have served to blur the distinctions even more. Hence Jonson can claim in a discussion of poetry that "the Study of it (if wee will trust *Aristotle*) offers to mankinde a certaine rule, and Patterne of living well, and happily; disposing us to all Civill offices of Society."[16] Aristotle in fact says no such thing: Jonson is here following the common Renaissance practice of appropriating in the name of one critic doctrines to be found only in another, and not necessarily altogether compatible with the authentic pronouncements of the first. When Jonson says that his objects of delight should not be suffered to pass without their admixture of profit, he does not, I think, mean merely that some form of instruction can be superadded to a diverting spectacle (he specifically discommends the writers of late Roman comedy for stuffing in sententiae).[17] The humanistic tradition in which Jonson stood was eclectic enough to permit a critic to intend a Platonic flavor in a Horatian recipe. When Sir Philip Sidney ever so quietly conflated Aristotle with Horace in writing that "Poesie therefore is an arte of imitation . . . with this end, to teach and delight,"[18] he did not suspend the Platonic principle that poetry should produce desirable moral effects. For although Sidney would have liked to live in a world in which all men acted according to their knowledge, he knew that he did not. Renaissance writers recognized that only the great minds can be counted on to respond properly to the instruction received through pure precepts; the rest of us must be prodded into reform, and it is at this point that rhetoric and poetry are welcomed into the commonweal. The editors of *Wits Commonwealth* at the end of the sixteenth century produced not one but three books of instructive reflections: the first was for philosophers and consisted of simple apothegms; the second, offered for the use of orators, was in the form of instructive similes; and the third contained didactic examples, which are most fit for teaching the more common sort of people.[19] Their assumption was that the rhetorical devices of simile and example are more effective than unadorned truth in moving the majority of people to a desire for virtue.

Renaissance poetic theory owed a great deal to such rhetorical assumptions. The critics of the sixteenth century inherited a rhetorical foundation for poetry and continued to interpret classical poetics in the light of rhetorical theory. As a result, the two were never far apart. "The *Poet*," Jonson observed in *Discoveries,* "is the neerest Borderer upon the Orator, and expresseth all his vertues . . . is his equall in ornament, and above him in his strengths."[20] The kinship is, in fact, so close that Jonson describes the qualities of the poet in words taken almost verbatim from Quintilian's description of the orator.[21] In the eyes of the humanists the primary task was the same for each: to persuade men to virtue. The justification for the element of delight in poetry is therefore not that it tickles the fancy agreeably but that it is an ethical instrument: "Poets," wrote Sidney, "delight to moue men to take that goodnes in hand . . . and teach, to make them know that goodnes whereunto they are mooued, which [is] the noblest scope to which euer any learning was directed."[22] In the best poetry, the affective component is inseparably wedded to the instruction rather than merely accompanying it; Sidney uses the example of heroic poetry in which "as the image of each action styrreth and instructeth the mind, so the loftie image of such Worthies most inflameth the mind with desire to be worthy."[23] Not sugared pills, but "nourishing and sound meates." The humanistic conception of poetry was nicely summarized by Henry Crosse in 1603:

The true vse of Poetrie standeth in two parts; the one in teaching the way to *Vertue;* the other to moue with delight therevnto: for honest delight stirreth vp men to take that goodnesse in hand, which otherwise would bee loathsome & vnpleasant: so that when it is bent to a good end, and euery thing laide out in his due annallgie, with some ioy the affections are thereby inuoked to a serious consideration, to imitate that goodnesse wherevnto it is moued ... So that Poetrie is no other thing, but a liuely presentation of things ingeniously disposed, whereby *Vertue* is painted out with fresh colours, that the mind is inflamed with her excellent properties.[24]

This is the tradition in which Ben Jonson wrote, and the spirit in which he approached his masques, which provided him striking new opportunities for painting out virtue and inflaming the mind. The aesthetic criteria which reveal the superiority of Jonson's masques to earlier examples of the form are not matters of indifference to Jonson, but they are nevertheless subordinate values: the mark which distinguishes "the true Artificer" is not aesthetic but ethical: "How he doth raigne in mens affections; how invade, and breake in upon them; and makes their minds like the thing he writes."[25] In short, "the wisest and best learned have thought her [Poetry] the absolute Mistresse of manners, and neerest of kin to Vertue."[26]

If Poetry is nearest of kin to Virtue, Knowledge stands high in the succession. Humanistic movements, particularly in England, continually emphasized the relationship between learning and virtue, generally promoting the idea that the former is a necessary condition of the latter. Indeed, in some more extreme writers, learning even seems to have been considered a sufficient condition. "The opposition to all *vertue*," Jonson wrote in a note on the *Masque of Queens,* "begins out of *Ignorance*";

in *Love Freed,* he repeats that there is "no folly but is borne of ignorance."[27] This Neo-Socratic position is clearly related to the problem of Jonson's pedantry, which Dekker felt had no place in the coronation entertainments and which Daniel and other unknown critics objected to in court masques.

In the prefaces to *Hymenaei,* the *Haddington Masque* and the *Masque of Queens* Jonson alludes to those whose ignorance has expressed itself in adverse judgments on the erudition of those masques.[28] But if Jonson's detractors balked at his show of learning, he was none the less secured by tradition against them. Renaissance scholars knew that meaning is not an easy achievement, and that worthy artistic efforts must soar above the vulgar. When Cicada, in Bruno's *De gl' Heroici Furori,* says of an emblem "I see that the interpretation is not easy," Tansillo replies "the more excellent the sense, the less common it is."[29] Jonson's master, Camden, observed this principle when he cautioned that in creating an *impresa,* composed of "the picture which is as the body; and the Motto which as the soul giveth it life," one should be careful that the motto be not "too plain."[30] Such devices were used for moments of mental ingenuity in pre-Jonsonian masques. I have already mentioned the use of such *imprese* on the shields of the knights who performed the "Masque of the Adamantine Rock."[31]

But in the "Masque of the Adamantine Rock," the presentation of the shields provided a moment of mental ingenuity in an entertainment otherwise quite simple and clear. Jonson made this kind of exercise characteristic of the masque as a whole. The resemblance between Camden's terms, in speaking of *imprese,* and Jonson's, in speaking of the coronation arches and the masques, is more than fortuitous. Jonson set out to unify the masque-form and to express through it meanings which could be attained only with difficulty and ample learning.

He could expect in his courtly audience a trained capacity for the unraveling of masques. The exercise of interpreting difficult symbolic constructs was a favorite Renaissance pastime, and produced not only countless *imprese,* emblems, allegories, riddles, and tendentious readings of the book of Revelation, but turned its voracious appetite even to the natural world to decipher the meanings hidden in the habits of beasts and the characteristics of plants. As a result, a Renaissance poet could assimilate for the purposes of his poetry a vast amount of culturally digested symbolism, and the poet who worked in cooperation with the visual arts had at his disposal traditions which made the infusion of poetic soul into bodily parts a much easier task.

One of the most interesting results of this Renaissance preoccupation is the change wrought upon classical mythology by a new wave of interpretation. There had been a great deal of energy expended in the Middle Ages on the interpretation of Scripture, and the application of the four-fold system of allegory to the exegesis of Biblical texts had produced grand structures of interlocking meanings in which an essentially historical episode in the Old Testament could be seen to figure a universal moral truth, a forecasting of the Church of the New Dispensation, and an eschatological doctrine. This elaborate technique was occasionally applied in composition as well as interpretation, most notably by Dante, but for the most part it was the special handmaid of hermeneutics and reserved for Holy Writ. Simpler allegorical techniques were applied to classical poetry, largely to disinfect it of its surface implications by establishing a moral meaning one layer deper. The process was usually one of simple moralization, by which, as Boccaccio pointed out in his mythographical treatise *De Genealogia Deorum,* edifying interpretations can be wrested from any old wives' tale (early English jest books frequently squeeze morals out of jokes). Plutarch himself had recommended this technique of interpretation for avoiding the dangers of poetry which might be morally deleterious on the literal level. The tradition of allegorizing the classics endured through the Renaissance, leaving its mark on the way in which poets employed classical mythology. The nature of the interpretive method left the mythological figures with the character of abstractions, and this is the genesis of the figures of Argus and Hercules in the "Masque of Peace": the MS. describing the show prefers their ticket-names, Circumspection and Valiant Courage, to their own.

Moralized, the classics were useful; but on the literal level they were not always well received. Plato's famous complaint about the damage done to the reputations of the gods by the myths of the poets was prophetic: Christianity not only repudiated them but scorned them, and their all too human behavior, which Plato feared would weaken piety, was invoked by Christian writers as proof of the superiority of their own religion and the foolish vanity of the one they were displacing. This tradition too endured. Stephen Batman published in 1577 a mythographical treatise whose essential attitude is clear from the title: *The Golden Booke of the Leaden Goddes, wherein is described the vayne imaginations of Heathen Pagans.* A similar stance is found in Richard Linche's dedication of a similar work, *The Fountaine of Ancient Fiction,* in 1599. Linche apologizes to his patron that "this matter so stuft and compacted of poeticall and vaine fiction, is not altogether beseeming the countenance of so graue and so worthy a personage."[32]

But the classical myths were not regarded by everyone with such contemptuous hostility. Again Plato was prophetic, as well as historical, when he remarked that the ancients had concealed deep meanings in the myths in order to hide them from the ignorant and irresponsible multitude. This tradition was not altogether forgotten in the Middle Ages, but it was not until the Renaissance that it received its fullest appreciation, and then there grew into some popularity the notion that the myths held a great deal more than met the eyes of Batman and Linche, and that it was just such a misunderstanding as theirs about the nature of the myths that kept their secrets hidden so long.[33] By the time Ben Jonson wrote *The Alchemist,* it was fairly commonplace to observe that "the choicest *fables* of the *Poets,* / That were the fountaines, and first springs of wisedome, [are]

/ Wrapt in perplexed *allegories*."[34] That is, the myths are not merely tales which can be moralized, but attractive coded messages in which the ancients presented their wisdom in the way best calculated to instruct intelligent men and make them virtuous. Depending on the capacity of the explicator, they could be made to reveal, as George Chapman asserted, "either some dimme and obscure prints of diuinity, and the sacred history; Or the grounds of naturall, or rules of morall Philosophie."[35]

Chapman's reference to "the sacred history" would be startling, if not blasphemous, to Linche and Batman. The phrase nevertheless accurately represents the new pedigree which the ancient myths were now acquiring. Italian writers of the late fifteenth century (among them Ficino, Leone Ebreo, and Pico della Mirandola) gave wide publicity to the notion that the truths concealed in the writings of the ancient poets derived ultimately from divine revelation. The mediating links varied from writer to writer—some suggested that the myths were descended from a primitive revelation to Adam, others thought they derived from Moses, and still others maintained that there had been a separate revelation to the Gentiles. Some thought that the revealed truths had become somewhat corrupted in the process of transmission, but the consensus was that the profound secrets could still be recovered almost intact by the application of methods of interpretation derived from Biblical exegesis.

I have already cited examples of this practice in the readings given the story of Circe by Natalis Comes, the Sieur de la Chesnaye, and John Gordon. Fortunately, not everyone had to work out the myths by his own imagination. A good share of the work was done in mythographical handbooks such as Cartari's *Le Imagini dei Dei degli Antichi,* Gyraldi's *De Deis Gentium,* and most particularly the *Mytholgia* of Natalis Comes. It is no accident that the principal mythographers were Italians; it was in Italy, as I have pointed out, that the new excitement over the ancient myths was most notable. The Italian mythographers digested the myths with the aid of the Neoplatonic philosophy of Ficino and his followers, and purveyed them to all Europe. In consequence, as Schoell has observed, "the mythology which was assimilated by the poets and humanists of Spain and France, of Germany and England, was naturally Italian from the beginning, and remained Italian." And although they borrowed material from medieval speculations— especially from Boccaccio's *Genealogia Deorum*—the readings given the myths by the Renaissance mythographers were true to their Florentine inspiration and were "rather strongly imprinted with a Neoplatonism somewhat debased, but which could not but please in the sixteenth century."[36]

In England, the result of all this speculation was a new depth of respect for the classical myths—enough to permit the pious Abraham Fraunce in 1591 to conclude a versified version of Christ's temptation in the desert with the classical rebuke, "Get thee away Sathan to the burning lake of *Auernus,* / Woorship alone is due to the sou'raigne Lord of *Olympus.*"[37] Not many Englishmen joined Chapman in seeing in the classical myths traces of the sacred history, but by the accession of King James I, many educated men (including Francis Bacon) believed that they embodied at least the awesome wisdom of the ancient sages, in a manner which both concealed the great truths from the vulgar (who would profane them) and revealed them in a more memorable and inspiring manner to those wise enough to understand. Abraham Fraunce summarized this new attitude toward the myths in 1592:

Both poetry, a speaking picture, and paynting, a dumbe poetry, were like in this, that the one and the other are vnder an amyable figure and delightsome veyle, as it were, couer the most sacred mysteries of auncient philosophie. Nay, *Pythagoras* himselfe by his symbolicall kinde of teaching, as also *Plato* by his conceited parables and allegoricall discourses in his bookes called, Phoedrus, Timoeus, Symposium, may make any man beleeue, that as the learned Indians, Æthiopians, and Ægyptians kept their doctrine religiously secret for feare of prophanation, so the Grecians by their example, haue wrapped vp in tales such sweete inuentions, as of the learned vnfolder may well be deemed [w]onderfull, though to a vulgar conceit, they seeme but friuolus imaginations. ... He that cannot conceaue any sufficient cause which might induce antiquitie to deale thus warilie in matters of such importance, let him knowe, that *rerum* εἰκασία, the picturing, fashioning, figuring, or, as it were, personall representing of things in verse after this manner, is most effectuall and auayleable, to moue mens mindes, to stirre vp delight, to confirme memorie, and to allure and entice our cogitations by such familiar and sensible discourses, to matters of more diuine and higher contemplation. ... They, whose capacitie is such, as that they can reach somewhat further then the external discourse and history, shall finde a morall sence included therein, extolling vertue, condemning vice, euery way profitable for the institution of a practicall and common wealth man. The rest, that are better borne and of a more noble spirit, shall meete with hidden mysteries of naturall, astrologicall, or diuine and metaphysical philosopie, to entertaine their heauenly speculation.[38]

Backed by such dignifying theories, classical myth became so popular with poets that an anonymous book called *Apollo Christian, or Helicon Reformed* was published in 1617 in attempt to woo poets from mythological subjects to Christian ones. Many poets, of course, continued to use mythology merely to add "ornaments, beauties, graces, and delicacies"[39] to their verses, but the mythographers had firmly established at least the option of more ambitious uses. The court for which Beaujoyeulx presented the *Balet Comique* contained persons who had absorbed both the new mythographical studies and the new versions of Platonic philosophy with which the myths were there combined, and his story of Circe successfully exploits their preparedness. In the treasuries from which he drew his materials, Circe was already a more removed mystery, and the gods reflected the authentic powers of nature and providence. A poet who wished to provide a court entertainment with profundity as well as grace could not do better than to follow Beaujoyeulx's example and make use of those gods and heroes who, as Abraham Fraunce reminds us, were employed by the ancient sages as the best means of teaching and moving, and thus informing men with virtue.

This is, of course, the way in which Ben Jonson worked. In sympathy with the demand for classical authenticity, Jonson found in mythographical handbooks a mine of information on the various ways in which the ancients had represented their gods, together with glosses on the meaning of their deeds and of their attributes. As recent scholars have shown, Jonson made extensive use of dictionaries and compendia of mythology as short-cut recollections of classical literature, and exploited the allegorical and symbolic possibilities which were far more clearly suggested in the Renaissance redactions than in the original poetry.[40] The author of the Queen's entertainment at Bissam in 1592 was not being unclassical in spirit when he represented Pan as "an eie-sore to chast nymphes," attempting to seduce two shepherdesses and boasting of his skill on "a Pipe that squeeketh like a Pigg"[41]—but this is the antipodes of the awesome Pan of Jonson's *Pan's Anniversary* who, as Jonson probably read in Natalis Comes, is the governing power of nature itself: "Pan is our All, by him we breath, wee live, / Wee move, we are."[42] By applying to the classical Pan St. Paul's words about God, Jonson is taking a daring step which simultaneously reveals the dignity which the myths could possess for a cultured audience and the kind of uses to which Jonson put them.

The nature of the gods in Jonson's masques is suggested in two ways. On the one hand, they were identified by traditional attributes. The classical poets, and the mythographers after them, had established conventional props—Mercury's caduceus, Jove's thunderbolt, Cupid's bow—which made the identification of principal gods an easy task. Minor figures were more difficult. Cesare Ripa's extremely useful and popular *Iconologia*[43] was frequently consulted by Jonson particularly for the costuming and furnishing of abstractions; the figures from the coronation arches, cited at the beginning of this chapter, are partly drawn from this book. Ripa, like the other encyclopedists of the time, drew on classical sources for the attributes of his symbolic figures, augmenting them from emblem literature and studies of the symbolism of the hieroglyphics. Thus Jonson had two basic sources of material for the furnishing of these figures: purely conventional attributes (e.g., the peacocks which were associated with Juno in classical antiquity), and independently significant symbols through which a new figure could be defined (or which could be appropriately annexed to a figure with its own set of conventional attributes). Jonson drew on both. Of the witches in the *Masque of Queens,* he says "I praescribd them they[r] *properties, . . .* out of the authority of antient, & late *Writers.*"[44] It was important, given Jonson's view of the masque, that the symbolic figures be intelligible; to that end, their presentation had to be through attributes which had either conventional or meaningfully appropriate signification. The result need not be banally clear—as Jonson says, "a *Writer* should always trust somewhat to the capacity of the *Spectator,* especially at these *Spectacles*"[45] —but it must be intelligible. One of the things that annoyed Jonson about Inigo Jones, who attached more importance than he to the spectacular part of the masque, was his willingness to

> Attyre y[e] Persons as noe thought can teach
> Sense, what they are! which by a specious fyne
> Terme of y[e] Architects is called Designe!
> But in y[e] practisd truth Destruction is
> Of any Art, besyde what he calls his![46]

Conventional attributes do not necessarily suggest anything about the nature of the gods, though they serve to identify them. Jonson was occasionally quite pedantic in his use of attributes and did not always insist that they contribute to the meaning of the masque as well as to the identification of the figures. In the presentation of Juno in *Hymenaei,* for instance, he prescribes among her symbols the lion-skin, which has a part to play in the ancient myths of Juno[47] but absolutely nothing to do with her role in the masque. But, of course, Jonson was well aware

that many of the flatly conventional attributes had been glossed
and philosophized into a new kind of appropriateness, and that
the philosphical flavor would cling even if he were not particularly busy about it, making its own contribution to the atmos-
phere of the masques. The lyre was an old and hackneyed attribute of Apollo, and appears in his hand on the title page of the
early folio editions of Jonson's works. Jonson's descriptions of
Neptune's Triumph and *The Fortunate Isles* are not ample
enough to mention a lyre associated with the Apollo who appears in those masques, but that it was there and that it carried
a symbolic value can scarcely be doubted. The lyre could, like
Juno's lion-skin, be used to serve merely as an identifying mark,
but the way was thoroughly prepared for it to be something
more if presented in the right way. To take only three representative mythographical texts, Cartari remarks that "Apollo
had in his hand a lyre, to show the exquisite harmony which the
heavens make."[48] Natalis Comes likewise observes that Apollo
"is placed in the midst of the other planets as their lord—the
Pythagoreans thought that their motion produced an incredibly
sweet harmony, on account of which Apollo is considered the
originator of music. The invention of the lyre is attributed to
him: the earlier form had seven strings . . . corresponding to
the number of the planets."[49] And Abraham Fraunce makes the
same connection, writing that Apollo "is also Musicall; and
therefore *Mercurie* gaue him a Lute; whereon he playeth; alluding to the harmonie of the coelestiall Globes."[50] Hence, when
Ben Jonson introduces Apollo sitting in the heavens with "the
Goddesse *Harmony*" and "the spirits of *Musique*,"[51] we can
hardly doubt that he intends the god and his instrument to
symbolize the harmony of the planets, and of the universe,
whether or not he makes specific comment about it. Jonson
expects the properly well-read members of his audience to be
aware that some of the mysteries exist ready-made.

The understanding of Jonson's symbolic figures, however,
depends not upon their identification through conventional at-

tributes but upon the way in which they are employed in the masques. When seen from this vantage point, Jonson's gods take on another dimension of glory. Jonson's Juno, despite the irrelevant lionskin, appears enthroned in the clouds with concords of sacred music, brightening the air around her; and her powers, who descend to communicate her blessing "onely moue / About th'harmonious sphaere of *Loue*" and wear masks to hide their brightness, "Lest, dazeling *mortalls* with their graces / As they approach them, all *mankind* / Should be, like *Cupid*, strooken blind."[52] Jonson contrives, with the aid of the devices of the scene and in the poetical presentation, to present Juno not as an abstraction or as a mere figure for marriage but as an authentic deity, with all the glory appropriate to a goddess—with all the glory bequeathed her by Neoplatonized mythography.

In the presentation of his gods, Jonson frequently draws on the more glorious side of their interpretations, and if we grant that his audience was prepared to understand the ways in which the classical myths could be exploited for philosophical purposes, it will readily be seen that the usual manner in which the masques present them in glory would remind the audience of the more removed mysteries toward which the masques strive. Indeed, not even this special form of presentation was always necessary. The Cupids in the *Masque of Beauty* appear at first to be merely *putti,* ornamental to the scene rather than functional. They do, in fact, represent little domesticated loves, expressed in the charming songs after the second dance.[53] But Jonson is here using the option which the mythographers had established quite clearly: the figures can have more than one meaning. The operation of the Cupids in this manner does not prevent their being used as the instruments of a farther-reaching philosophical purpose. The first two songs of the masque are devoted to comparing the beauty of the masquers' entry and dance to the beauty given the world by Love's act of bringing the primal order out of the original chaos. This Neoplatonic doctrine of love is amplified in the notes—mostly derived from the mythographical handbooks—which Jonson appends to the text, and is clearly intended to affect the meaning of the Cupids who serve as torchbearers for the masquers. If one is alert to the more awesome interpretations of the myths, Jonson's manner of presenting his mythic figures will usually be seen to be deliberately reminiscent of them.

Jonson's clever exploitation of the gods therefore permits him to enhance both the splendor of the masques and the meanings embodied in them. But even this is only part of the story. From the point of view of the audience, the gods are not the fulcrum of the masque, no matter how much they may add to it. The masque existed for the sake of the masquers, who were the great persons of the court; the gods were merely professional actors. Throughout the gradual elaboration of the basic masque-forms, the entry and dance of the masquing courtiers always remained the high moment. Jonson could not afford to forget this. In fact, he turned it to advantage. One of the principal means by which he managed this was through his use of the gods and demigods to communicate meaning to the masquers within the scheme of the masque.

Jonson's masquers are not the highest powers represented in the masques; they are something more than ordinary mortals, but they are clearly subordinated to a god or a demigod. Jonson's masques make this appear to be such an obviously appropriate formula that it perhaps needs to be pointed out that it does not exist in any known English masque before Jonson, though it can be found in the *Balet Comique*. In their subordination, the masquers are exalted, because they are presented in some form of participation in the glory of the superior powers. Sometimes the masquers are the votaries of the presiding gods: the ladies of the *Masque of Blackness* are the worshippers of Diana-Æthiopia, and the Princes of *Pleasure Reconciled to Virtue* are the pupils of the goddess Virtue. In other cases, the masquers are the direct representatives of the gods they serve, expressions of their power; the ten courtly virtues of *Love Restored* are manifestations of the Cupid who presides over that masque, and the ladies who masque in *Hymenaei* figure the powers of Juno as goddess of marriage. Frequently, the very appearance of the masquers is made to depend on the intervention of some protecting god—as Saturn and Venus must intervene to bring forth the masquers of *Time Vindicated*—and sometimes the gods rescue the masquers from some threat, most notably in *Lovers Made Men,* where Mercury bestows an exemplary humanity on men dehumanized by un-reasonable love. And repeatedly Jonson exploits the real relation-ship of the courtiers to their king, representing the King as Neptune or Jove or Pan and giving the masquers roles of special devoted subordination to him, perhaps the most obvious example being *Pan's Anniversary.* In various manners, the masquers are presented in some form of meaningful relationship with the gods who preside over the scene, and for the purposes of the masques, it is this relationship that largely determines their meaning and function.

To make this clearer, compare for a moment the use of gods and heroes in Jonson's masques with their employment in the "Masque of Peace," described in the last chapter. The "Masque of Peace" is primarily on the order of emblematic tableaux: there is a static solidity in its characters and its actions, which expresses itself in the ticket-names of the classical figures and in the notably undramatic character of the show. The entire scope of the three nights' entertainment could be re-expressed in a set of five em-blems with little omission of detail. The first two parts of the "Masque of Peace," in fact, are merely processional emblems glossed by a presenter and amplified only in the giving of tokens by the presenter to the watching Queens. Even the third night's dramatic action is cut to the minimum: a presentation of tokens, a symbolic arming, and a symbolic fight. The masquers have no apparent relationship to this action or to the gods and virtues and heroes who perform it, and presumably no relationship was expected by the audience (or there might have been raised eye-brows among the Scots when the English ladies of the masque were drawn into the scene on the third night by Disdain and

Prepensed Malice). The lady masquers are not involved with the gods, and the gods themselves are more workmanlike creations than their equivalents in Jonson's masques: Jupiter remains thoroughly outside, communicating with the world only by messenger, and his power is expressed in the "Masque of Peace" only in terms of achieved ethical entities and stable moral equations. Everything is predefined, which accounts for the solidity and classically emblematic nature of the show. With its orientation toward a more rationalistic ethics, the "Masque of Peace" follows a common allegorical practice of the time in transforming the higher powers to the likeness of the lower.

The equivalents of that Jupiter in Jonson's masques, on the other hand, approach the arena of action more immediately. In and through them, there is present in the masque-world a mystery of providential and perfecting power which does not cease to be mysterious in being communicated to the mundane sphere but rather, by its controlled relationship to the masquers, transfigures the world to its likeness.

The glorification of the masquers as achieved through their participation in the glory of the gods is reinforced by another strategy which constantly reappears in Jonson's masque—the use of contrasting forces. These appear in embryonic form almost from the beginning: *Hymenaei* is disrupted by the disorderly conduct of the humors and affections, to set off the harmonious order into which they are subsequently brought by the intervention of reason; the *Barriers* following that masque introduces a conflict between Truth and Opinion in order to glorify Truth in the end; and the bright daughters of Niger in the *Masque of Beauty* are imprisoned by Night at the beginning of the masque, being finally rescued by the intervention of their tutelary goddess. Jonson continues to use this kind of symbolic threat throughout his masques, but early in his career a special version of it began to take shape, a phenomenon which played an enormously important part in the history of the masque: the antimasque.

Although the idea had been anticipated in part by devices in earlier masques, Jonson's first full-blown antimasque occurs in the *Masque of Queens* (1609), apparently by request:

> her Matie (best knowing, that a principall part of life in these *Spectacles* lay in they^r variety) had commaunded mee to think on some *Daunce,* or shew, that might praecede hers, and haue the place of a foyle, or false-*Masque;* I . . . therefore, now, deuis'd that twelue Women, in the habite of *Haggs,* or Witches, sustayning the persons of *Ignorance, Suspicion, Credulity,* &c. the opposites to good *Fame,* should fill that part; not as a *Masque,* but a spectacle of strangenesse, producing multiplicity of Gesture, and not vnaptly sorting wth the current, and whole fall of the Deuise.[54]

Jonson's qualifying clause is significant: "not as a *Masque,* but a spectacle of strangenesse." A masque, being the presentation of courtiers, in symbolic roles, was a dignified spectacle: an antimasque (the term was Jonson's invention) is a kind of parody or "false-Masque," which could be used as a "foyle" to set off the principal masque with more emphasis. This is precisely what Jonson attempts in the *Masque of Queens*: the malicious efforts of the grotesque hags to war against fame and virtue prove futile and powerless, and provide an effective contrasting ground against which the grace and beauty of the glorious queens, who represent virtue and fame, show all the more splendidly. In this and in other vicious antimasques,[55] Jonson heightens the contrast and the power of the virtuous main-masque by avoiding direct conflict: the mere advent of the main masque or its agents suffices to scatter the impotent forces which presumed to challenge it.

The court preferred more fanciful antimasques, however. It was not the main masque but the "anticke-maskes" that King James wished to see again after the performance of the "Masque of Flowers" in 1614, and they were composed of whimsical figures who had nothing to do with the masque itself—a Pantaloon, Usurer, Bawd, Midwife, Chimney-sweep.[56] Unlike James, Jonson was not happy with this kind of antimasque. In the introductory part of his *Neptune's Triumph,* the Cook expresses incredulity when the Poet, after declaring that he has prepared no anti-masque, adds

> neither doe I thinke them
> A worthy part of presentation,
> Being things so *heterogene,* to all deuise,
> Meere *By-workes,* and at best *Out-landish* nothings.[57]

But the court would have them, and apparently complained if they were not forthcoming.[58] Jonson therefore complied, though clearly with reluctance, and introduced these outlandish nothings frequently in his later masques. He did, however, contrive ways of keeping the antimasques from interfering with the nobility of his design. Perhaps his cleverest method was to create an absurd presenter for the antimasque and treat it accordingly as a foolish parody of a real masque. The *Masque of Augurs,* for instance, is preceded by a brief dramatic scene in which foolish servants try to organize a masque worthy of the court, and the result is a collection of outlandish ideas and two actual burlesque antimasques with which the crude inventors are well pleased. Vangoose, the chief inventor, criticizes Jonson and Jones for the naturalness of their masques, insisting that he himself is not so barren of wit and would "bring in some dainty new ting, dat neber vas, nor never sall be, in de *rebus natura.*"[59] When Vangoose proposes an "antick-masque" of pilgrims which seems to have no pertinence to the other devices, the Groom of the Revels politely enquires about the relevance of it and receives the assurance that "vor an Antick-maske, de more absurd it be, and vrom de purpose, it be ever all de better. If it goe from de *Nature* of de ting, it is de more *Art.*"[60] The introduction and anti-masques of *Time Vindicated* are likewise made a clever parody of the popular notions of entertainment and of one of the themes of the main masque, fame. Nose, Eyes, and Ears, expressing "the Curious" (i.e., popular taste), hope for a Saturnalia entertainment of license and disorder and express pleasure and satisfaction with the foolish Satirist and the absurd antimasques which are accordingly presented, for they "only hunt for novelty, not truth."[61] By contrast, the real Saturnalia is presented with great dignity—implicitly, the kind of dignity which distinguishes great courtiers from foolish commoners—and expresses not novelty but truth, revealing something about the nature of authentic fame.

In general, Jonson used the antimasque, where he could, as a direct foil to the themes and the dignity of the main masque, exemplifying his principle that virtue is "more seene, more knowne, when Vice stands by."[62] His last attempt is in his penultimate masque, *Love's Triumph,* in which an antimasque of Depraved Lovers provides the vicious contrast to the Perfect Lovers of the masque itself. Where the antimasque does not provide an anticipatory parody or threat to the main masque specifically, Jonson makes it a fatuous parody of true masques in general, an airy and fantastic whimsy worthy of deranged or inferior minds, and sharply contrasts it with the dignity and truth of the main masque. Occasionally, he underscores the point by having an agent of the main masque dismiss the antimasque with a contemptuously patronizing rebuke:

> Giue place, and silence; you were rude too late:
> This is a night of greatnesse, and of state;
> Not to be mixt with light, and skipping sport.[63]

Vanish with thy insolence, thou and thy Imposters, and all mention of you melt, before the Maiesty of this light. . . . Vanish, I say, that all who haue but their senses, may see and iudge the difference betweene thy ridiculous monsters, and his absolute features.[64]

Faith, your folly may deserve pardon, because it hath delighted: But, beware of presuming, or how you offer comparison with persons so meere Deities. Behold where they are, that have now forgiven you, whom should you provoke againe with the like, they will justly punish that with anger, which they now dismisse with contempt. Away.[65]

Through their participation in the glory and mystery of the

gods, and their opposition to the contrasting antimasque, the masquers are raised to a position of vast dignity, and their dances take place under circumstances which greatly enhance them. Jonson's techniques are excellently suited to the purposes for which verses were first joined to the masque—to provide a suitable fiction to occasion and to heighten the costumed dance. But Jonson was not one to miss further opportunities. The masquers were at the heart of the masque, and could therefore be appropriately employed at the heart of the poetic design that formed its soul.

Jonson uses them in the service of ethical poetry: the masquers are presented not merely as exalted figures, but as persons exalted in particular and meaningful ways, within a framework of themes and ideas. The following chapters will discuss at greater length the ways in which the masquers are made symbolic of an ideal virtuous order, realizing and resolving poetically the themes with which the masques repeatedly are involved—as the courtly virtues who represent, in their harmonious gathering under the leadership of the god of Love, the ideal conduct of a courtier under the law of love that binds him to his king; and as the blessed souls of Elysium, raised to demigods for their great virtue and brought forth by the command of Pallas to sustain a new Golden Age; and as the great Arcadians who express the virtue and the harmonious commonwealth which they have achieved through the imitation of Pan, their king and their All. In the masquers, Jonson epitomized the masque itself; and in the masques he epitomized not only the gods and music and dance and light which helped create them, but the great themes of beauty and love, virtue and glory, and that divine order, imaged especially in a commonwealth ruled by a virtuous king, in which all things find their perfection. In the masques, Jonson epitomized the ideals of his time, creating a symbolic vision designed to teach and to inspire, for, like Beaujoyeulx, Jonson desired his spectator to rise a wiser, and a better, man.

Chapter III · Music

The masque, even if primarily a poem, is a "harmony of the arts," and in Jonson's poetic texts a certain self-consciousness about this status lies between the lines. The performance of a court masque was a festive occasion, and enormously expensive; considering this, along with the fact that its main constituent elements—music, dance, costume, poetry—were generally popular among courtiers and matters in which they possessed respect-

57

able skill, it was inevitable that the masque should exploit the possibilities of its component arts.

This is not merely to say, of course, that the music should be played as skillfully as possible and the costumes should be lavishly splendid; that is only minimum standard. Music, which occupies a central place in all of Jonson's masques, had possibilities other than acoustical ones. The range of metaphorical music from the harmony of the soul to the harmony of the spheres has often been recounted, and everyone is now quite aware that music carried for the Renaissance a great metaphorical force that it no longer possesses. But it is important to see what kind of associations could be evoked through music and supported by music toward the building of a certain sort of poetic world in a masque; and therefore we must retrace some of the old steps, both in the Renaissance and in the antiquity with which it allied itself. Jonson's bias for authenticity forced him to do the same.

I. MEANING

Music was allied to the cosmos from the beginning. Although harmony was undoubtedly attributed to the stars through analogy with some musical instrument, the process was quickly reversed in Western thought; the Pythagoreans, deferring to the apparently superior celestial order, considered the lyre to be an imitation of the harmony of the universe, pointing to the heptachord of Terpandros as a plain imitation of the seven planets. It is not difficult to see how the close relationship between music and mathematics, which apparently existed among the Pythagoreans, should result in a confusion between the mathematical regularity of the heavens and that of the vibrating string. At any rate, the resulting concept of a musical world harmony, comparable to audible music, remained a standard piece of furniture in the European mind for two thousand years.

In this idea lay many of the seeds of the analogous universe which was later to dominate Western thought. It was, Leo

Spitzer observes, probably Pythagoras himself who originated the overwhelmingly important idea of the fourfold harmony, "the harmony of the strings (and of the string), of the body and soul, of the state, of the starry sky; and this idea has been alive wherever the influence of Pythagoras was felt, from Plato and Ptolemy and Cicero to Kepler, Athanasius Kircher and Leibniz."[1]

Whether or not Pythagoras meant this to be taken literally, it was given more than metaphorical force by his successors. And this clearly makes an immeasurable amount of difference in the cosmic status of human music; it is not only *comparable* to the greater harmony of the cosmos, but an *active participant* in it. "It is plain to me also," wrote Athenaeus, "that music should be the subject of philosophic reflection. Pythagoras of Samos, with all his great fame as a philosopher, is one of many conspicuous for having taken up music as no mere hobby; on the contrary, he explains the very being of the universe as bound together by musical principles. Taking it all together, it is plain that the ancient wisdom of the Greeks was given over especially to music."[2]

Because music is brother to the stars, it may be used to restore to accord with the greater harmony the soul which has fallen into discord. "Music," says Timaeus,

in so far as it uses audible sound, was bestowed for the sake of harmony. And harmony, [ἁρμονία] which has motions akin to the revolutions [περίοδοι] of the Soul within us, was given by the Muses to him who makes intelligent use of the Muses, not as an aid to irrational pleasure, as is now supposed, but as an auxiliary to the inner revolution of the Soul, when it has lost its harmony, to assist in restoring it to order and concord [συμφωνία] with itself.[3]

Spitzer points out the cosmic overtones of the language in this passage: "περίοδοι are the periods in the life of the soul that are comparable to those celestial revolutions which produce the harmony of the spheres; συμφωνια is the order introduced into the soul by music, an order which re-establishes the order of the cosmos; αρμονια is the result of being well-joined, well fitted together ... and the soul which really understands music, does not 'enjoy' hedonistically alone, but understands the *Nous* of the Muses, the beauty of order."[4] The immediacy of the order of music and its fidelity to cosmic order also make it, of course, an important aspect of the Platonic educational scheme. In the *Laws*, it is established that the name "music" is properly given to "the vocal actions which pertain to the training of the soul in excellence" for there was, to antiquity and to the Renaissance, an undeniable relationship between excellence and order.[5]

The preoccupation of the Greek mind with the principle of order and a metaphorical "harmony" between psyche on the one hand and logos or cosmos on the other was thus on more than a metaphorical level: soul, stars, and state were bound up with music in an essentially meta*physical* way. In fact there were those who, like Plato's Simmias in the *Phaedo*,[6] (and like Dowland and, at least hypothetically, Burton,[7] in a later age) identified the soul with harmony. The identification of the world-soul with cosmic harmony was an obvious and simple step; and once made, it had natural repercussions on the rest of "harmonic" existence, reinforcing the mind's conviction of the essential importance of the harmonic principles of things. Harmony was now an ultimate, both immanent and transcendent, and thought of with sufficient literalness to allow Aristotle (and after him Castiglione, among others) to use in his argument for the natural limitation on the number of one's true friends, the observation that it is harder to tune three instruments together than two.[8]

Music was also known to the ancients as a cure for physical ailments, and proponents of music well into the seventeenth century pointed to cures of this nature effected in antiquity. The fables of Orpheus and Amphion further testified to both their literal and their metaphorical readers over a period of two thousand years, the remarkable ability of music to give order.

The ideas of music which appeared at one time or another in Greek antiquity, and which were to survive nearly intact into the seventeenth century in England, accorded to music an extensive power and a broad significance: as a master of animals and of the human passions, as a restorative for illnesses of soul and body, as an image—and yet more than an image—of psychological order, of friendship, of political order, of world harmony itself.

These ideas were retained by the Romans, and can be found particularly in the works of Cicero;[9] and they were thus fully available to Latin Christianity as well as to the Greek Church. It was, of course, inevitable that Christian thinkers would capitalize on the ideas of harmony to reinforce the specifically Christian vision. Throughout Christian Europe, the Pythagorean concepts of harmony were not only preserved and perpetuated, but in some respects augmented and strengthened as well. The proverbial formula "qui cantat bis orat" largely determined the character of the Christian liturgy at least to the Renaissance, and in many areas well beyond. The liturgy became music's mansion to the Middle Ages; the Church used music in such a way that it was both an illustration of the New Harmony and a participation in it. Music as worship necessarily solidified through practice the idea of pervasive harmony in the universe, especially that of the New Order of grace, of which music was at once an image, an affirmation, and an act of response.[10]

The place of music in medieval education, the multitude of moral, theological, and philosophical analogies which were drawn from it, the liturgical position of music, and the growing appropriateness of it as an illustration and microcosmic member of an ever-expanding theological and philosophical harmony and order—these factors alone would have been quite enough to imbed music in the fibre of thought by the time of the Renaissance. This music-consciousness is, at any rate, certainly abundantly present when the Renaissance does present itself. Mrs. Gretchen Finney has shown how extensively the writers of the

English Renaissance employed the imagery of musical instruments for the representation of nearly all imaginable things;
Crashaw was representative of his time in referring to

> All Things that Are,
> Or, what's the same,
> Are Musicall.[11]

By use of such musical figures, the poets and rhetoricians testify
to the existence of a deep-rooted tradition of musically-derived
thought, in their very act of extending and perpetuating it. The
same pattern is also reinforced from the other direction through
the *laudes musicae* poetical tradition, in which music receives
praise in terms of the principles I have just surveyed. James
Hutton's article "Some English Poems in Praise of Music" ex-
amines this tradition in England and demonstrates that the cosmic implications and associations of music which Pythagoras
had begun were most definitely alive in the early seventeenth
century; the idea of music was still able to evoke the associated
ideas and images which had grown about it from antiquity.[12]
One illustration will suffice, a poem omitted by Mr. Hutton but
of particular relevance to the present discussion: Ben Jonson's
epigram to Alfonso Ferrabosco, the primary director and composer of music in his early masques.

> To vrge, my lou'd ALPHONSO, that bold fame
>   Of building townes, and making wilde beasts tame,
> Which *Musick* had; or speake her knowne effects,
>   That shee remoueth cares, sadnesse eiects,
> Declineth anger, perswades clemencie,
>   Doth sweeten mirth, and heighten pietie,
> And is t'a body, often, ill inclin'd,
>   No lesse a sou'raigne cure, then to the mind;
> T'alledge, that greatest men were not asham'd,
>   Of old, euen by her practise, to be fam'd;
> To say, indeed, shee were the soule of heauen,
>   That the eight spheare, no lesse, then planets seauen,
> Mou'd by her order, and the ninth more high,

> Including all, were thence call'd harmonie:
> I, yet, had vtter'd nothing on thy part,
>   When these were but the praises of the Art.
> But when I haue said, The proofes of all these bee
>   Shed in thy Songs; 'tis true: but short of thee.[13]

The praises which Jonson gives the art of music come not from the inventive power of his own wit, but from the accumulation of many centuries of tradition: Jonson is speaking of music's *fame*.

The Enlightenment and the period of positivistic bias which intervene between our own time and that of the Renaissance Englishman make it quite impossible for our sensibilities to recover the sense of the harmony of the universe which was not only habitual but connatural to the minds of that age. This gap makes it also somewhat risky to speculate on the intellectual character of the period's music imagery; but it can hardly be doubted that such typical examples as Lorenzo's musical image for proper human attunedness, or Ulysses' use of a musical figure for social and civil harmony,[14] or Shylock's more subtle but no less evident relationship between musiclessness and gracelessness, are meant to be understood if not literally at least with more than metaphorical force. The harmony of order was one of the central preoccupations of the Renaissance thinker, as it had been for the Greeks; and the way in which such a mind entertains the nature of music does not altogether depend upon whether a man thinks of the music of the spheres with the literalness of Lodge's "Looke vppon the harmonie of the Heauens? hange they not by Musike?"[15] or with the greater intellectual reserve of Sir Thomas Browne:

For there is a musicke where-ever there is a harmony, order, or proportion; and thus farre we may maintain the musick of the spheares; for those well-ordered motions, and regular paces, though they give no sound unto the eare, yet to the understanding they strike a note most full of harmony.[16]

The point is that the vision of musical order was not merely a fanciful figure, but rather a description with such a strong philosophical basis that it was almost universally accepted either literally or in a metaphorical way which was so strongly metaphysical as nearly to blot out the difference between the two.[17]

This habit of mind has an important effect upon the poetic possibilities of human music, for it means that the poet, by alluding to music or introducing music into his work, was employing a harmony which was not simply analogous to the order of the passions under reason or of the state under the king, but was rather a different example of the same kind of harmony. This identification could be exploited for the purposes of extending the significance of a poetic point, or reinforcing an idea of order, or helping to elevate the action of a poem both morally and cosmically. This is not to say that the first five bars of "Back and Side Go Bare" would strike piety into the hearts of revelers (although there will be a suggestion of such a notion in a moment, when the quotation from Sir Thomas Browne is completed); but simply that these connections of music with essential order and cosmic and divine significance could be evoked when desired with far less effort and explicitness than would be required in our own time. It is not unlikely, in fact, that given the right set of circumstances no explicit reference at all would be needed to set them into poetic operation. Music was often heard in this way even without such reference.

Lodge refers to music as "this heauenly concent, which is ful of perfettion, proceding from aboue, drawing his original from the motion of y⁰ stars, from the agreement of the planets, from the whisteling winds & from al those celestial circles, where is ether perfit agreement or any *Sumphonia*," and he says of it: "O Lorde howe maketh it a man to remember heauenly things, to wonder at the works of the creator."[18] Hooker found in music "the very image and character euen of vertue and vice," and thought music quite capable of moving the mind to love of virtue.[19] And consider these further words of Sir Thomas Browne:

Whosoever is harmonically composed delights in harmony; which makes me much mistrust the symmetry of those heads which declaime against all Church musicke. For my selfe, not only from my obedience, but my particular genius, I doe embrace it: for even that vulgar and Taverne Musicke, which makes one man merry, another mad, strikes mee into a deepe fit of devotion, and a profound contemplation of the first Composer; there is something in it of Divinity more than the eare discovers. It is a Hieroglyphicall and shadowed lesson of the whole world, and the Creatures of God, such a melody to the eare, as the whole world well understood, would afford the understanding. In briefe, it is a sensible fit of that Harmony, which intellectually sounds in the eares of God. It unties the ligaments of my frame, takes me to pieces, dilates me out of my self, and by degrees, me thinkes, resolves me into Heaven. I will not say, with *Plato,* the Soule is an Harmony, but harmonicall, and hath its neerest sympathy unto musicke.[20]

Direct poetic exploitation of this habit of mind is most certainly not out of the question, even without explicit reference to these properties of music. In his description of the *Balet Comique,* Beaujoyeulx tells us that "ten consorts of music" were contained in a vault which was called "Golden, as much on account of its great splendor as for the sound and harmony of the music that was sung there," and that when the music was played, those of the audience who were "more learned in Platonic studies thought that it was the true harmony of the heavens, by which all things that exist are preserved and sustained."[21] Many pages further, at the entry upon the scene of Minerva, the music is reported to have sounded "with such sweetness and harmony that the astonished audience thought they heard, at the arrival of that goddess, some portion of the harmonious melody of the heavens."[22] Allowing for exaggeration, there is still a striking poetic effect here contributed by the music—and this is without explicit references, the music being allowed to make its effect by its own power in the poetic context.

Jonson also exploited this implicit association, and even more often made it explicit. The poetry of his masques often makes use of musical metaphors, in which the associations of music are evoked to enhance the other half of the metaphor, and often in conjunction with actual music. In *Time Vindicated,* the arrival of the masquers as "glories of the time" is greeted in song with "What harmony their presence makes," referring at once to the audible harmony and to the metaphorical harmony of the order of the Golden Age; the Cupids in the *Masque of Beauty* are said, again in a song, to "strike a musique of like harts;" and Hymen in *Hymenaei,* asserts that Union "eu'rie discord in true musique brings." *Love's Triumph* announces "a world of chast desires, / Which may produce a harmony of parts!"; while the *Masque of Beauty,* reaching to the absolute attunement, claims that the women in the dance "moue each heart, and eye, / With the *worlds soule,* true *harmony.*" These last two quotations are sung, and the literal musical harmony naturally not only underlines the metaphorical one, but for poetical purposes makes it tangibly present to contribute its force to the action of the poetry: although an actor may be behind Apollo's mask, it is Apollo's work that he does before the audience. Some of Jonson's uses of this musical device pertain to a political version of harmony. *Pan's Anniversary* emphasizes the role of James by means of a musical figure:

> And come you prime Arcadians forth, that taught
> By PAN the rites of true societie,
> From his loud Musicke, all your manners wraught,
> And made your Common-wealth a harmonie,

and in *News From the New World,* the masquers are assured that the music derived from James is "pure harmonie." The latter quotation was certainly sung, and the former probably so, thus again giving an actuality to a metaphorical music.

The text of Jonson's masques often creates a special role for music by using it as a means of praise or ritualistic celebration. In *Hymenaei*, Reason says at Juno's unveiling, "Harke how the charming tunes doe beate / In sacred concords 'bout her seate!" and in the *Masque of Beauty* the spirits of the ancient Greek musicians live again to behold the beauties of the masque and "Sing hymnes in celebration of their worth." Indeed, in *Neptune's Triumph*, the whole masque becomes metaphorically a music of praise.[23]

Music is thus linked, both metaphorically and actually, with praiseworthiness, and (as the masques repeatedly remind us) the praiser of the worthy, be it music or a poet, has an important position in the order of the world. The relationship of music to proper order is, however, made even more plain in such direct uses of music as occur in the *Masque of Queens,* where the sound of a "loude triumphant musicke" serves in itself to scatter the hags who had been dancing grotesquely to a diabolical "strange and sodayne Musique": the use of music here is plainly allegorical, and denotes, to quote the plot-summary, "that the sounde of a virtuous fame is able to scatter and affright all that threaten yt." In *Love Restored,* music plays a similar role: it is to the actual music that the text gives the office of ordering the masquers, who

> figure the ten ornaments,
> That do each courtly presence grace.
> Nor will they rudely striue for place,
> One to precede the other; but,
> As *musique* them in forme shall put,
> So will they keep their measures true,
> And make still their proportions new,
> Till all become one *harmonie,*
> Of *honor,* and of *courtesie,*
> True *valure,* and *vrbanite,* (etc.).

Here the power which brings virtuous order to civil society, and which preserves and perfects that order, is given dramatic existence in the form of music: music is made to figure, through Jonson's metaphor, a more perfect power—but a more perfect power of which it is, by nature, actually the image and potentially the representative. Such an allegorical extension of the significance of music is certainly Jonson's intention in his placing and dressing the musicians in *Hymenaei* so as to make them seem "*airie* spirits," thus making their music more cosmic, mysterious, and other-worldy. In *Neptune's Triumph*, the musicians themselves are "*Apollo,* with *Mercury*, some *Muses*, & the Goddesse *Harmony*," and are revealed in the heavens as they play their instruments and sing. Nature sings in *Mercury Vindicated,* Apollo in *Masque of Augurs;* and *The Fortunate Isles* opens another heaven, "and APOLLO with *Harmony,* and the spirits of *Musique* sing." We are to recognize in these cases an allusion to world harmony, even though there is no overt verbal declaration: Jonson was not working with words only. And such an invocation of world harmony is clearly to Jonson's poetic advantage here, where his masques are concerned with the excellence and the transcendent beauty of right order.

These explicit uses of music are significantly numerous in Jonson's masques; but perhaps still more important for Jonson's construction of ideal and celestial masque-worlds is the closeness of music's operation in all the masques. Given an attitude toward music such as I have cited in Lodge, Hooker, and Browne, it is plain that the society of gods, allegorical figures, and virtuous heroes, which Jonson manipulates with other elements in an attempt to create an inspirational vision of order and harmony in a confrontation of men by the celestial order, cannot fail to have its intended effect underlined, poetically strengthened, and extended by the continual close association with music which is given them. Even without explicit references, the presence of a "diuine rapture of *musique*" (to use Jonson's description) would serve not only to support but to contribute as well to a masque's "Hieroglyphicall and shadowed lesson of the whole world,"[24] bringing the spectator to a deeper contemplation and clearer vision of that greater harmony "by which all things that exist are preserved and sustained,"[25] which "the whole world well understood, would afford the understanding ... that Harmony, which intellectually sounds in the eares of God."[26]

II. METHOD

The significance of music was not limited to its poetical-metaphysical connotations; it had a practical application as well among the ancients, and the Renaissance did not forget the stories of Orpheus, Amphion, Timotheus. There were few in either age who doubted Orpheus' taming of beasts or Timotheus' control over the passions of Alexander. The more incredible feats of Orpheus and those of Amphion were usually, if not taken literally, read as figurative of similar ethical powers: "by virtue of their Musick, and their wise and pleasing Musical Poems the one brought the Savage and Beast-like *Thracians* to Humanity and Gentleness; the other perswaded the rude and careless *Thebans* to the fortifying of their City, and to a civil Conversation."[27] The preface to Claude LeJeune's *Le Printemps* (1603), to which I shall return later, observes that the ancients' concentration on one of the elements of their music brought it "into such perfection that they performed marvelous effects with it— moving the souls of men thereby to whatever emotions they wished: which they represented for us under the fables of Orpheus and Amphion, who softened the savage tempers of the most savage beasts, and stirred trees and stones even to motion."[28]

Antiquity indeed seems not to have questioned the direct ethical power of music. When Homer has Agamemnon leave with his wife a musician to protect his interests, there is apparently felt to be no need for explanation. Certain spiritual effects of music are still quite obvious, of course, although our age is disinclined to discuss their relationship to art and to life: but the ancients naturally considered this feature of primary importance, giving music a definite role in education for this reason, and the Renaissance, with its ethical preoccupations, naturally followed suit. Mrs. Finney has observed that

Many classical ideas about music were accepted in the seventeenth century without controversy. That music could influence morals and govern passions, that it could temper man's mood by increasing joy or assuaging sorrow, that it could, by promoting amity, improve his relationships with other men—these possibilities were seldom questioned.[29]

These "effects" are the corollaries of the ideas which I considered earlier—moral order as harmony, the harmony of friendship, of society, of passions ordered by reason. That order of which music is the image can be restored or sustained through its use. When the men of the Renaissance turned to antiquity, just as they could find ideas of harmony shared by both eras, so they could find evidence of the practical application of these ideas in stories of the "effects"; and as Dr. D. P. Walker has shown, among the musical humanists of the sixteenth and early seventeenth centuries, "a firm belief in the historical truth of most of the effects of ancient music was ... almost universal."[30]

Agrippa derives the effects of music, as one would expect, from music's participation in the harmony of the stars and thus from its ability to provoke celestial influences.[31] But he also (quoting Ficino without acknowledgement) credits a more direct process to vocal music:

Singing can do more than the sound of an Instrument, is as much as it arising by an Harmonial consent, from the conceit of the mind, and imperious affection of the phantasie and heart, easily penetrateth by motion, with the refracted and well tempered Air, the aerious spirit of the hearer, which is the bond of soul and body; and transferring the affection and mind of the Singer with it, It moveth the affection of the hearer by his affection, and the hearers phantasie by his phantasie, and minde by his minde, and striketh the mind, and striketh the heart, and pierceth even to the inwards of the soul. ...[32]

Now this part of the theory, the philosophical superiority of song over instrumental music for the production of ethical

effects, accords nicely with the historical approach to the ancients'
musical effects: for the Renaissance humanists believed firmly in
the virtual inseparability in antiquity of poetry and music. As
Beaujoyeulx succinctly noted, "Antiquity simply did not recite
verses without music, and Orpheus never played without
verses."[33] When Ben Jonson, in the *Masque of Beauty*, speaks
of "*Poets* and *Singers*" of the ancients and their "knowledge
musicall," he glosses the latter term, "So *Terence* and the Ancients calld *Poesy, Artem musicam*."[34] Thus the Renaissance
search for the recovery of the effects of ancient music was also
by necessity involved with literary matters.

The effects were most assuredly sought by the Renaissance.
Indeed, it is almost inconceivable that the Italian critics of the
sixteenth century would make nothing of Aristotle's discussion
of the purging *katharsis* of the soul involved in music, especially
when Aristotle himself points out that he uses the same term for
poetry's effects.[35] As a result of their attentions, a double movement grew in Italy: the musical humanists strove to recover the
ethical character of ancient music, and the litterati worked on
the recovery of the effectiveness of antique poetry through the
restoration of music's place to what had been the *ars musica*.

The two streams merged almost at once. The musical humanists, following the example of the ancients, needed poetry to
give definition and particularization to the power of their music,
while those whose aim was poetry needed a new music to replace
the polyphonic style which was already causing dissatisfaction
with the madrigal and which almost universally blurred and
distorted lyrical poetry. Giulio Caccini, in recalling his experi-
ences with the Florentine Camerata, Italy's foremost group for
the practice of the ideas of humanistic music, says that

these most understanding gentlemen always encouraged me and convinced me with the clearest reasons not to follow that kind of music
which . . . ruins the conceit and the verse . . . but to hold fast to that
manner so much praised by Plato and other philosophers, who declare that music is nothing other than the fable, with the rhythm and
the sound coming last, and not the other way around, in order that it

might penetrate into the minds of others and produce the marvelous effects which the writers admire and which cannot be produced by the descant in modern musical compositions.[36]

This view was characteristic of the musical humanists, who in general reacted to polyphony; "all writers of the period," Dr. Walker points out, "except Salinas, Doni, and perhaps Mersenne, believed that the music of the ancients was monodic," and some (e.g., Zarlino) suggested that monody was the most decisive feature in the achievement of the *effetti*.[37] Few, however, insisted that modern music ought to become *simply* monodic; for although monody achieves values lost to polyphony, harmony on the other hand has virtues unknown to classical antiquity. Thus there were, among the humanists, two primary styles: monody and homophony.

The concentration of the humanists was on dramatic music, that is, both the music of the theatre, the *stile rappresentativo* or *recitativo,* and a more dramatic version of song, the monodic "ayre" which appeared in the works of English masque-composers shortly after Caccini had created a taste for it in Italy.[38] Pietro de'Bardi, in recounting to Doni the history of his father's Camerata, said that Caccini, the author of *Le Nuove Musiche,*

completely under the instruction of my father, began to sing to the accompaniment of a single instrument various ariettas, sonnets, and other suitably intelligible poems, to the amazement of those who heard him. Jacopo Peri, . . . working together with Giulio, sweetened this style [the *stile rappresentativo*] and made it capable of moving the affections in a rare manner, as they both eventually succeeded in doing.[39]

Caccini had acknowledged his debt both to the Camerata and to the antique ideal which inspired the group; in dedicating his *L'Euridice* to the elder Bardi in 1600, he says of the *stile rappresentativo* in which it is composed that

this is likewise the manner which Your Lordship, discussing it in the days when your Camerata was flourishing in Florence, said—

along with many other noble virtuosi—had been used by the ancient Greeks in the representation of their tragedies and other fables.[40]

Humanistic music in Italy was almost entirely a dramatic music; the theorist Vincenzo Galilei (whose son also showed empirical tendencies) "even advises his readers to go to the theatre and observe the exact manners of speech" used by good actors, in order that the *stile rappresentativo* might be a total, not merely a vocal, dramatic achievement.[41] It must be noted that this dramatic style was not designed for solo voices only. The humanists also dealt with choral singing, usually homophonous, and their backward glances at the Greek theatre brought choral dancing as well; this union was achieved in the Rinuccini-Peri *Euridice* in the form of a dancing chorus, an idea obviously taken from the Greeks. Rinuccini himself nearly equates the new achievements with the drama of the ancients: "It has been the opinion of many, Most Christian Queen," he says in the dedication of *Euridice* to Maria Medici,

that the ancient Greeks and Romans sang their tragedies throughout when they staged them; but this noble manner of recitation has not only been revived by no one, but to my knowledge has not even been attempted until now—and I used to believe that this was due to the deficiency of modern music, vastly inferior to the ancient.[42]

But he confesses that upon beholding the performance of his own *Dafne* with the music of Peri (the first staging of the *stile rappresentativo* and a performance which the younger Bardi still remembered with awe forty years later), he changed his mind and now foresaw such a perfection of modern music that the ancients, so much praised by the old writers, need no longer be envied.[43]

The declamatory style ("which, surpassing that of ordinary speech, yet came sufficiently short of the melody of song that it took an intermediate form" to use Peri's description of ancient dramatic music)[44] was the primary achievement of Italian musical humanism, and is the direct result of the attempt to recover the ethical effects of the ancient *ars musica,* the poetry of the ancients; the accounts suggest that they were convinced of their success.

There was a parallel movement in France, centering primarily in Baïf's *Académie de Poésie et de Musique* founded in 1570. The Letters Patent for this academy give the principles which were to dominate its efforts: "first, that music and verse are to be firmly united; secondly, that this union is to produce a revival of the ethical effects of ancient music."[45] It is true of the theories of the French as well as the Italians that "the keystone of nearly all these theories is the problem of the 'effetti,' i.e., the desire to revive the ethical power of ancient music"; Baïf's *Académie* was attempting "the recreation of an art which should arouse and control passions, inculcate and preserve virtue, even cure disease and ensure the stability of the state."[46] The Pléiade, too, was affected; Ronsard "was deeply interested in the 'effects' of the union of word with sound,"[47] and believed with everyone else that this was a leading characteristic of ancient music. The ethical effects were the prime object in France as in Italy, and although no theoretical work by the poets and musicians of the French school survives, the characteristics of their work can largely be accounted for by the prevailing humanistic theories of the time.[48]

French humanistic music is not simply a copy of the Italian work. The French emphasis was more on rhythmic problems than declamatory ones, and instead of *stile recitativo* they produced *musique mesurée.* Probably the foremost name to be associated with *musique mesurée* is that of Claude LeJeune, who, although not a member of Baïf's *Académie,* may be supposed to have accepted its main tenets.[49] LeJeune's *Le Printemps* was published posthumously in 1603 and was, interestingly, dedicated to King James I of England. In the preface to this work it is observed that of the two ancient divisions of music, "Harmonique, & Rythmique," the moderns had perfected the former greatly; but the latter, which was the principle by which the "effects" had been achieved in antiquity, the moderns had almost entirely neglected—"until Claude LeJeune, who is the first stalwart to revive this poor Rhythm from the tomb in which it had lain so long, to match it with Harmony." The result of LeJeune's reinstatement of rhythmic principles is that his music is "not only equal to that of the ancients, but much more excellent and more capable of beautiful effects"; for to the perfection of harmony, which "can strike wonder into even the most subtle minds," is now added "Rhythm...which can animate, move, lead where one pleases, by means of the gentle violence of its regulated movements, any soul, no matter how rude and gross."[50] LeJeune's achievement was sufficient to inspire an anecdote, recorded by Artus Thomas, in which he was said to have duplicated the feat performed upon Alexander by Timotheus.[51]

Baïf's *Académie* was certainly not less ambitious than its Italian counterpart in its formal intentions; and as Dr. Walker points out, the *Académie* was involved in other projects not mentioned in the Letters Patent: among these was an attempt at "reviving Greek drama in its entirety, complete with music and choreography *mesurés à l'antique*."[52] How far this venture progressed within the *Académie* is unknown. But there was a similar effort which "owes a great debt to Baïf's Academy":[53] the *Balet Comique de la Royne* by Balthasar Beaujoyeulx.

Beaujoyeulx (or Belgiojoso, for his Italian origin may not be irrelevant) apparently regarded the music in the *Balet Comique* as something of a revival of ancient music: "I was of the opinion," he remarks, "that it would not be indecorous to mix the one and the other together, and vary the music with poetry, and interlace the poetry with music, and still more often combine them both together: since antiquity simply did not recite verses without music, and Orpheus never played without verses."[54] The poems prefixed to the published text commend him for just such an accomplishment:

My mind, Beaujoyeulx, wanders in bewilderment
Within your high and learnedly contrived projects
And the old monumènts, uprooted from Greece
To entertain our kings with such a rare spectacle.[55]

An examination of the characteristics of the music written for the *Balet Comique* reveals the same features found in the ideas of the humanists. The songs are either monodic or homophonic, even in the larger choruses—precisely the practice recommended by the Italian humanists and the theorists of *musique mesurée*. The rhythmic characteristics which are superadded to the homophony in the dance tunes are perhaps derived from the same attention to rhythmic effects given by LeJeune. As Dent describes them, "the dance tunes are harmonized continuously in five parts with no attempt at counterpoint or variety of any kind. . . . There are constant changes of rhythm which are most bewildering to anyone who reads them merely as music."[56] Beaujoyeulx was apparently making deliberate use of humanistic music, and undoubtedly for the ethical impact for which the humanists themselves were attempting to exploit it; the *Balet Comique* is built upon a moralized foundation, and Beaujoyeulx seems to have used developments in music to intensify the message of his moral fable.

We cannot be sure what was going on in England while the continental humanists were striving for the instauration of ancient music. England was, as I have pointed out, not lacking in friends of music, and even friends with humanistic leanings. There may have been some connection between Baïf's *Académie* and the English *Aereopagus* in the late sixteenth century, and Thomas Campion may have worked with the ethical notions behind the new music with which he dealt as a reformer of poetry and music.[57] But an English theoretical treatise on specifically ethical music is apparently not to be found.

This does not mean, of course, that there were no comparable musical experiments in England. One must remember that even in France "no theoretical work by any of the poets and musicians of *musique mesurée* survives,"[58] although there is not the least doubt of their interest, ideas, or industry. It is unlikely that England produced a Camerata or an *Académie de Poésie et de Musique;* in England, unlike Italy, the masters of music remained conservative, and the traditional strongholds of music were unlikely to allow any experimentation. "But," Parry observes,

there was a form of entertainment which just supplied the framework required to introduce parallel experiments to those of the Italian promoters of the 'Nuove Musiche,' which at the same time remained characteristically English. The popularity of masques at Court and among aristocratic classes . . . almost compelled composers who were called upon to supply music for them to consider their art from a different point of view from that of the old church composers and composers of madrigals; . . . . Their productions . . . are really of great historical interest, as representing the counterpart to the first experiments of the Italians in genuine stage music.[59]

It is in the masques that the new music reached England—the newly perfected dramatic form embraced the newly developed dramatic music. Of Alfonso Ferrabosco, son of the great Elizabethan master of the same name and long Jonson's collaborator in masque writing, J. A. Fuller Maitland says,

From the internal evidence of the second Alphonso's music it is clear that he imbibed none of his father's "deep skill," and that he attached himself definitely to the new school of music which sprang up in Italy at the beginning of the seventeenth century. It is not known whether he was actually one of the musical revolutionaries who met at the house of Giovanni Bardi in Florence, and who ultimately changed the massive polyphony which had been the chief glory of the previous century to the slight and easy monody, which gave free scope for the portrayal of dramatic situations. It is certain, however, that he was one of the first who brought the new music into England.[60]

It seems unlikely that Ferrabosco was in Italy at the time of Bardi's Camerata, although his history is extremely confused by the fact that he was the second of three Alfonso Ferraboscos attached to the English court in a musical capacity. There is, however, a direct connection between the two lands in the person of the Italianate Englishman John Coperario (*né* Cooper), another masque-composer, of whose sojourns in Italy there is no doubt:

his importance in the history of English music lies in the fact that he must have been in Italy at the very time when the homophonic school arose, and that though his own bent was clearly towards the earlier school, yet his compositions for solo voices are written in the new manner, which was afterwards so astonishingly developed by his pupils, William and Henry Lawes. Coperario, in fact, with Ferrabosco and Laniere, forms the connecting link between Italy and England at the period when the musical drama originated.[61]

"Laniere" is, of course, Nicholas Laniere or Lanier, author of the music for Jonson's *Vision of Delight* and *Lovers Made Men*. His name is primarily known among music historians as that of the man who first introduced into England, in a masque by Ben Jonson, the *stile recitativo*—that style which was the fruit of the most severe forms of Italian musical humanism.[62] Coperario and Lanier worked together on a Campion masque in 1614, and it was very shortly after this that Jonson and Lanier produced the *Vision of Delight* with its Italian style of dramatic music.

Coperario probably never worked in a Jonson masque; but he was involved in masque-composition, and is associated in his musical ideas with two others, Ferrabosco and Lanier, the two leading musical associates of Jonson. It is plain that all three borrowed from the new humanistic music of Italy; it seems most unlikely that they could have remained ignorant of the theoretical premises and primarily ethical design of this music, especially considering Coperario's immediate connection with it. Mr. Pattison maintains that the theories of the Camerata were discussed in England as well as put into practice, and cites Coperario and Ferrabosco as the men who accepted them most completely.[63]

The evidence is not quite enough to allow the direct assertion that Jonson knew and used the music of the "effects" as the French and Italians did, for the purpose of heightening the ethical impact of his masques. The evidence does, however, make this extremely likely. France and Italy were enthusiastic about their recovery of the music of the ancients and the ethical power which goes with it; this is most assuredly an event which would interest Jonson, and it is impossible to believe that it would never have come to his attention when he was writing for the English court the counterparts of the new French and Italian musical dramatic shows.[64] Jonson's insistence upon the *prodesse,* the uplifting ethical character of his masques, would make the music of the "effetti" the perfect musical vehicle for them; and we know that he used the music which originated for this purpose in Italy. It is not necessary for us to be stopped, though we may be given prudent cause, by the fact that Jonson does not declare his use of the music of the effects. Jonson's descriptions of the collaborators are notoriously scanty, and in fact even Beaujoyeulx, whose attachment to the music of the effects cannot be denied, does not mention the effects or even suggest that a radical departure in the realm of music is taking place in his ballet. There may be more than an extravagant compliment involved in Jonson's lines to Ferrabosco describing music's "knowne effects,"

> That shee remoueth cares, sadnesse eiects,
> Declineth anger, perswades clemencie,
> Doth sweeten mirth, and heighten pietie,
>
> .   .   .   .
>
> But when I haue said, The proofes of all these bee
> Shed in thy Songs; 'tis true: but short of thee.[65]

How far Jonson exploited the "effects" cannot be determined; but there seems to be good reason to believe that he employed for its specifically dramatic and psychological values that humanistic type of music which, being primarily a dramatic music, would support the dramatic-poetic "soul" which Jonson breathed into his masques, and which, with its psychological power, would give his message an additional attractiveness and ethical impact, and his songs additional force:

Which Art being excellent and naturally delightful, doth then become admirable, and entirely wins the love of others, when such as possess it, both by teaching and delighting others, do often exercise it and make it appear to be a pattern and true resemblance of those never ceasing celestial Harmonies, whence proceed so many good effects and benefits upon earth, raising and exciting the minds of the Hearers, to the contemplation of those infinite delights which Heaven affordeth.[66]

Chapter IV · Dance

Jonson's exaltation of the poetic part of the masque over its visual components and the pique with which he decried the court's—and eventually, Inigo Jones's—emphasis on spectacle may easily appear to suggest that Jonson regarded the visual elements as merely the clumsy members of a body in which the poetic soul was unfortunately imprisoned. His terms are actually more Aristotelian in this case: the soul perfects the body and

81

finds its expression through it. Jonson was well aware of the value of the visual side of the masque and carefully used it to advantage. In the Jonsonian masque, spectacle is made animate in the service of poetry.

At the centre of the masque spectacle is the dance; and it was therefore plainly in Jonson's interest to discover and exploit whatever was available to a student of antiquity and a man of the Renaissance that might serve to bring the dance into a more intimate association with the poetry of the masque. The ancient writers and the ideas of the Renaissance provided him and his choreographers with excellent opportunities, and as a result the Jonsonian masques make rich use of the dance to extend, emphasize, and intensify the operation of their poetic souls—indeed, following even in this the example of the ancients, for

from the very beginning, the poets arranged dances for freemen, and they used dance-figures only to illustrate the theme of the songs, always preserving nobility and manliness in them. . . . But if any one arranged his figures with undue exaggeration, or when he came to his songs said anything that did not correspond to the dance, he was discredited.[1]

I. MEANING

Jonson most often employs the dance as an image of order, particularly the order of the heavens. The dance was commonly thought to have arisen as an imitation of the regularity of the stars and planets, and neither Greek antiquity[2] nor the Renaissance ever lost sight of this origin. Claude Menestrier, in a history of the dance that serves as an excellent compilation of classical and Renaissance thought on the subject, writes that

The Egyptians, who were sages disciplined in minute detail, made the first of their dances hieroglyphics in action, as they had among them figures to express their Mysteries. Plato, who was their disciple and their admirer, could not sufficiently praise the mind of the one who first put into concert and into dance the harmony of the universe and all the movements of the stars, and concluded that he must have been a god or a divine man. The interpreters of Sophocles, Euripides, and Aristophanes have revealed to us the mysteries which Plato did not explain: they say that all the dances which the Egyptians made represented the celestial movements and the harmony of the universe.[3]

The natural result of this idea of imitation was an enhancement of the idea of cosmic order through the projection of the dance, and an enhancement of the dignity of the dance through its association with the awesome order of the heavens. Caelius Rhodiginus found exactly this in his reading of the ancients:

Therefore, after many and various investigations, the truest account appears to me to be that the beginnings of the dance sprang forth through a divine power, simultaneous with the creation of the world and with that love that is most ancient. To be sure, this exquisite chorus of the stars and of the heavens, and the interweaving of the planets with the fixed stars, and the elegant and harmonious organization and wonderful order all bear witness to this. If anyone thinks these things to be the cradle and origin of the dance, he is in my opinion very close to the truth.[4]

The alliance of dance with music resulted in a further mutual reinforcement of each art's ability to suggest celestial order to the Greek mind. Plutarch observes in the *Moralia*[5] that dance was intimately connected with poetry as well as with music, and Menestrier points out that the poetic forms connected with dance further emphasized the celestial imitation. The strophes, he says, "express the movements of the heavens," while antistrophes were "to represent the movements of the planets," and "Epodes represented the stability and immobility of the earth."[6]

The dance achieved another dimension of meaning through its association with religious rites. As Caelius Rhodiginus observes,

one can find considerable evidence that the dance was held by the ancients to be no mean or contemptible thing—note especially that there were no older ceremonies or consecrations in which the dance was not employed.[7]

Pythagoras is named by Menestrier as the source for the philosophical backgrounds of the religious dances of Greece, with the additional comment that "These dances were not merely religious observances—they were, in fact, Mysteries, since they expressed the characters of the divinities for whom they were performed"[8]—another way of imitating the celestial order and symbolically raising the mundane to a higher mode of existence:

> Blessed are the dancers and those who are purified,
> who dance on the hill in the holy dance of God.[9]

Religious dancing remained in the early Christian era, often with a backward glance at the dancing in the Old Testament (though more probably imitating the Greek tradition than attempting to reconstruct the Hebrew). St. Basil recommends holy dancing as an imitation of the dances of the angels, for, according to Menestrier, he and certain other philosophers "believed that these intelligences had no other way of conversing than by signs and movements arranged in the form of a dance."[10]

Earth dances in consonance with heaven: this is the underlying understanding throughout the history of the dance in the ancient Greek world. The dance of the stars, of the Graces, of Apollo and the Muses[11] are echoed in the chorus in which music, poetry, and dance combine in a ritualistic act of potentially profound significance. It is against this background that one must read the curious passage in the Gnostic *Acts of John,* where Jesus leads his disciples in a choral hymn in his leavetaking:

> Grace danceth. I would pipe; dance ye all. Amen.
>
> . . . .
>
> The number Twelve danceth on high. Amen.
> The Whole on high hath part in our dancing. Amen.
> Who danceth not, knoweth not what cometh to pass. Amen.[12]

It is therefore far from surprising to find Plotinus seizing the chorus as a metaphor for the proper attunement of man with the Supreme:

We are always in the presence of it [the Supreme], but we do not always attend it. But like a singing chorus: keeping order around the leader, it might turn away from him whenever it turns about, yet it sings with beauty and keeps order truly around him. Thus we are always in its presence—and if ever we are not, there will be our total dissolution and we shall no longer exist—although we do not always attend it: but when we do see it, then our completion and our repose and our cessation of displeasing all dance truly around him a God-filled dance.[13]

Nowhere is the idea of the dance as an image of cosmic order made more clear than in Lucian's general encomium of the dance, his dialogue *Peri Orcheseos,* to which Renaissance writers on the dance turn frequently for support. The dialogue shows that the dance could be philosophically apprehended somewhat after the better known manner of music. Nor does Lucian forget the cosmic origins and implications of his subject:

Those historians of dancing who are the most veracious can tell you that Dance came into being contemporaneously with the primal origin of the universe, making her appearance together with Love—the love that is age-old. In fact, the concord of the heavenly spheres, the interlacing of the errant planets with the fixed stars, their rhythmic agreement and timed harmony, are proofs that Dance was primordial. Little by little she has grown in stature and has obtained from time to time added embellishments, until now she would seem to have reached the very height of perfection and to have become a highly diversified, wholly harmonious, richly musical boon to mankind.[14]

Thus the metaphorical implications of the dance, as formed in antiquity, greatly resembled those of music: both were primarily suggestive of the harmony and order of the cosmos. The Renaissance, of course, picked up these associations. Thoinot Arbeau writes at the end of his treatise, *Orchesography* (1588), "practise these dances carefully and you will become a fit companion of the planets, which dance of their own nature."[15] Shakespeare plays with this association on a broader scale in *Midsummer-Night's Dream*: the disastrous and disordering weather described

in Titania's long speech in II, i, is said to be the direct result of
Oberon's interruption of the dances of Titania and her followers.
By implication, the orderly dances which close the play indicate
the restoration of nature's order. Even the moral but inept poetry
of Anthony Sherly, although basically severe about dancing,
admits that

> The Heauens do tread quicke measures, to the Spheares,
> The Planets *Dance,* obseruing time and numbers;
> Trees trip before the Winde: thus *Dancing* weares
> His badge from Heauen. . . .[16]

But the *locus classicus* for the poetry of the dance is Sir John
Davies' *Orchestra, a Poem of Dancing* (1596), in which the
dance penetrates through the complete range of the universe. At
the beginning of the poem the sun descends to a masque in
Ocean's court, and most of the remainder of the poem is taken
up with the attempts of Antinous to woo Penelope to dance by
means of an exaltation and universalization of dancing. "Imitate
heau'n," he begs her,

> whose beauties excellent
> Are in continuall motion day and night.
> And moue thereby more wonder and delight.[12][17]

> Dauncing (bright Lady) then began to be,
> When the first seedes whereof the world did spring
> The Fire, Ayre, Earth, and water did agree,
> By Loues perswasion, Natures mighty King,
> To leaue their first disordred combating;
>   And in a daunce such measure to obserue,
>   As all the world their motion should preserue.[17]

This is the same doctrine which Lucian culled from his "historians." The dance thus remains not only an image of cosmic
harmony and order, but also, since Love devised "this wondrous
myracle" [18] of dance and instructed the world to follow it,
the dance is also an image of love:

> Kind Nature first doth cause all things to loue,
> Loue makes them daunce and in iust order moue.[56]
> . . . .
> Thus Loue taught men, and men thus learnd of Loue
> Sweet Musicks sound with feete to counterfaite.[76]

The heavens make music and dance to it, and this is the explanation of their "goodly Architecture" [20]; hence, noble persons should "imitate the starres caelestiall" [60], and aspire through the dance to the heaven which is itself a dance: for dancing is "The heau'ns true figure, and th'earths ornament" [96].

All is dance. Antinous finds speech to be a dance of air [43–44], and music to be air's perfect dance [46]. The sea dances with the earth [50], the air and wind are masquers [47], and beauties should note the example of streams, which stay fresh by dancing [54]. Ritual, rite, ceremony, weddings, parliaments all bear the mark of the dance [77]. The trivium is a dance, and so is poetry [92–93]. And of the excellent dance of virtues in Penelope's soul, Antinous says, "Could I now see as I conceiue thys Daunce, / Wonder and Loue would cast me in a traunce" [108].

It is against this background that Ben Jonson saw the dances in his masques, and found in them metaphorical possibilities which he exploited to enrich the poetic power of the masque.[18] In the *Masque of Beauty,* for instance, after making it quite plain that he is imitating the motions of the heavens in the device of a turning throne,[19] Jonson celebrates the first dance of the masquers with this song:

> So beautie on the waters stood,
> When *loue* had seuer'd earth, from flood!
> So when he parted ayre, from fire,
> He did with concord all inspire!
> Add then a *motion* he them taught,
> That elder then himselfe was thought.
> Which thought was, yet, the child of earth,
> For *loue* is elder then his birth.[20]

The poetic purpose of the song is, in the context of the performance, clear enough: the spectator is to be made conscious of the idea of cosmic order and true harmony derived from love, and is to see it expressed and figured in the movements of the dance, thus elevating, intensifying, and expanding the scope of the masque as a poetic effort.

Or consider the song after the second dance in *Love Restored,* which echoes the same theme:

> Haue men beheld the Graces daunce,
> Or seene the vpper Orbes to moue?
> So these did turne, returne, aduance,
> Drawne backe by doubt, put on by loue.
> And now, like earth, themselues they fixe,
> Till greater powers vouchsafe to mixe
> Their motions with them. Doe not feare,
> You brighter planets of this spheare. . . .[21]

Likewise the planets are invoked in a song sung by Nature in *Mercury Vindicated,* as an introduction to a dance; the dancers are to "shew they are the creatures of the Sunne, / That each to other / Is a brother," and to study the motion of the soft heavens of ladies' eyes, where "more orbes and Planets are then seuen."[22] The main dance in *Vision of Delight* presents a still more complex idea of the harmony of nature, being reminiscent of Zephyr and Flora, of Venus, of the spring itself.[23]

The association of the dance with the harmony of the heavens or with the celestial order or the order of nature need not be explicitly mentioned in the text of a masque to be operative. In *Hymenaei,* the masquers are revealed in the heavens, in conjunction with Jupiter, Juno, Iris, and a whirling "region of fire," and then descend in two clouds to dance.[24] In the *Haddington Masque,* the dancers, attired as signs of the zodiac, appear first on a huge sphere which figures the sphere of heaven.[25] James is referred to as Hesperus in *Pleasure Reconciled to Virtue,* and the Prince, the chief masquer, is one "of the bright race of *Hesperus*" and "only a lesse Light then He."[26] In *News From the New World,* the masquers are said to have been "rapt above the Moone" for some time, and after their dance are told that they "take / The Suns reflected light" (that is, of course, James's), and derive from him a motion that is "pure harmonie," an obvious allusion to the planets.[27]

Thus it is clear that in his handling of dance, Jonson emphasizes and exploits the image of celestial harmony and order which the art is capable of presenting to minds which are prepared by traditional associations and stimulated by specific allusions. Jonson's use of the dance underlines ideas of other orders as well. *Hymenaei* introduces Order, as Reason's servant, to conduct the masque-dance—in allegorical reply to an earlier antimasque-dance in which the four humours and four affections disturbed the progress of the ceremony to "a kind of contentious Musique."[28] Jonson considered the allegory "very cleare," but reluctantly glossed it as follows:

First, as in *naturall bodies,* so likewise in *minds,* there is no disease, or distemperature, but is caused either by some abounding *humor,* or peruerse *affection;* after the same maner, in *politick bodies* (where *Order, Ceremony, State, Reuerence, Deuotion,* are parts of the *Mind*) by the difference, or praedominant will of what we (*metaphorically*) call *Humors,* and *Affections,* all things are troubled and confused. These, therefore, were *tropically* brought in, before *Marriage,* as disturbers of that *mysticall bodie,* and the *rites,* which were *soule* vnto it; that afterwards, in *Marriage,* being dutifully tempered by her *power,* they might more fully celebrate the happinesse of such as liue in that sweet *vnion,* to the harmonious lawes of Nature and Reason.[29]

Note especially the concluding expression, "the harmonious lawes of Nature and Reason," by which Jonson refers to a proper order in which the health of a natural body, a mind, a body politic, a marriage can be figured: every kind of order is a fulfillment of these "harmonious lawes," and as such can be imaged in music and dance. In *Love Restored,* the dance is to represent an ordering of virtues by presenting

> *one harmonie*
> Of *honor,* and of *courtesie,*
> True *valure,* and *vrbanitie,*
> Of *confidence, alacritie,*
> Of *promptnesse,* and of *industrie,*
> *Habilitie, Realitie.*[30]

And in *The Golden Age Restored,* the dance is said to be appropriate to that state in which "peace, and loue, faith, ioyes, all, all increase. / And strife, and hate, and feare, and paine, all cease."[31] That is, the dancers in their order are to display the order of the Golden Age.

It was, according to Lucian, and to Davies, and to Jonson, Love that originally imparted order to the universe; and love remains the ordering principle ever since. The dance of virtues in *Love Restored* is to display love, for love is the power which orders virtue:

> This motion was of loue begot,
> It was so ayrie, light, and good,
> His wings into their feet he shot,
> Or else himselfe into their bloud.
> But aske not how. The end will proue,
> That loue's in them, or they'are in loue.[32]

Even the courtier's love images the great power, Love. In *Love's Triumph,* Jonson deals with another allegorical dance which is a figure of right love: again, the masque dance is preceded by an antimasque of "deprau'd Louers" whose dance, not deriving from right love, is incapable of showing "any motion eyther of order or measure."[33] But the masque-dance itself presents the King as Heroic Love, surrounded by other proper loves who make a circle around him while he receives "all the lines of loue in one," probably ribbons held by the other dancers; the resulting circle represents "those glories ... / Fit to be sought in *Beauty,* found by *Loue,*" for "The circle of the will / Is the true spheare of *Loue,*" and "Where *Loue* is mutuall, still / All things in order moue."[34] The dance reveals that one harmony, that basic "harmonious lawe of Nature and Reason" which makes the King the center and orderer of the commonwealth, heroic love the ordering power of the loves, the will the source of love's order, and mutual love the basis of all order. The Christian tradition in which Jonson stood has always emphasized love as the great sustainer of order, and it is that order to which Jonson alludes in the masque-dance. What we see on the stage is the image of a philosophical absolute:

> Kind Nature first doth cause all things to loue,
> Loue makes tham daunce and in iust order moue.[35]

II. METHOD

The possibilities of the dance are not exhausted, however, by using it as an illustration and metaphor for order. Just as the ancients had found in music both an image of order and an effector of it, so dance too had its powers over the soul in addition to its symbolic properties. Antiquity found the dance full of moral possibilities; Menestrier recalls Plato's prescription of dance as "a kind of study and a practical exercise" and as a means of counteracting "dangerous passions."[36] Plato felt that the purpose of the dance was primarily to aid the harmony of the soul, and to that end he made an important place for it in his ideal *paideia*.[37] Dance as an exercise (as distinguished from dance as a spectacle) recovered a serious place in education in the Renaissance; one need only think of Elyot or Mulcaster. Even John Locke strongly recommends that children be taught to dance as early as possible, since "it gives children manly thoughts as well as improving their carriage."[38]

But still more pertinent to the study of the masque is the reputation of the dance as a perfector not merely of the participants, but of the spectators as well. Dance was considered in antiquity to be not only a moral exercise, but also a means of imparting moral improvement to the beholder by enlightening his understanding and moving his affections. Caelius Rhodiginus writes of this side of the dance:

The most serious authors have declared that it reaches to the very top of excellent disciplines—not only music but rhythm, not to mention geometry: and above all, philosophy, both natural and ethical; nor is it unacquainted with rhetoric, seeing that it reveals the character and affections which the rhetoricians are concerned with moving.[39]

Menestrier observes that Agamemnon presented dances to his wife in which "he represented to her all the virtues of illustrious women, and by this means aroused in her mind a regard and a love for virtue, and by these worthy diversions he kept all scheming thoughts from her mind."[40] Any enlightenment, to a mind with a Platonic bent, has necessary moral consequences; and to that extent there are ethical as well as intellectual effects involved in the revelations brought about by the "Choruses which, besides the singing and the narrations, had allegorical and representational dances, which Athenaeus calls modest songs and philosophical dances, since everything in them was regulated and since they were for the most part ingenious allegories."[41] All instruction, all the elements of the *paideia* contribute to the moral wholeness of man, and the dance was a means of genuine enlightenment. Lesbonax of Mytilene, according to Menestrier, praised his dancers highly for their skill in revealing "the most hidden mysteries of nature";[42] and of the religious dances founded on the thought of Pythagoras, he adds, "these dances were not merely religious observances—they were, in fact, Mysteries, since they expressed the characters of the divinities for whom they were performed."[43] Lucian's dialogue on the dance expresses largely the same position concerning moral enlightenment achieved through the dance, which "brings not only pleasure but benefit to those who see it; how much culture and instruction it gives; how it imports harmony into the souls of its beholders."[44] "I have come back to you from the theatre," says Lucian's defender of the dance, "with far more wisdom and more insight into life."[45]

The classical theatre, as Lucian points out, involved dancing as an integral part, and a part which, like the others, perfected the characters of the spectators.[46] The Renaissance humanists did not forget this. Sir Thomas Elyot notes that "the olde maner of daunsinge was forgotten" when all things declined along with the Roman empire, but that with proper study of "the sciences liberall, and . . . histories," one could "reuiue the auncient fourme . . . of daunsing . . . whereof they mought take nat only pleasure, but also profite and commoditie."[47] Baïf's *Académie de Poésie et de Musique,* dedicated to the recovery of the theatrical art of antiquity, had extensive projects for the perfection of dance in hopes of restoring its ethical powers; and the Italian humanists were likewise engaged in an attempt to recover the choral dance of the ancients, for the same purposes.[48]

The records of Italian developments in the restoration of the ancient virtues of the dance are scanty, but there is evidence that the theorizing of the humanists did not go entirely unnoticed. In 1581, Fabritio Caroso published *Il Ballarino,* a collection of dances which, although scarcely to be considered a direct product of the humanistic investigation of the dance, bears some marks of the climate of such theorizing in Caroso's prefatory remarks invoking the estimation in which the dance was held by the ancients[49] and in the almost predictable compliment of Francesco Guglia's commendatory poem describing Caroso's dances as "the harmony below of the spheres above."[50] But these minor suggestions are far less significant than those that appear in the revised edition of Caroso's collection, which was printed in 1600 under the title *Nobiltà di Dame.*[51] The later edition demonstrates a considerably greater concern for the theory of the dance than is evident in *Il Ballarino,* of which Caroso says in the preface to *Nobiltà di Dame* "I have corrected it with precise rules and with true theory . . . so that where it was imperfect, I have now brought it into true perfection."[52] The section describing the "rules" of the dance is expanded in *Nobiltà di Dame,* and the descriptions of individual dances frequently conclude with references to their theoretical respectability, occasionally with a disparaging allusion to the ruder versions found in *Il Ballarino:* "And this is done with true theory";[53] "Made with true rules and with perfect theory, and is exactly right";[54] "everyone should scorn it [the earlier version] since it is contrary to the rules and badly made. However, to do it in accordance with theory and with proper finish, one should do it thus. . . ."[55]

But an even more important suggestion of the impact of the humanists' efforts can be found in yet another addition in *Nobiltà di Dame:* the attempt to unite dance with poetry, which was perhaps the chief goal of the humanists in their investigations of the dance. An engraving on sig. HhI illustrates "Il Contrapasso made with true mathematics to the verses of Ovid." The illustration is simply a diagram of the paths of movement that the dancers are to follow; but there also appears on the diagram a spondee and a dactyl marked in musical notes after the humanistic manner of setting poetic metres to music. The verbal description of this dance—which concludes with the words "this dance made with true rules, perfect theory, and mathematics"[56] —does not depart from the normal format observed in the other descriptions; but there is a brief passage in the prefatory section on rules that provides a partial gloss. Caroso there describes the ways in which dactyls, spondees, Sapphics, and distichs are to be rendered in dance, taking as an example of his method Ovid's *Hanc tua Penelope, lento tibi mittit Ulisses:*

> There are in this verse four dactyls and two spondees, and therefore take note, if you wish to dance properly and according to true rules, that in the movements that you make, the left foot must have as many steps as the right; that two dactyls and one spondee must have a foot each; and thus observing these rules of mine, all the dances which you perform will be just right.[57]

There is virtually nothing more on the subject in the rest of the book; but if Caroso had only partially digested the efforts of the humanists, he at least testifies to their effective presence in Italy, and provides some potentially fruitful hints about "vera Theorica" from which an English choreographer might profit in his efforts to achieve the most authentic and effective form of dance.

The humanists in France were, in the meantime, following the same paths; and in 1581 was performed the work which best represents, although indirectly, the kind of project they were attempting: the *Balet Comique de la Royne.*[58]

As the title implies, the dance was as important in the *Balet Comique* as it had become in Jacobean masques, and Beaujoyeulx took special pains with it. As Miss Yates has pointed out, he regarded the dances of the *Balet Comique* as a revival of ancient dancing.[59] "As for the dance," he writes in an address to the reader, "although it is a modern invention—or at any rate repeated so long after antiquity that one may so style it...."[60] The commendatory verses prefixed to the published text single out the dance for special praise:

Beaujoyeulx, who first brings back to the light of day, out of the ashes of Greece, the design and skill of the formal dance proportioned in its turns....[61]

Your Circe, Beaujoyeulx, does not charm me nearly so much as the subtle turnings of your dance, just as the art of your Circe yields to the celestial Moly. But in such sweet pleasure I feel my soul become so enchanted, and my senses so ravished....[62]

The confused order of the dance, revealing by a mystical effect the harmony of the heavens....[63]

The exact nature of the choreography in the *Balet Comique* is impossible to determine, but Beaujoyeulx's general description implies that it was primarily an interweaving and interchanging of geometrical figures, "geometrical combinations of several persons dancing together to a varying harmony of several instruments."[64] At the climactic point of the description, he offers a little more detail: "before His Majesty ... the main dance was performed, with forty changes or geometrical figures ... now in a square, and then in a circle ... and yet again in a triangle, accompanied by another little square, and other little figures."[65] Such geometrical choreography appears to have been a general

European phenomenon, and was very likely characteristic of Jonson's masques as well as the *Balet Comique*. If Jonson's descriptions of dances in "curious *Squares,* and *Rounds*" ending in "the figure of a *Diamant*" suggest to a modern reader a rather dull performance, he must remember the effect which the authors of commendatory verses ascribed to the geometrical dances of the *Balet Comique*.[66]

It is worth a brief pause to observe that despite the particular and definite value which Beaujoyeulx himself and the authors of the commendatory poems placed upon the dancing of the *Balet Comique,* we are given only the inadequate descriptions quoted above. Subsequent French ballets, and English masques as well, preserve hardly as much choreographic description; this is not in itself evidence that their dances were not ambitiously conceived. Perhaps the most nearly adequate, and possibly the most intriguing, account is that preserved in the text of the *Ballet de Monseigneur le Duc de Vandosme,* produced January 17–18, 1610.[67] This ballet apparently began with a sort of antimasque in the form of a "dance of green *magots,* which they danced in ten ways, always keeping time, with different leaps, bounds, gestures, and grimaces."[68] Later came a "letter dance" in which "the twelve nymphs dance the spelling of the name *Alcine*"[69]—a device occasionally used by Jonson as well.[70] The climax of the dancing in the *Ballet de Vandosme* came when the music altered and "the said Knights, changing their step and measure, went into their first figure, which, following the alphabet of the ancient Druids (found a few years ago on an old monument), represented a character of this alphabet made with twelve points, signifying *Powerful Love*."[71]

After forming this figure, they proceed to other symbols from the same alphabet, signifying "Ambitious Desire," "Virtuous Scheme," "Immortal Renown," "Greatness of Courage," "Pleasing Pain," "Tested Constancy," "Known Truth," "Fortunate Destiny," "Loved By All," "Crown of Glory," and "Supreme Power."[72] The figures are all shown in the text, and each is

represented as an arrangement of twelve points, joined with
lines. It appears that the lines must have had some counterpart
in the dance, such as ribbons held between one dancer and another (compare the dance in Jonson's *Love's Triumph* or that
in *Pleasure Reconciled to Virtue,* which seem to involve the
same kind of procedure), since the distribution of points—i.e.,
of dancers—is identical in "Vertueux Dessein" and "Couronne
de Gloire," which are distinguishable only by the different line-
combinations among the points. It also appears that these figures
must have been glossed, either by an interpreter or by a written
key of some sort provided for the spectators. The latter seems
more likely. There is no provision in the text for an interpreter,
and although this in itself means little, the introduction to
Lacroix's *Ballets et Mascarades de cour,* in which the *Ballet de
Vandosme* is printed, points out that "the majority of these
ballets are only programs, printed exclusively for the performance; they were given out from hand to hand, to the spectators
and to the actors."[73] But Lacroix unfortunately does not indicate
whether or not the *Ballet de Vandosme* is an example of this
kind of libretto.

At any rate, the spectators were most likely not left ignorant
with respect to the "meanings" of the dances, and the value of
the dance was probably thought to rest heavily upon the elevation of the beholder's mind and soul as he watched with pleasure
and admiration the graceful execution of a figure with a moral
meaning. Perhaps he was to contemplate the fitness of a given
figure for the expression of its title;[74] and perhaps he was merely
to be pleased by the grace of the dancing and have the morality
creep in only as an unconscious recognition of the fact that the
thing which delighted him had a moral name. Whatever the
case, the dances in the *Ballet de Vandosme* are intended to carry
an ethical weight of some kind, directly and in themselves.

This is admittedly a special case in many ways. Although
Jonson worked closely with his choreographers, and although it
is by no means impossible that among the forms given the

dancers in his masques were hieroglyphical figures analogous to the druidical characters in the *Ballet de Vandosme* (Jonson is certainly using an allegorized dance-figure in *Love's Triumph,* for instance), still there is no specific evidence that such a practice of hieroglyphic choreography is characteristic of the Jonsonian masque, and it is thus at best a vague possibility. The main pertinence of invoking the *Ballet de Vandosme* is the way in which it illustrates a Renaissance characteristic which does have an undeniably valid application to Jonson: the attention to the intellectual exercise of the dance spectator.

Laneham wrote of the entertainment of Elizabeth at Kenilworth in 1575 that Sunday afternoon was occupied "in excelent muzik, of sundry swet instruments and in dauncing of Lordes & Ladiez, and oother woorshipfull degrees, vttered with such liuely agilitee & commendabl grace: az whither it mought be more straunge too the eye, or pleazunt too the minde, for my part indeed I coold not discern: but exceedingly well waz it (methought) in both."[75] We are not accustomed consciously to regard a dance as it is pleasant to the mind, although we certainly experience this in a well-conceived ballet; but the Renaissance mind seems deliberately and consciously to have attended to this aspect, even in the relatively impromptu dancing of the sort Laneham describes. Again, this is not to say that a galliard was considered primarily an object of intellectual contemplation. But the poetical-philosophical associations of the dance with all order, from cosmic harmony to psychological order, were always there to be remembered either explicitly or implicitly: and the dance accordingly retained in the Renaissance its original status as an expressive and imitative art. "The interpretours of Plato," wrote Sir Thomas Elyot,

do thinke that the wonderfull and incomprehensible ordre of the celestial bodies, I meane sterres and planettes, and their motions harmonicall, gaue to them that intentifly, and by the deepe serche of raison beholde their coursis, in the sondrye diuersities of nombre and tyme, a fourme of imitation of a semblable motion, whiche they called daunsinge or saltation; wherfore the more nere they approched to that temperance and subtile modulation of the saide superiour bodies, the more perfecte and commendable is their daunsinge, whiche is moste like to the trouthe of any opinion that I have hitherto founden.[76]

Elyot further observes that in the dances of the ancients "there was a concinnitie of mouing the foote and body, expressing some pleasaunt or profitable affectes or motions of the mynde": one dance showed "the maiestie of princes," and "also there was a kynde of daunsinge called *Hormus,* of all the other moste lyke to that whiche is at this time used; wherin daunsed yonge men and maidens, the man expressinge in his motion and countenance fortitude and magnanimitie apt for the warres, the maiden moderation and shamefastnes, which represented a pleasant connexion of fortitude and temperance."[77] Caroso's *Il Ballarino* likewise observes of the dance,

Nor is such a quality a minor grace; since it is joined with poetry and with music, a faculty most worthy among the others—and it is part of that imitation which represents the affections of the soul with the movements of the body. Besides that, it is quite appropriate to a noble person ... and, in short, joins grace, beauty, and decorum in the presence of the beholders.[78]

The dance teaches both dancer and spectator, the former by giving order and discipline to expressive movement, the latter by drawing the attention and admiration to the same; both are perfected in the thing expressed through the order and excellence of the expression:

And who is unaware that by the dance, as by an ingenious master, the noble movements of the person are learned; how one should bow more gravely, how to turn more gracefully, and how, with many other comely attitudes, one can silently attract the souls of others—which things I consider to be of no small moment. And since our soul is composed of certain proportions, or secret harmonic numbers, which it would be out of the question to discuss, it shows itself necessarily more or less perfect as it discloses itself to the eyes of the beholders moving with its body more or less measuredly.[79]

Sir Thomas Elyot points out that "in every daunse, of a moste auncient custome, there daunseth to gether a man and a woman, holding eche other by the hande or the arme, whiche betokeneth concorde,"[80] and that if men dance according to manly qualities and women according to womanly, the conjunctions will figure virtues: "And in this wise *fiersenesse* ioyned with *mildenesse* maketh *Seueritie; Audacitie* with *timorositie*, maketh *Magnanimitie; . . . Couaitise of Glorie,* adjourned with *benignitie* causeth honour,"[81] and so forth.

These qualities, in this wise beinge knitte to gether, and signified in the personages of man and woman daunsinge, do expresse or sette out the figure of very nobilitie; whiche in the higher astate it is contained, the more excellent is the vertue in estimation.[82]

The resemblance of this last quotation to the ideas of Caroso is notable, and becomes even more so when we consider the dances which Caroso devised, in which the proper movements of the man and the woman are set forth for dances in honor of Italian noblewomen and bearing such titles as "Amor Costante," "Fideltà," "Gloria d'Amore," "Nobiltà," as well as "Ardente Sole," "Chiara Stella," and "Le Bellezze d'Olimpia."[83]

The external grace of the dance is always, in the Renaissance, to be a sign of an internal grace of virtue and excellence, and this is an "allegorization" which obtains even when the dance does not have Caroso's or Elyot's deliberate and specified emblematic design. The ballet is by its *nature* emblematic of virtuous and right order in general, and if the spectator should choose to find further specific emblems, he may: they are virtually contained in the general significance of the dance, and thus really present to the man who can read them. The same is true in reverse of deliberately awkward dances, such as Jonson uses for antimasques; the depraved lovers in *Love's Triumph* dance "expressing their confus'd affections," and perhaps even portray them individually,[84] but antimasque dances in general give a general portrayal of vice or deformity and leave any specification to the observer. "Now," Elyot says,

by cause there is no passe tyme to be compared to that, wherin may be founden both recreation and meditation of vertue, I haue amonge all honest passe times, wherin is exercise of the body, noted daunsinge to be of an excellent utilitie, comprehendinge in it wonderfull figures, or, as the grekes do calle them, *Ideae,* of vertues and noble qualities, and specially of the commodiouse vertue called prudence, whom Tulli defineth to be the knowledge of thinges whiche oughte to be desired and folowed, and also of them whiche ought to be fledde from or exchewed.[85]

Elyot does not refer to a specifically allegorical dance, but to a habit of mind which sees the enlightening image and ethical action which is potential and latent in *every* dance. Playford, in *The English Dancing Master,* commends "The Gentlemen of the Innes of Court, whose sweet and ayry Activity has crowned their Grand Solemnities with Admiration to all Spectators."[86] It is this admiration which holds in itself the power of an ethical effect similar to that sought by the humanistic theorists of music in the Renaissance, for it draws the spectator into an attitude well disposed towards enlightenment and perfection: and Elyot says that

I have deuised howe in the fourme of daunsinge, nowe late used in this realme amonge gentilmen, the hole description of this vertue prudence may be founden out and well perceyued, as well by the daunsers as by them whiche standinge by, wyll be diligent beholders and markers . . . Wherfore all they that haue their courage stered towarde very honour or perfecte nobilitie, let them approche to this passe tyme, and either them selfes prepare them to daunse, or els at the leste way beholde with watching eien other that can daunse truely, kepynge iuste measure and tyme.[87]

The climax of Davies' *Orchestra* displays precisely Elyot's ideal manner of perceiving the dance: Penelope is enabled to see, in a

mirror, the dance of Elizabeth's court, which appears to be of
stars circling about the moon; the sight "sooth'd her minde with
sweet enchanting pleasure," and

> when she had view'd
> The strange-eye dazeling-admirable sight,
> Faine would haue praisd the state and pulchritude,
> But she was stroken dumbe with wonder quite,
> Yet her sweet mind retayn'd her thinking might:
>> Her rauisht minde in heau'nly thoughts did dwel,
>> But what she thought, no mortall tongue can tell.[88]

The intimate relationship between dance and virtuous harmony thus serves a double purpose: it teaches the dancers the
excellence of such harmony by making them participate in it
through a harmonization of their actions and movements, which
are thus "attuned" to the higher harmony reflected and micro-
cosmized in the music to which they dance as well as in the
dance itself (for, Mulcaster reminds us, dance is an imitation of
musical harmony as well as celestial);[89] and it presents to the
audience the pleasing spectacle of noble persons imitating, in
an ordered motion which is worthy of admiration, that higher
order of virtuous concord which it is the nobility's duty to reflect
and everyone's obligation to admire and imitate. A dance was
not inevitably read in this fashion; Elyot complains that too
few seek for virtue and wisdom in their recreations.[90] The possibility, however, was there. And the dance was joined to the idea
of virtuous harmony with sufficient philosophical literalism to
allow Jonson to introduce into *Cynthia's Revels* the following
exchange between Arete (Virtue) and Crites (Judge):

AR.   CRITES, you must prouide strait for a masque,
        'Tis CYNTHIAS pleasure,
CR.   How, bright ARETE!
        Why, 'twere a labour more for HERCVLES.
        Better, and sooner durst I vnder-take
        To make the different seasons of the yeere,
        The windes, or elements to sympathize,

> Then their vnmeasurable vanitie
> Dance truely in a measure. They agree?
> What though all concord's borne of contraries?
> So many follies will confusion proue,
> And like a sort of jarring instruments,
> All out of tune: because (indeede) we see
> There is not that analogie, 'twixt discords,
> As betweene things but meerely opposite.[91]

The examples given earlier in this chapter amply illustrate Jonson's use of the dance as a visual metaphor complementary to the poetry and therefore extending its instructive force; it will suffice here to add examples of the way in which Jonson used other instructive possibilities of the dance. The simplest level, on which the physical grace of the dance is to express an internal grace, is reflected in *Oberon,* where the masquers are directed to dance "figures, to expresse / The grace of him [Oberon],"[92] or in *Pleasure Reconciled to Virtue,* where the spectator is "instructed to y^t height⟨n⟩ing sence / of dignitie, and reuerence, / in your true motions found."[93] Dance as a winner of love is a common theme in Jonson's masques,[94] and has a potential social-political significance, since the dancers are of the nobility. *Love Restored* contains a striking use of the dance as an image of virtuous harmony which bears quoting in full:

> See, here are ten,
> The spirits of Court, and flower of men,
> Led on by me [Cupid], with flam'd intents,
> To figure the ten ornaments,
> That do each courtly presence grace.
> Nor will they rudely striue for place,
> One to precede the other; but,
> As *musique* them in forme shall put,
> So will they keep their measures true,
> And make still their proportions new,
> Till all become one *harmonie,*
> Of *honor,* and of *courtesie,*
> True *valure,* and *vrbanitie.*

Of *confidence, alacritie,*
Of *promptnesse,* and of *industrie,*
Habilitie, Realitie.
Nor shall those graces euer quit your Court:
Or I be wanting to supply their sport.[95]

The penultimate line is literal in two ways: not only shall the virtues listed remain in the members of the court, but also the "graces" who dance them, the ten courtier masquers, shall continue to live in court, to be bearers and examples of virtue, and to image in their workings together that virtuous harmony now figured by their dance—and Cupid, Love, will always go with such conditions. As such, this dance functions not only as an inspiration to the spectator to admire and imitate, but also to the masquers themselves to live up to the condition which they are describing in dance—to do in soul what they have learned to do using the body as a metaphor; or, as Jonson puts it in *Hymenaei,* "And as, in *circle,* you depart / Link'd *hand in hand;* So, *heart in heart,* / May all those *bodies* still remayne."[96]

As examples of an intellectually more complex use of dance as an inspirational or enlightening image, I have already considered the allegorical dance in *Hymenaei* which Jonson himself glossed thoroughly,[97] and that in *Love's Triumph,* where the dancers, as perfect lovers ranged in the "circle of the will," turn their attention to the centre of the circle, where stands the King personifying Heroic Love.[98] The latter dance can be read as an expression of the relationship of loves to Heroic Love, of loves to the King, of courtiers to Heroic Love, or of courtiers to the King, and Jonson does not exclude any of these readings—rather he seems to be encouraging them all. A more difficult example is found in the *Masque of Augurs,* where the augured secrets are revealed in dance, perhaps in such a way that the audience could read them with or without a guiding program,[99] and perhaps in a way decipherable only by the augurs themselves, who explain them to the audience;[100] but at any rate, it is a dance in which enlightenment is said to reside. Another difficult example occurs in *Pleasure Reconciled to Virtue*, where, guided by Dedalus and his "sacred harmony," the masquers dance the "laborinth of love" and "laborinth of Beauty," weaving a "curious knot" as they dance:

> Then, as all actions of mankind
>   are but a Laborinth, or maze,
>   so let your Daunces be entwin'd,
>   yet not perplex men, vnto gaze.
> But measur'd, and so numerous too,
>   as men may read each act you doo.
> And when they see ye Graces meet,
>   admire ye wisdom of your feet.[101]

The wisdom and enlightenment which the observer is to find in these labyrinths become much more clear when one has examined more of the ideas with which Jonson deals repeatedly in his masques; but it is sufficient here to observe that this is another example of the familiar use of the dance: an allegory of the way in which knowing and virtuous men follow pleasure in the complexity of human action without compromising their virtue, and in pursuit of good.

It is certainly clear that, in general, Jonson expected his audiences to be aware of what the dance is, what it imitates and images, and how it can teach. Such an awareness, it may be suggested, can be exploited even without explicit reference: an art laden with such associations releases them into the poetic stream when the context makes them pertinent. And when the context deals with love, with virtue, with order; when the participants are gods and muses and virtues and heroes; when the progress of the scene moves through a disrupting and disordering antimasque to a restorative vision of harmony, then a dance in such a context could scarcely fail to exist in the perception of the audience as an image of harmony, and perhaps even as a compelling allegory of the proper concord of courtier-masquers in their courtly occupations. We cannot tell how much automatic response Jonson relied upon from his audience. But we know that these associations were available to its members, and that Jonson often evokes and uses them; and through them, he gives the audience, and the masquers as well, a glimpse into a higher harmony, and a deeper wisdom:

> For Dauncing is an exercise
>   not only shews y^e mouers wit,
> but maketh y^e beholder wise,
>   as he hath powre to rise to it.[102]

Chapter V · Light

Ben Jonson once celebrated Cynthia as "Goddesse, excellently bright," and presumably even the dullest of the audience at *Cynthia's Revels* detected something more than astronomical fact in this lovely line. But what exactly the line means is difficult to say, because it does not have a simple independent meaning —it is a symbolic summation of all the excellencies attributed directly or indirectly to Cynthia: her beauty, chastity, majesty, virtue, and all other qualities by which she makes "a day of night."

The epithet "bright" is a convenient and frequent device in English poetry, and is found repeatedly in Jonson's masques. The symbolism of light upon which it draws has been a more continuous tradition than that of music or dance, and is therefore more immediately accessible; but it is also a more amorphous tradition. All the languages of Europe associate light with understanding and knowledge, and all their philosophies and literatures employ the symbolism of light in the representation of goodness, beauty, truth, excellence, life.

One might therefore expect that Jonson might use light metaphorically in the masques to represent almost any kind of perfection or value, and this is in fact the case. Beauty shines in an eternal day,[1] love brings the world to light,[2] and reason has a "bright and numerous flame";[3] there is a valor which is "wont to giue / Light to the world,"[4] and both honor and fame are bright;[5] marriage so perfects a bride as to make her bright as Hesperus,[6] virtue herself "in darknes shines. / 'tis she yᵗ still hirself refines, / by hir owne light, to euerie eye"[7]—and of course even the minor sorts of heavenly powers have faces bright enough to dazzle mortals.[8]

There is nothing novel about such a poetical use of light. To this extent, Jonson is merely exploiting a conventional opportunity and employing the metaphor of light as a convenient, if highly indefinite, kind of eulogy. But although convention permitted him to settle for disconnected occasional drafts on the metaphorical treasury, Jonson was happily a more systematic investor, frequently organizing his light-imagery in a consistent and fairly intricate way to enhance the movement and meaning of the masques. The first instance is the first masque.

The central conceit of the *Masque of Blackness* is that the daughters of Niger, the masquers, are beautiful despite their blackness. The opening song celebrates their father, the river Niger,

> With all his beautious race:
> Who, though but blacke in face,
> Yet, are they bright,
> And full of life, and light.[9]

Black beauty is a paradox which Niger defends by arguing that blackness is a sign of the "feruent'st loue" of the sun for the Aethiopes—and Niger also points out that the sun is "the best iudge. . . . Of all dames beauties," and since its fervent shining on the daughters of Niger suggests a special devotion, it must be that "in their black, the perfectst beauty growes."[10] The Daughters of Niger are not satisfied with this sophistry and cannot be satisfied with their blackness. But Jonson does not find it necessary to abandon the metaphor of light—he merely extends it. The black ladies are visited by a face "all circumfus'd with light" and told to seek out a land where the sun which blackened them

> doth neuer rise, or set,
> But in his Iourney passeth by,
> And leaues that *Clymat* of the sky,
> To comfort of a greater *Light,*
> Who formes all beauty, with his sight.[11]

Their search is unsuccessful, until the moon appears and with her "pure, auspicious light greetes vs": since the Ethiopians have long adored her "generall brightnesse," Niger begs her to show them the blessed land for which they are searching. She reveals that she was that "bright face" who first gave the command, and that they are now arrived in the place where the Daughters of Niger can be beautified—Britania, "Rul'd by a *Sunne,* that to this height doth grace it: / Whose beames shine day, and night, and are of force / To blanch an *Æthiope.*"

> Inuite them, boldly, to the shore,
> Their beauties shall be scorch'd no more:
> This *sunne* is temperate, and refines
> All things, on which his radiance shines.[12]

They are given final instructions to bathe, in the light of the moon, with rosmarine and that foam "Whereof bright Venus" was born, and then to dry themselves "in the beames of yond' bright *Sunne,*" whose "light scientiall is, and (past mere nature) / Can salue the rude defects of euery creature."[13]

The symbolism of light is thus quite consistent on the poetic level. It is an attribute of the sun as judge and cause of beauty, of the consequent beauty of the Daughters of Niger, of the moon as the goddess Diana-Ethiopia, and of the King as a greater and more temperate sun. That is, light is here made expressive of the characteristic excellence celebrated in the masquers, the two chief powers which govern them, and the power to which they are ultimately referred in order to achieve an even greater perfection. Light goes hand in hand with the structure of the fable on which the masque is formed.

And there is still another dimension of appropriateness beyond the internal coherence of the plot. The link, for instance, between the light of the sun and the brightness of beauty may appear arbitrary on the surface of the lines which establish it:

> he (the best iudge, and most formall cause
> Of all dames beauties) in their firme hiewes, drawes
> Signes of his feruent'st loue; and thereby shewes
> That, in their black, the perfectst beauty growes.[14]

But it is not arbitrary: it is an exploitation of the philosophical reflections on light, prominent in the Neoplatonic thinkers, which considered light the formal cause of beauty on the grounds that its intervention is required for beauty to be grasped at all. "For light," Patritio insists in Annibale Romei's *Courtiers Academie,*

is the greatest of all beauties sensible, as that which is no other but a beame & influence of diuine essence, dispersed ouer the w[h]ole world (as I haue said) this being graunted to the most perfect, of all bodies sensible, which is the sun, to the end that by it, it might not only be beautifullest of all other creatures, but that it should also bee the meane and principal cause, of the apparance of all other beauties.[15]

If the sun is cause of beauty, it is judge of beauty as well; poetical conceit need not stretch very far to contrive the rest of Niger's argument about blackness and beauty.

There is still another link revealed in the quotation from *The Courtiers Academie*. If light is "no other but a beame & influence of diuine essence" then the light of the divine moon, Diana-Æthiopia, is congruent with the light of the sun—Jonson attributes to the moon her own divine light rather than having her borrow it from the sun—and this in turn not only justifies the attribution of light to James once he is represented as a sun, but even justifies that representation itself: for a King too is "a beame & influence of diuine essence," and his quasi-divinity can be expressed as a kind of light. Note the properties of the King's light. Like the light of the sun, it is a cause of beauty; its beams

> shine day, and night, and are of force
> To blanch an *Æthiope,* and reuiue a *Cor's*.
> His light scientiall is, and (past mere nature)
> Can salue the rude defects of euery creature.[16]

This is almost distressingly extravagant, but there is a germ of propriety in it. The power of the King is constantly present in his kingdom, shining day and night. His favor does make a difference: those on whom it shines may meet a gracious reception far beyond the desert of their defective natures, and may be beautified with the honors which James bestowed so freely. He can, by virtue of his office, cure victims of the King's Evil. Further, the virtuous King is a paradigm for his kingdom, and by his example draws the thralls of vice into virtue, a regeneration which may be compared to reviving the dead or whitening the black. I do not mean to suggest, of course, that the passage cited above is an allegorical statement of precisely these ideas. The commonplaces of kingship which I list are merely parts of the body of standard received ideas which made the symbolic statement intelligible to Jonson's court audience. That audience did not have to translate, for the passage would have appeared to them not as an outrageous compliment which can be theoretically justified, but as a symbolic representation appropriate to any king considered in the ideal quality of his office. The representation of the King as a sun is one of the oldest commonplaces of poetry. By a carefully controlled use of the poetry of light, Jonson here manages to breathe new life into it and even to make it illuminating.

Jonson shows comparable ingenuity in applying the symbolism of light to other themes as well. In the *Haddington Masque,* light is put at the service of love and marriage. Venus begins the masque with a search for Cupid, who has lately been seen in that same place "with diuers of his brethren, lending light / From their best flames, to guild a glorious night"[17]—alluding to the loves in the *Masque of Beauty* who had lighted the beauties of that masque just a month previously. Cupid appears, calling his companion loves to "Aduance your light" because "This same night / Is *Cupid's* day."[18] Venus is concerned that her son may be up to no good; but he refers her to Hymen ("He can giue you farther light") and slips away, telling his companions that they may remain "Till I call, to light the *Bride.*"[19] Hymen then chides Venus for abandoning her star on such a night, "Which should be crown'd with your most chearing sight."[20] As Venus looks upon the chair of state and "What Crowne there shines," Hymen speaks the praises of James and of the bridegroom; and Venus forgives Cupid for his absence for such an honorable purpose. Now Hymen informs her that Vulcan is preparing "Some strange, and curious peece, t⟨o⟩'-adorne the night, / And giue these graced *Nuptials* greater light," which gift Vulcan then presents to Venus "To grace the chaster triumph of her *sonne.*" Venus responds:

> And for this gift, will I to heauen returne,
> And vowe, for euer, that my lampe shall burne
> With pure and chas⟨t⟩est fire; or neuer shine,
> But when it mixeth with thy *spheare,* and mine.[21]

And the masque concludes with the singing of an epithalamion which claims that Hymen's "hallowed *rites* / Could neuer boast of brighter lights," with the refrain "Shine, *Hesperus,* shine forth, thou wished *starre.*"[22]

Here light is consistently a function of love and marriage. It belongs to Cupid in his chaste office of love between the prospective bride and groom, to Venus as goddess of their love, to Hymen as god of their marriage, to James as the new Æneas under Venus' favor, and to Vulcan (as Jonson's note explains) as *"Præses luminis:"* "the god of *fire,* and *light.* Sometime taken for the purest *beame:* and by *Orph. in Hym.* celebrated for the *Sunne* and *Moone.*"[23]

Vulcan's gift is to "giue these graced *Nuptials* greater light." It does so not only in its representation of the "Zodiac of Marriage," the perfections which are to form the marriage here being celebrated; but also in that the gift itself is a marital gift, presented by Vulcan to his wife as a token of love, and in that Venus' response is to return to heaven to shed her benign influence on the marriage in an ideal marital way—for she vows to shine only in conjunction with her husband's sphere, which literally implies that this marriage will be faithful and figuratively implies that it will be fruitful.[24] Again, light is used as a structural correlative, being used as the brightness of love made brightest in marriage and consistently attributed to the characteristic excellence celebrated in the masque and to the powers which govern that excellence.

The *Barriers* of *Hymenaei* uses symbolic light to resolve the central conflict, the contention between Truth, who salutes the light through the mist, and Opinion, made by "the black sorceresse *night*" out of "these drie, and empty fumes."[25] The contention is finally resolved after an angel of light introduces Truth in triumph, claiming that "Eternall *Vnitie* behind her shines," and the brightness of Truth undoes the charms of misty opinion.[26] The *Masque of Queens* solves an analogous contention between Fame and Anti-Fame by the use of light. The hags who personate "the opposites to good *Fame,*" offended by "these bright Nights / of Honor," attempt to "blast the light" with charms; but at the appearance of Heroic Virtue and the bright

House of Fame, they "fly the light," leaving the scene to the "bright Beuie" of famous Queens who form the masque and to James, "that light, from whence [the Queen's] truth of spirit / Confesseth all the lustre of her Merit."[27] *Prince Henry's Barriers* celebrates the renascence of the old light of British chivalry, once glorious under Arthur (who has been made a star) but since fallen into decay until the coming of James, who outshines Arthur and revives the glories "brighter farre, then when our *Arthur* liu'd." James's bright fortune, Merlin prophesies, will grow brighter, and his princely son is instructed to "Looke on this throne, and in his temper view / The light of all that must haue grace in you"[28] *Love Freed From Ignorance* creates still another kind of inspiration out of the poetry of light. Love, threatened by the Sphynx of Ignorance, must solve an obscure riddle in order to win from the "prison of the night" the bright beauties whom he is leading to the palace of Phoebus. His own wit is inadequate to solve the riddle, but when the Muses' Priests advise him to "looke / In the brightest face here shining, / And the same, as would a booke, / Shall helpe thee in diuining,"[29] he looks upon the face of the King and is inspired with the right answer. Love's light and the brightness of the beauties he guides are thus saved; they dance in honor of love and in the bright presence of "that glorious starre, / For whose loue you came so farre," and the mutual attraction of Love, Beauty, and the divine Sun-King shines out to banish all trace of ignorance, folly, and night.

These examples are far from exhaustive, but they do indicate the versatility of Jonson's poetic use of light as expressive of excellence and perfection of various kinds. This versatility permitted Jonson to organize the poetry of light in a complex fashion conformable to the structure of the masque in general, thereby enhancing and unifying the main components. Where the masques are threatened, the threat is usually cast in terms of an opposition between light and darkness.

The metaphorical light is often used to represent the virtue and glory and excellence of the King. This too is a traditional practice: *"Kings, Rulers* and *Magistrates,* and others eminent in *Charge,* are called *lights,* as hauing relation to *supreme light."*[30] In Jonson's masques, its value and effectiveness as a poetic strategy are particularly great; in the poetry of the masques the symbolic properties of light introduce an oblique and almost hypothetical quality into eulogies which might well be ludicrous if applied directly to a king like James. When Jonson celebrates the light of excellence which streams from the King, even when it is represented as James's own light and not that of The-King-as-Phoebus or The-King-as-Neptune, its symbolic value communicates to the king a role which fits within the framework of the masque, thereby endowing him with an idealness which reduces the chance of shipwrecking the fable upon unaccommodating realities. What the masque says, through the metaphorical light, is that this power (or personal excellence or magnificence or majesty or whatever) is ideally one of the concomitant qualities of kingship, and with the masque's discovery of this quality in the office of the English king, the matter is appropriately concluded. Some of the masques become precariously personal in their praise of the king, but none of them quite breaks the veil of the ideal world, in which such eulogies are unquestionably deserved. When transfigured by Majesty, personal weaknesses are largely irrelevant. The words of Edward Forsett serve well as a summary of Jonson's attitude in dealing with the royal light:

when the person of a Prince is looked vpon (wheron we doe seldome gaze enough) our inward cogitations filled with a reuerence of the regall maiestie seated in that flesh (otherwise as infirme and full of imperfections as other is) ought to surmount all sensuall conceits (scant thinking of any humane nature) but making an infinit difference betweene that body, so (as it were) glorified with the presence, representation & in dwelling of that supreme or exalted eminencie, and other ordinarie persons, which yet doeth consist materially of the same substance, and perhaps endued by nature with equall graces. Doe you desire a brighter displaying of the illustrious maiestie shining in soueraigntie? doe but obserue how much it surmounteth the person it selfe thereof possessed, like a brittle glasse all illightened with the glorious blaze of the Sunne.[31]

And if there always remains a hint and an innuendo on the less ideal level of "sensuall conceits," this too works to the advantage of the masque as a serious mirror of men's lives: if the King's splendor is not visible, there is a failing either in the King or in the beholder—and it needs to be mended. If the King's virtues do not shine out, let him take note; but if the subject cannot see that light of majesty by which the masques symbolize the mystery of sovereignty, demanding devoted allegiance and reverent homage, then let him mend his defective eye. It is the literal world which is on trial here, not that of the masque; and if the masque finds both real and ideal excellence as visible as light and as beautiful, the literal world must judge itself and perhaps revise its values and habits of response.

This may appear to be setting an outrageous weight upon a metaphor, though I think the weight of evidence suggests that Jonson could expect his courtly audience to follow the intricacies of his poetic light and realize these implications in it. At any rate, the pure metaphor of light will bear a heavy burden before collapsing, perhaps even as much as I have here assigned to it; and that is all I wish to establish with respect to the metaphor by itself, because it is not in this case the last court of appeal. Jonson's masques do not leave the metaphor unassisted. They constantly reinforce it by the use of visible light, and the complex signification of light which is at least accessible in the poetry of the masque is thereby almost inescapable in the performance.

Thus, when the humors and affections who perform the anti-masque in *Hymenaei* have disturbed the wedding there in progress, Hymen turns to the globe (or microcosm) whence they had emerged and begs help through the metaphor of light:

> If there be
> A Power, like *Reason,* left in that huge Bodie,
> Or little *world of Man,* from whence these came,
> Looke forth, and with thy bright and numerous flame
> Instruct their darknesse, make them know, and see,
> In wronging these, they haue rebell'd 'gainst thee,

and Reason descends to put things right, bearing a lamp and a bright sword, and "crowned with lights."[32] Visually, her instructing flame is obvious and dazzling, her power and supremacy self-evident; the rebellious humors and affections submit promptly and retire "amazed" to the sides of the stage. The "pure, auspicious light" whose brightness the daughters of Niger adore in the *Masque of Blackness* is revealed with equal glory to the audience when Aethiopia makes her initial appearance on a silver throne "crown'd with a *Luminarie,* or *Sphaere* of light."[33] The loves who were in the *Masque of Beauty* "lending light / From their best flames, to guild a glorious night" did this literally as well as figuratively;[34] and the Venus who so describes them in the *Haddington Masque* visibly executes her vow to shine her benevolent influence on the bride and groom, for as the epithalmion reiterates the refrain "Shine, *Hesperus,* shine forth, thou wished *starre,*" Venus sits above the scene in her chariot, crowned with her "flaming" star.[35] Arthur, stellified for his virtue in *Prince Henry's Barriers,* appears in the scene "as a starre aboue"[36] to shed his influence and light on the court. In the barriers of *Hymenaei,* Truth is visually presented on the scene just as the Angel has described her:

> Vpon her head she weares a crowne of starres
>
> .   .   .   .
>
> And you may see her heart shine through her brest.
> Her right hand holds a *sunne* with burning rayes,
> Her left a curious bunch of golden kayes,
> With which *heauen* gates she locketh, and displayes.
>
> .   .   .   .
>
> And squint-eyd *slander,* with *vaine-glory* backt,

> Her bright eyes burne to dust: in which shines fate.
> An *angell* vshers her triumphant gate,
> Whilst with her fingers fans of starres shee twists,
> And with them beates backe *Error,* clad in mists.
> Eternall *Vnitie* behind her shines....[37]

And after the brightness of Truth has undone the charms of false Opinion, we see her transferring her splendid attributes symbolically to the King,

> To whose right *sacred highnesse* I resigne
> Low, at his feet, this *starrie crowne* of mine,
> To shew, his rule, and iudgement is diuine;
> .   .   .   .   and these *rayes,*
> To shew his piercing splendor; these bright *keyes,*
> Designing power to ope the ported skyes,
> And speake their glories to his subiects eyes.
>   Lastly, this *heart,* with which all hearts be true:
>   And *Truth* in him make *treason* euer rue.[38]

The symbolic splendor of kingship has rarely been made more visible than this.

In addition to these special effects, which vary from masque to masque, there were two standard features of lighting whose symbolic possibilities Jonson repeatedly exploited in the composition of his masques,[39] or, to place the priority where Jonson would have preferred, which he repeatedly used to reinforce the metaphorical use of light in the masque's poetry.

The first is the appearance of the hall itself, which was illuminated with an unusual and striking intensity for the performance of a masque. Jonson frequently gives the brightness of the hall a symbolic value. The hags of Anti-Fame in the *Masque of Queens* are resentful that "these bright Nights / Of Honor blaze, thus, to offend oʳ eyes."[40] In *Prince Henry's Barriers,* the gleam of the hall is the splendor of revived glory and valor, outshining even Arthur.[41] In *Love Freed* it is an expression of beauty, "For where such *Beautie* shines, is euer day,"[42] and in *The Golden Age Restored* "This, this, and onely such as this, / The bright

Astraea's region is."[43] Most frequently, the brightness of the hall is tied symbolically to "the Maiesty of this light,"[44] the King, "whose eyes doe dart *Promethean* fire / throughout this all."[45] In *Love's Triumph*, he is told that the hall is "by the splendor of your rayes made bright,"[46] and in *Love Restored* the hall is illuminated "by the vertue of this Maiestie, who proiecteth so powerfull beames of light."[47] *Oberon* is lighted by the moon reflecting "a greater light" than usual—the King.[48] And in *News from the New World,* the brilliance of the hall is amazing and dazzling, and is a function, as the Herald informs James, "of the pietie, wisedome, Majesty reflected by you . . . from the Divine light, to which onely you are lesse."[49] Jonson's frequent characterization of James as a sun is in part a means of giving a symbolic value to the light in which the masque was performed, and the presence of that light in turn helps to justify that characterization.

The second recurring feature is a massing of light around the figures who form the dramatic core, the main-masquers, at their first revelation. So constant and important is this feature of the masques that Jonson apparently has a technical term for it, allowing him to give the laconic marginal note in *The Golden Age Restored:* "The Scene of light discouered."[50]

The appreciation of the "scene of light," and of the lighting of the hall as well, requires at least a little effort. Just as the changed intellectual ambience makes it difficult for us to understand the metaphorical powers of music and dance in Jonson's day, so the triumph of electricity impedes our proper appreciation of the impact of the scene of light in a Jonson masque; the Venetian ambassador who wrote about the *Masque of Beauty* that "the abundance and beauty of the lights [was] immense,"[51] singled out a particularly impressive feature of the entertainment.

Jonson seems to have beeen impressed as well. Although ordinarily tending to begrudge any praise merited by the designers and builders of the scenes, he often gives some favorable notice to the scene of light: "a glorious beame" illuminated the masquers in the *Masque of Blackness*;[52] the *Masque of Beauty* had "a Mine of light";[53] "an illustrious *Concaue*, fill'd with an ample and glistering light" adorned the *Haddington Masque*;[54] "all store of light" circles the masquers' throne in the *Masque of Queens*,[55] while the central scene of the *Masque of Oberon* is "a bright and glorious Palace,"[56] and that of *Mercury Vindicated* "a glorious boure."[57] Such descriptions are not burning with enthusiasm, but they do seem to imply that as far as Jonson was concerned, the scene of light was a striking effect. And considering the nocturnal setting of the masques and the apparent care with which light was used, the scene of light must have been remarkably beautiful, and effective.

Effective: as the patient reader knows by now, this word is intended to carry more than aesthetic meaning. By now, it should be amply clear that (to make only the minimum claims) Jonson was decidedly interested in the philosophical and ethical significance of his masques, and that he was a sufficiently careful craftsman not to have missed the opportunity of capitalizing on the possibilities of the particularly striking scene of light. A look at the masques will reveal that the scene of light is generally used to intensify and epitomize what Jonson considered the "soul" of their meaning.

An analogous phenomenon occurred in continental art near the beginning of the seventeenth century, and I think the comparison valid and revealing. Religious subjects which had been painted in a relatively naturalistic manner were reorganized to emphasize the awesome and transcendant qualities of the scene. In the early sixteenth century, the Annunciation, for instance, was regularly rendered with only two figures in the scene, Mary and the angel Gabriel, both firmly planted on the floor and provided with only natural illumination. By the end of the century, the angel hovers in the air, bathed in a light of supernatural glory (and often accompanied by other members of the heavenly host, breaking splendid through the clouds), and beams his message upon the woman below. A comparable change took place in the representation of the Nativity. And alongside these alterations grew yet another kind of subject: the ecstatic vision, in which a glorified figure, wreathed in clouds and streaming with light, confronts a blessed mortal below, who receives the sight in a posture of wonder. Whatever the particular causes may have been for this minor revolution in art history,[58] the motives seem clear enough: the more naturalistic treatment of these religious subjects had deprived them of some of the glory and mystery which rightly belonged to them by theological standards. A greater glorification of the heavenly powers, by means of a dramatically exaggerated use of light, permitted the restoration of mystery and transcendence in the representation, in a way designed to amaze and awe the beholder in giving him an imitative glimpse of the splendor of heaven and the miracle of its communication to earth. It is in this spirit that Jonson used the scene of light to glorify the masquers under the aegis of the gods.

The main-masquers are usually first presented in a scene of light. I have remarked earlier upon the relationship between the masquers and the superior powers whom they serve. This relationship, in which the masquers are usually portrayed as deriving their order and excellence through their subordination to the higher powers, is emblematically represented in the scene of light.

In some cases the masquers appear in the scene of light along with the gods, and in visually evident close subordination to them; in other cases the higher powers appear first, disclose their relationship to the masquers, and command their revelation in the scene of light; and sometimes the gods are presented in the heavens above the scene in their own scene of light, from which they shine down their blessing on the masquers.

In *The Golden Age Restored,* for instance, Pallas, having banished the antimasque and having called Astraea and the Golden Age back to earth, wakes the poets and instructs them to aid her in recalling to earth the heroes of virtue who will be able to sustain the new Golden Age: these virtuous men, who are, of course, the masquers, are revealed when Pallas "throwes a lightning from her shield,"[59] at which the masquers appear in the scene of light. The dramatic subordination echoes a philosophical one—virtue is a product of wisdom—and the glory of the scene of light and consequently of the masquers as the virtuous "semigods" is dramatically rendered the gift of the gods, and the emblem of virtue. The revelation of the scene of light in the *Masque of Beauty* is even more visually emblematic, and is preceded by a description which establishes and clarifies its significance: the goddess Hecate has freed the masquers from the night's power and has brightened them: they now sit upon a throne of Beauty,

> and are, like Heauen, whirl'd
> About the Earth; whil'st, to them contrarie,
> (Following those nobler torches of the Skie)
> A world of little *Loues,* and chast *Desires,*
> Doe light their beauties, with still mouing fires.
> And who to *Heauens* consent can better moue,
> Then those that are so like it, *Beautie* and *Loue?*[60]

The scene is revealed as described, while the poetry of the masque continues to reinforce the point that the beauty of the masquers must be understood in terms of the transcendent light of that celestial power of love represented by the torch-bearing Cupids:

> When *Loue,* at first, did mooue
> From out of *Chaos,* brightened
> So was the world, and lightened,
> As now![61]

Hymenaei presents an even plainer case: the masquers are the powers of Juno and are seated by the throne of Juno when the scene of light is revealed, while Jupiter ("figuring the *heauen*"[62]) reigns above. As the audience beholds this scene,

Reason provides a gloss which identifies the masquers and underlines the obvious implications of the visual allegory: the splendor of the scene is the splendor of Jupiter and Juno, and the
brightness of the masquers derives from their participation in
these higher powers, and is to be communicated from them to
the bride and groom.

In like manner, the "bright Beuie" of masquers in the *Masque
of Queens* appear on a throne along with Heroic Virtue, who
then descends to introduce them, making it clear that the brightness of the scene derives ultimately from him, as their fame is
the result of their virtue.[63] In *Time Vindicated,* Saturn has prom-
ised Venus to free "certaine glories of the Time" from "yond
darkness," and with Saturn's words "Looke, have you seene such
lights as these?"[64] the masque is epitomized with the discovery
of the masquers—the bright gift of providence to James's court,
made on behalf of Love. The gods' gift in the scene of light is
sometimes made in conjunction with their representative—and
incarnation—the King. In *Neptune's Triumph,* Apollo appears
in the heavens to proclaim the triumph as the masquers are discovered, representing "all the Heau'ns consent"; but the light
of the triumph itself belongs more specifically to another representative of heaven, King James as Neptune:

> I! now the Pompe of *Neptunes* triumph shines!
> And all the glories of his great designes
> Are read, reflected, in his sonnes returne![65]

Love Restored discovers the masquers, as "The spirits of
Court," guarding the chariot of Love and thus subordinated to
him; but although Love has a light of his own, it shines now
only because the light of the King has intervened to rescue him
from the dark clutches of Mammon:[66] the bright masquers are
thus divine Love's gift to the King. The King occasionally stands
alone as the divine source of the masquers' glory in the scene of
light. In *Pan's Anniversary* the "Fountaine of light" in which
the masquers are discovered as they prepare their homage to

Pan is said to be a distant version of his brightness, as their harmonious Arcadian commonwealth is an imitation of his great
order of nature;[67] and the scene of light in *News from the New
World* shines on the devoted masquers from the King, who reflects the divine light.[68]

All these examples reveal Jonson's consistent exploitation of
the brilliant and beautiful scene of light, which is one of the
highest moments of the masque, to emphasize the excellence of
the masquers (or of the figures they personify) and the powers
which reign over them and to remind us that this excellence is
first the property of those powers and secondarily the property
of the masquers, by participation. The scene of light is itself
beautiful and Jonson treats its beauty as a more removed mystery of excellence, thereby impressing upon the beholders the
splendor of the perfections which it signifies. Through the
visible light of the masque and through the poetic image of light
which defines and sustains its implications, the masques not
only allege but demonstrate that one becomes splendid by relating oneself properly with the powers of heaven, with nature,
with virtue, with wisdom, with love, with the divinely instituted
and perfecting order of the king. And through the light thus
acquired, men may, as the masquers do, resemble the heavens
whose order they imitate, and become, like the masquers,
"lights,"[69] "planets,"[70] and "stars,"[71] "to burne / On earth, / For
others good."[72] For "*Good men,*" as Jonson says in *Discoveries,*
"are the Stars, the Planets of the Ages wherein they live, and
illustrate [i.e., brighten] the times."[73] In the masques, this illustration is a literal one, and its metaphorical sense is therein af-
firmed and strengthened. For as Jonson observes, "if wee will
looke with our understanding, and not our senses, wee may
behold vertue, and beauty, . . . in their brightnesse":[74] in the
masques, he makes the eye of sense see with the eye of understanding; the brightness of virtue and beauty is beheld, and its
sources known.

Chapter VI · Beauty and Love

Love, the Christians have always maintained, is from the beginning; for God is Love, and the Third Person of the Trinity is pre-eminently so. And Beauty, the Platonists and Neoplatonists assert, is an aspect of the Ultimate, the Idea of Ideas. The marriage of love and beauty is one of Platonism's first gifts to Christian theology, and it is hardly surprising to find in the work of even so hard-headed a philosopher as Thomas Aquinas that Beauty is one of the transcendentals, coextensive with Being, and a fitting title for the Second Person of the Trinity. Renaissance thought gave a place of even greater importance to the related concepts of beauty and love. The Italian Neoplatonic movement elevated them to the main cosmic principles and offered to all Europe a new foundation for philosophy and theology:

All we see is a perpetuall circle of God to the world, and of the World to God; This circle beginning in God by inestimable perfections, full of charmes, and attractiues, is properly called Bewty: & when it comes to extend it-selfe in the world, and to draw to it-selfe, it is called loue.... So loue is a circle, which turnes from good to good by an euerlasting reuolution.[1]

Few writers, however, succeeded in applying these ideas systematically to a detailed philosophy, and Platonism did not succeed in becoming for the Renaissance the kind of general philosophical foundation that Aristotelianism had been for the late Middle Ages. Instead, the original Platonizing of Marsilio Ficino and Leone Ebreo was popularized in fragmentary form by the flood of sixteenth-century Italian *trattati d'amore* and by the discussions which they engendered. Neoplatonism became essentially a new spiritualized view of love, considerably more attractive (and flattering) than the more harshly moral view with which it competed, and in that form it became extremely popular among European courtiers. It is by that path that it reached England. Few Englishmen read Leone and Ficino, or even Pico della Mirandola, let alone Plato himself; many more read Thomas Hoby's translation of Castiglione's *The Courtyer* (1561) with its brief but suggestive discussion of love in the fourth book, and learned there what attitudes were stylish as well as "Very necessary and profitable for yonge Gentilmen and Gentilwomen abiding in Court."[2] Others went to Italy and read *trattati d'amore* and heard discussions like the one represented in *The Courtyer*. English writers copied the Platonizing poetry of Europe from

Petrarch on, and invented more on the same themes. By the time Spenser wrote the *Fowre Hymnes,* Neoplatonic thought in England was fashionable and far from rigorous, and consequently the specific sources of Spenser's ideas about love and beauty cannot be identified. Some of them are undoubtedly several times removed from the Florentine Academy.[3] By the time Ben Jonson wrote his first masques, he could assume that general Neoplatonic notions were widely diffused in the English court. This is not the sort of advantage he would ignore. His audience knew that where love fixes its attention, there is beauty; and that where there is beauty, love cannot but respond.[4] Between these two propositions, there is room for many a masque.

"It was for *Beauty,* that the World was made" says a song in the *Masque of Beauty,* to which Jonson appends a note: "An agreeing opinion, both with *Diuines* and *Philosophers,* that the great *Artificer* in loue with his owne *Idaea,* did, therefore, frame the world."[5] This beauty, inherent in the divine idea, was then expressed—as well as the material allowed—in the artifact, the universe. This too is standard Neoplatonism,[6] and is echoed in another song from the *Masque of Beauty,* a song occasioned by a pause after an intricate dance:

> So beauty on the waters stood,
> When *loue* had seuer'd earth, from flood!
> So when he parted ayre, from fire,
> He did with concord all inspire!
> And then a *motion* he them taught . . .[7]

The harmony of the stars, of the elements, of the universe in general is, then, the offspring of love and beauty, ordered by the divine Mind in "the *worlds soule, true harmony.*"[8] This is a doctrine of central importance in the patterns of thought that lie behind the masques, because in it is the great paradigm of all the versions of order with which they constantly deal. Behind the figure of Truth in the Barriers of *Hymenaei* shines "Eternall Vnitie,"[9] bringing all things into that state of harmony on which their truth depends. And to the Neoplatonic initiate, an alternative name for both the ultimate unity and the harmonies which participate in it, in whatever form they may appear, is *Beauty*.

One of the problems of Renaissance Neoplatonic thought was the way in which the beauty of the body was related to the higher beauty of the soul. Analogously, one of the occasional embarrassments of Neoplatonic poetry was the relationship between beauty and goodness. Where the two are present together, it is charming to be able to suggest that they are intimately bound together by nature—Jonson alludes to three common explanations of such conjunctions in his dedication of the *Masque of Queens* to Prince Henry.[10] But the extreme forms in which such doctrines were often proposed by Neoplatonic poets are clearly silly. What is pretty is not necessarily what is excellent, but many a poem awkwardly insists that the two are inseparable and that to praise one's mistress' loveliness is to say the conclusive word on the subject of her character. "For all that faire is, is by nature good,"[11] wrote Spenser, perhaps thinking of Castiglione's justifying argument: ". . . beawtie commeth of God, and is like a circle, the goodnesse whereof is the Centre. And therefore, as there can be no circle without a centre, no more can beawty be without goodnesse."[12] They both hedge, perforce. Spenser goes on to explain that a beautiful person may sin, but that this is the fault of the person, not of beauty—as if that solved the problem. Castiglione goes on to say, "Whervpon doeth verie sildome an ill soule dwell in a beawtifull bodye," without bothering to explain how, given his theoretical explanation, it can ever happen at all. Jonson gets out of the difficulty in *Love Freed* by taking the logical step of qualifying the first principle: "How neere to good is what is faire!"

Proximity is more easily defended than identity. Jonson's song proceeds to develop an argument which, if a bit more sensible than those of Spenser and Castiglione, is no less Neoplatonic: beauty causes love, and that love in turn moves the lover toward a state of goodness:

> How neere to good is what is faire!
> > Which we no sooner see,
> But with the lines, and outward aire
> > Our senses taken be.
> We wish to see it still, and proue,
> > What waies wee may deserue,
> We court, we praise, we more then loue.
> > We are not grieu'd to serue.[13]

"For shame frightens men away from evil deeds," says Ficino, "and the desire of being superior summons them to good deeds. Nothing lays these two before men more sharply and clearly than Love."[14] The same process of self-improvement can be inspired by one's own beauty as well as that of another, which Castiglione also points out[15] as another instance demonstrating the close affinity of the beautiful and the good. Socrates, according to an anecdote often repeated in the Renaissance,

> would very often aduise his Schollers and followers, to make a continuall vse of looking themselues in a glass, to the end, that he who perceaued his shape to be comly and well beautified, might thereby learne to shunne all turpitude in manners, which would much deforme and blemish so goodly an appearance.[16]

Beauty is near to goodness because, for one thing, it tends to inspire it. That, of course, is still only part of the matter. Beauty's relationship to goodness is seen to be far more intimate once we distinguish between higher and lower forms of beauty. The highest human beauty is more than physical, which is one of the more obvious points behind the two Florimells in the *Faerie Queene*. Just as true love is differentiated from false love by the rule of reason in the lover, holding his love in harmony, so true beauty is differentiated from false beauty by "the mindes inward vertues & more splendant graces" which Socrates' less lovely pupils were moved by the mirror to acquire as a compensation.[17] True beauty, that is, is the beauty worthy of true and reasonable love and, therefore, as an earlier English Platonist suggested, is possessed only by one who has achieved goodness in "forme of lyuinge, countenaunce, and gesture: which ioyned all to gether maketh one hole and perfecte harmonie, which sendeth in to the hartes of the beholders and herers a voluptie or feruent dilectation."[18]

It is with this higher beauty that Jonson's masques are primarily concerned, and his emphasis reminds the audience that he is paying the Queen the higher kind of compliment in *Love's Triumph* when he has Euphemus address her as

> The top of beauty! but of such an ayre,
> As, onely by the minds eye, may bee seene
> Your enter-wouen lines of good, and fayre![19]

Likewise, in the *Masque of Beauty*, after one song expresses the fear that the many Cupids and the many beautiful women in the scene might do some amorous damage to the hearts of the gentlemen beholders, another song denies the danger on the grounds that these are loves and beauties of the higher sort:

> Yes, were the *Loues* or false, or straying;
> Or *beauties* not their beautie waighing:
> But here, no such deceipt is mix'd,
> Their flames are pure, their eyes are fix'd:
> They doe not warre, with different darts,
> But strike a musique of like harts.[20]

"Or *beauties* not their beautie waighing"—for their kind of beauty is an office of high order, demanding an exercise of *noblesse oblige:* the "Elements of Beauty," as depicted upon the "Throne of Beauty" on which these masquers and their Cupids entered the scene, are climaxed with Dignity, Perfection, Harmony. This is, as Jonson says, a vision of chaster loves and "a more diuine beautie."[21] And when such powers meet, the conclusion is harmony—"a musique of like harts"—for just as this higher beauty "grows out of goodness, so it leads those who love it to the good."[22] Jonson writes to a beauty in *Epigrammes* that Cupid, "finding so much beautie met with vertue, / ... hath not onely gain'd himselfe his eyes, / But, in your loue, made all his seruants wise":[23] love of true beauty moves to goodness, and there are found "like harts," wisdom, and harmony, "And who to Heauens consent can better moue, / Then those that are so like it, *Beautie* and *Loue?*"[24]

Are Cupid's arrows then perpetually banished from the world of the masque? Hardly. Sheer practicality alone would suffice to keep them in. Marriages were often the occasion of masques in the sixteenth century and continued to be so in the seventeenth; Jonson remarks in the introduction to the *Haddington Masque* that "The worthy custome of honouring worthy *marriages,* with these noble *solemnities,* hath, of late yeeres, aduanc'd it selfe frequently with vs."[25] On such an occasion, Jonson could hardly pretend that the bride and groom were meeting on the level of statesmanlike good will.

In the "Citty of *Beauty* or *Goodnes*" in which *Love's Triumph* is set, it seems, indeed, as if Cupid is outlawed—at least that Cupid "which they fayne, *caecum cupidine,* or *petulantem*" as Jonson distinguishes him in the *Masque of Beauty;*[26] for, as in the *Masque of Beauty,* the Cupids who appear in *Love's Triumph* are "a world of chast desires, / Which may produce a harmony of parts."[27] The "deprau'd Louers" who form the antimasque in *Love's Triumph* are the victims of the other Cupid, "their whole life being a continew'd *vertigo,* or rather a torture on the wheele of *Loue,* then any motion eyther of order or measure,"[28] and they are accordingly banished from this ideal city of Love and Beauty.

This is a sort of Last Judgment of love, however, and does not necessarily exclude a Redemption; and Jonson does, in *Lovers Made Men,* provide for a redemption which does not have to exile even the lesser Cupid, although finding it necessary to tame him.

The framework of the whole dramatic movement of *Lovers Made Men* is implicit from the beginning of the masque: the scene opens with a triumphal arch, auspicious of a victorious conclusion for the figure who sits reigning over it, Humanity, who scatters flowers and holds a golden chain, "to shew both the freedome, and the bond of Courtesie."[29] The emblematic figures of Cheerfulness and Readiness on the sides of the arch complete the allegorical presentation of that state of graceful virtue which is the perfection of courtly love.

It is within this frame that the "ghosts" of men,

> Drown'd by love,
> That drew them forth with hopes as smooth as were
> Th'unfaithfull waters he desir'd 'hem prove,[30]

appear in silent and slow procession, guided by Mercury into the realm of shades. They are the victims of the tyrannous Cupid of the sonnets. But the Fates insist that their death is not real, and Mercury causes them to drink from Lethe that their true forms may be restored to them. After dancing an antimasque expressive of their love-wrecked state, they depart, to reappear restored and reformed within the sacred grove of myrtles at the back of the scene. Thence they emerge in dance, expressive of their new order, to hold as 'twere a mirror up to others,

> And warne a world,
> That now are hoorld
> About in tempest, how they prove
> Shadowes for *Love*.[31]

Thus far the allegory is clear: men blasted by love can, through "wit" (for this Mercury is essentially the same as that of the *Balet Comique*), overcome the effects of love and be restored to their fuller order and perfection, in which they become examples "For others good."[32] The point is more completely made when Cupid appears, claiming their service again: Mercury protects them with his caduceus, as in the *Balet Comique*, and the order shown in their subsequent dance testifies that they are proof against that distemper of love which has previously produced the disorder of their antimasque. Cupid challenges them, saying that the reign of Mercury is not enough, that "They doe, indeed, like dead men move, / That thinke they live, and not in love!"[33] They then dance with the ladies; but the discipline of that dance as well seems intended to show the continuity of ordered love, for Cupid protests the hegemony of Mercury again and offers to surrender his weapons rather than be banished. Yet this is not enough: Mercury recognizes the value of love but insists that it be governed by his rule, and accordingly makes Cupid swear "Never to force them act to doo, / But what he will call HERMES too."[34] Cupid thanks Mercury, and the chorus rejoices that the lovers have the good fortune to remain lovers, but under the governance of wit. Cupid is controlled, but not banished.

But there are even conditions under which Cupid can be allowed to retain his weapons without endangering harmony. One of the favorite Renaissance conceits is the production of harmonious results from discordant sounds; and Cupid is allowed to participate in this paradox when the influence of the benevolent powers so governs a relationship of love as to make the cupidinous contribution a factor in the total harmony of love. This happens, of course, only in marriage; and it is the theme of one of Jonson's lovely wedding-masques, the *Haddington Masque.*

The opening set of the *Haddington Masque* is a grand emblem of the reign of love in the noble marriage here celebrated: a "high, steepe, red cliffe" which was to represent not only the family of the bride, Elizabeth Radcliffe, but also "a note of *height, greatnesse,* and *antiquitie.*"[35] Before the cliffe stand "two *pilasters,* chardg'd with spoiles and *trophees,* of *loue,* and his *mother,* consecrate to *marriage,*" the elements of the decor effecting the symbolic meaning: "old and yong persons figur'd, bound with *roses,* the wedding garments, rocks, and spindles, hearts transfixt with arrowes, others flaming, *virgins* girdles, gyrlonds, and worlds of such like."[36] And overhead, as an arch, are the figures of Triumph and Victory, holding a garland of myrtle. This much is fairly obvious: it remains for the masque to demonstrate what is meant by such a triumph of love.

Now, emphasized—and, to some extent, characterized—by a "solemne musique," the celestial Venus appears adorned with a star, drawn in "a triumphant chariot" by doves and swans and accompanied by the three Graces. This is plainly an emblematic expression of the highest love, in contrast with that love which "hates none like to Reason,"[37] the disordered love represented by the Cupid whom Venus has come to seek, the love suffered by the victims in *Lovers Made Men*. It soon appears that this triumph of love belongs in fact to Cupid rather than to the celestial Venus, for Cupid appears on the scene accompanied by a dozen "anticks" and claims that this affair is his work. His claim is shortly confirmed by Hymen, who informs Venus about the marriage at hand. But Cupid's is not necessarily the last word; Venus retains her controlling influence and is accordingly chided by Hymen for leaving "your starre, / Without your influence" "and, on such a night, / Which should be crown'd with your most chearing sight."[38] Venus then hears the praises of the bride and groom, promising to aid the latter as she did Aeneas, views with approval Vulcan's magnificent contribution to the feast, and returns to the heavens vowing "that my lampe shall burne / With pure and chas⟨t⟩est fire," under the auspices of Hymen, for ever—for this is, as Vulcan observes, not a victory for the disordering power of Cupid, but his "chaster triumph."[39]

For Cupid is subsumed under an order more complete than he alone can provide. The heavens themselves will protect this marriage. Venus will shed her influence and protection as the Venus of marriage, conjunct with Vulcan; and their union is itself an allegory, for Jonson's declaration that he is here employing Vulcan to symbolize, among other things, "*calor naturae*"[40] universalizes the marriage of Vulcan and Venus to the union of love with the natural heat through which procreation is made possible. Under these stars, Cupid's contribution is made a positive one. For the tricks of his twelve anticks and the stings of his arrows are disciplined and brought into a

greater order through the perfection which these universal forces
achieve in marriage; and this is the significance of the "heaven
of marriage" which Vulcan has made. It is "In due proportion
to the *spheare* of heauen, ... the perfect'st forme" and carries like
the heavens its own zodiac, in this case consisting of the "twelue
sacred powers, / That are praesiding at all *nuptiall* howers,"[41]
fertility, mutuality, youth and beauty, strength and manliness.
These forces are to work in harmony and bring the marital
state into a perfection of order like that of the stars themselves.
And just as Venus vows to reign always as Vulcan's loyal spouse,
so Vulcan considers his "heaven of marriage" a successful creation "if it but please my wife, / And she commend it, to the
labor'd worth."[42] And thus through the universal harmony expressed in Venus and Vulcan, the harmony of marriage expressed by Vulcan's sphere and zodiac descends upon the marriage here celebrated. Within that zodiac there is room even for
the "*iarres,* / And *stings* in wedlock; little *strifes,* and *warres,*"[43]
because there are other forces which remove their effects and
retain harmonious love. There is room for Cupid and his train,
because the governance of Venus with Vulcan gives effective
force to the influence of this heaven of marriage; and it is this
truth which is acted out at the end as the zodiac-masquers dance
their various dances "full of elegancy, and curious deuice"[44] to
a music interspersed with verses of an epithalamion, sung by
Hymen's priests, with the refrain: "Shine, HESPERVS, shine
forth, thou wished *starre.*"[45] For the nature and harmony of
things is such that there is a place for every phase and kind of
love, if it is brought into the framework of true order. Cupid
may be blind still; whether or not he is interested in chastity,
his is a "chaster triumph" when heaven and earth cooperate to
that end.

The subject of love is not exhausted in the story of Cupid's
fortunes, of course. To confine the matter to the restraint and
discipline of love would be to misunderstand and cheapen love's
position in the order of things. Love is, to the Neoplatonists, the

primary force by which the cosmos is organized, and for the human sphere to be a proper mirror of the divine, prescription is as important as proscription; apathy where there should be love is as serious an obstacle to harmony as a love disordered. *Lovers Made Men* establishes a sort of social love between masculine and feminine courtiers, a nonexclusive love built upon respect and upon the virtues represented in the emblematic arch with which the masque begins—Cheerfulness, Readiness, "freedome, and the bond of Courtesie," all subsumed under the reign of Humanity. *Love Restored* deals with love as a courtly virtue also, but in a more universal manner, embracing a much wider variety of acts and relationships in which love properly should be in control. This is, in fact, the main dramatic movement of the masque: to restore to Love's control those offices which rightfully belong to him but which are now governed by Plutus, who has frozen Cupid into helplessness and now fraudulently impersonates him:

> that Impostor PLVTVS, the god of *money,* who ha's stolne LOVE'S ensignes; and in his belyed figure, raignes [i'] the world, making friendships, contracts, mariages, and almost religion; begetting, breeding, and holding the neerest respects of mankind; and vsurping all those offices in this Age of gold, which LOVE himselfe perform'd in the golden age.[46]

Love here is not the same Cupid encountered in the previous discussion, of course; yet in another sense, he is. He is the Cupid of proper love, which under varying circumstances is the *eros* of marriage, the *philia* of friendship, the *agape* of piety, and, in fact, the universal force that must be expressed in every sphere according to its nature, in order to hold the whole in harmony.[47]

Love Restored deals primarily with the operation of love within the sphere of the court. When Love is restored and appears, his chariot is guarded by masquers who are styled "The spirits of Court, and flower of men" and who represent "the ten ornaments, / That do each courtly presence grace."[48] Their

dance is an image of love's harmonious power in general, but
most particularly of the harmony of courtly virtues and of men
in a court governed by love:

> Nor will they rudely striue for place,
> One to precede the other; but,
> As *musique* them in forme shall put,
> So will they keep their measures true,
> And make still their proportions new,
> Till all become one *harmonie,*
> Of *honor,* and of *courtesie,*
> True *valure,* and *vrbanitie,*
> Of *confidence, alacritie,*
> Of *promptnesse,* and of *industrie,*
> *Habilitie, Realitie.*
> Nor shall those graces euer quit your Court....[49]

And herein is displayed, for the dancer-courtiers and the spec-
tator-courtiers alike, a metaphorical image of the ideally harmonious court, so that they might see and understand the beauty
of it.

It is not simply to each other than the courtiers are related in
this dance, however; as the last line quoted above indicates, the
song—and the courtly virtues cited in it—is directed to the king,
who is the true center of the court and gives it the final perfection of order. Love lay frozen as this masque opened, and we
are told how he is to escape his bondage: "the vertue of this
Maiestie, who proiecteth so powerfull beames of light and heat
through this Hemisphere, [shall] thaw his icie fetters, and scatter the darknesse that obscures him."[50] The restitution of the
proper place of love in the world derives from the king's having
awakened love. Love of the king is the main axis of proper love
in human affairs.

It is a startlingly hyperbolic conceit; but the really astonishing thing is that Jonson was apparently serious. Both his seriousness and the justification for it can be seen in the following passage in *Discoveries:*

After God, nothing is to be lov'd of man like the Prince: he violates nature, that doth it not with his whole heart. For when hee hath put on the care of the publike good, and common safety; I am a wretch, and put of[f] man, if I doe not reverence, and honour him: in whose charge all things *divine* and *humane* are plac'd.[51]

One must love the king or one violates nature. For the understanding of the position of the king in Jonson's masques, this is a matter of supreme importance. The king is not to be loved as an expedient for insuring political stability, but because, given his position, it is *in the nature of things* that he should be loved, and loved second only to God. In Jonson's repeated insistence in his masques upon love of the king, he does not always give the right reason, but it must not be forgotten that those failings are not instances of fraud or hypocrisy, whatever other charges may be laid upon them: Jonson genuinely believed that the achievement of the true and valid order which is virtuous life involves such a love for the king. When his masques argue poetically that we ought to love the king, and when they build an attempt to move us to love the king, we may freely question their success—but we may not doubt that their purposes are serious ones.

It is this consideration that saves from sheer absurdity the argument of *Love Freed from Ignorance,* in which

these Ladies [the masquers] being the perfect issue of Beautie, and of all worldly grace, were carried by *Loue* to celebrate the Maiestie, and wisdome of the King, figur'd in the Sunne, and seated in these extreme parts of the world; where they were rudely receiued by Ignorance [in the form of a riddling sphynx], on their first approach, to the hazard of their affection, it being her nature to hinder all noble actions.[52]

Love is baffled by the sphinx's riddle, and Jonson observes that "This shewes, that *Loues* expositions are not alway serious, till it be diuinely instructed; and that sometimes it may be in the danger of Ignorance and Folly, who are the mother, and issue:

for no folly but is borne of ignorance."[53] But before Ignorance can carry out her threat to destroy Love, the Muses' priests appear, sent to save him. Jonson again spells out the allegory:

Here is vnderstood the power of wisdome in the *Muses* ministers, by which name al that haue the spirit of prophesie are stil'd, and such they are that need to encounter Ignorance, and Folly: and are euer readie to assist *Loue* in any action of honor, and vertue, and inspire him with their owne soule.[54]

It is *Cynthia's Revels* and *Lovers Made Men* all over again—but with a difference. Jonson says in another place that "Loue is the right affection of the minde, / The noble appetite of what is best,"[55] and it is to find out the meaning of that *right* and *best* that the imposters in *Cynthia's Revels* are sent to Helicon and that Cupid is made in *Lovers Made Men* to recognize the sovereignty of Mercury. By the same token, we could perhaps expect the Muses through their priests to disabuse Love of his error and give him the answer that will save him from the sphinx's claws: but instead, the priests tell Love that

> they bid, that thou should'st looke
> In the brightest face here shining,
> And the same, as would a booke,
> Shall helpe thee in diuining.[56]

And, gazing into the face of the king, Love suddenly hits upon the solution. The king is here, as Jonson has explained, representing the sun—and that in turn is obviously a metaphor for something further: "*Loues* expositions are not alway serious, till it be *diuinely* instructed." One of the most overworked commonplaces of the Renaissance is the correspondence between the king on one hand and the sun and God on the other, and it is a commonplace with firm roots in classical antiquity.[57] Here the king is Phoebus—sun and God in one—and Love's discovery of the proper answer by beholding him is not simply due to the fact that he is part of that answer. It is his divine power as sun-god, which is the illumination attending right order. When Love turns to the King, it participates in that order of all things by virtue of which the king resembles God and is his earthly representative; and in this order lies the truth which conquers all folly.

In conclusion, let us turn to what is perhaps Jonson's most complex and difficult masque, *Hymenaei,* performed at the Essex-Howard wedding in 1606. Being occasioned by a wedding, it deals with the subject of marriage, but it treats this subject as a member and an image of more universal forms of order and harmony. This masque has been very thoroughly and capably dealt with in a long article by Professor D. J. Gordon[58] in which the reader may find detailed accounts of the roots and sources of the masque's elements, leading back inevitably to the mythographical handbooks and to Neoplatonic thought. As is suggested by the title of Professor Gordon's article, *Hymenaei* takes as its pivotal element the concept of *union,* through which he analogizes and unites the various themes touched in the course of the masque—marriage, the proper order in the soul, the kingdom, the universe. The force of union is identified with the celestial powers: the altar consecrated to Union with which the masque opens is made deliberately similar to an ancient altar dedicated to Juno,[59] and the two are later identified[60] through the Unio-Iuno anagram. The Juno of *Hymenaei* is, of course, not the pseudo-Homeric irascible Juno of the *Aeneid* but rather the pseudo-Homeric transcendental Juno of the Neoplatonizing mythographers.

The masque opens with a Roman marriage ritual, presided over by Hymen. Hymen's first speech glorifies James and his marriage under the theme of union, and then continues, saying that this "*king,* and *priest of peace*" knows

> how well it [union] binds
> The fighting *seedes of things,*
> Winnes *natures, sexes, minds,*
> And eu'rie discord in true musique brings.[61]

This "union" is that universal force described by Orpheus, Empedocles, and Natalis Comes, under the name of Love.

There then follows a bit of allegorical action. The model of a Roman wedding which is proceeding under the direction of Hymen is suddenly interrupted by eight dancers (symbolizing the four affections and the four humors) who emerge from a microcosm (i.e., man) to the accompaniment of "a kind of contentious Musique" and surround the altar, swords in hand. Hymen calls upon Reason, who descends from the top of the microcosm and puts the riotous humors and affections in order, explaining to them the symbolic value of the articles used in the Roman marriage. The personal allegory is, as Jonson claims, obvious: these eight rebels are "brought in, before *Marriage,* as disturbers of that *mysticall bodie,* and the *rites,* which were *soule* vnto it; that afterwards, in *Marriage,* being dutifully tempered by her *power,* they might more fully celebrate the happinesse of such as liue in that sweet *vnion,* to the harmonious lawes of Nature and Reason."[62] The other aspect of the allegory is not so obvious, and I shall return to it presently.

At this point, Reason having re-established order in the microcosm, the glorious Juno descends from heaven, accompanied by personifications of her powers as goddess of marriage, elaborately glossed and authenticated by Jonson's notes. Reason's servant, Order, arranges them according to Reason's instructions while Reason identifies them and their gifts to marriage. Again, the allegory is lucid: when Reason has established order, the divine influence and favor descend to bless marriage with the perfections possible to it.

And now they dance, while a song declares their harmony of motion to be an image of Union, and end with hands linked, which Reason compares to the Great Chain of Being. Here again is the triumph of the metaphorical power of song and dance, as Reason cries

> all is *peace,* and *loue,* and *faith,* and *blisse:*
> What *harmony* like this?[63]

But this harmony is not confined to the allegory of marriage. What is true of the microcosm is true also for the macrocosm. This again is not merely to say that the universe too retains a harmony, or that Venus and Vulcan shape the heavens to the same form worn by the ideal pattern of earth. There are intermediates as well. I have already noted that the allegory of the four affections and four humors has a second aspect, beyond that of the individual person: it is in the state. Jonson's note at that point, after speaking of the application of the allegory to *"naturall bodies . . .* likewise in *minds"* goes on to say

after the same maner, in *politick bodies* (where *Order, Ceremony, State, Reuerence, Deuotion,* are parts of the *Mind*) by the difference, or praedominant will of what we (*metaphorically*) call *Humors,* and *Affections,* all things are troubled and confused.[64]

And they are restored in like manner. At the conclusion of the last dance, the dancers fall into a circle around Reason, who praises their assumption of this "perfect'st *figure"* and asserts that the circle is here no accident but rather the logical result of their having retained Reason as their "guide, and *center."* Reason then, in his final speech, bids them pay homage to James as they depart, keeping all the while this perfect form which they have achieved through his guidance:

Now moue vnited, and, in gate,
As you (in paires) doe front the *state,*
With gratefull *honors,* thanke his *grace*
That hath so glorified the place:
And as, in *circle,* you depart
Link'd *hand in hand;* So, *heart in heart,*
May all those *bodies* still remayne
Whom he (with so much sacred payne)
No lesse hath bound within his realmes
Then they are with the OCEANS streames.
Long may his VNION find increase
As he, to ours, hath deign'd his peace.[65]

This is, as Professor Gordon has suggested, intended for ears other than those of the bride and groom. The theme of union, of love, here becomes one of central importance for the entire audience; and the masque is to show them not only how to achieve the harmony of reason's rule within themselves but also how to relate themselves to their King and to each other through the forces of union, of love. Essex is not the only one whose marriage is involved: it is also a matter of the marriage of England and Scotland, and of the king's marriage not only to his wife but to his kingdom. Professor Gordon has demonstrated that these specific issues are a part of the material of this masque, and that Jonson was attempting to create an image of proper solidarity in face of criticism arising over the union of Scotland and England, and over James's official styling of himself as husband to the realm. In short, this masque too brings its messages and metaphors to bear on a matter of more than frivolous import, and attempts to incarnate an image of union, of harmony, in which man, marriage, state, and universe are united in true order, to which the heavens let fall their blessings. The *Barriers,* held on the subsequent night, repeats the theme of the marriage of the kingdom:

> ... one *king*, that doth inspire
> *Soule*, to all *bodies*, in this royall spheare ...
> Is there a band more strict, then that doth tie
> The *soule*, and *body* in such vnity?
> *Subiects* to *soueraignes*?[66]

But the splendor of the spectacle and of the music, the artistic organization of the poems and dances, the marriage of thought and senses through the literal rendering to James of the symbolic "Order, Ceremony, State, Reuerence, Deuotion" must have made the effect of the masque something greater than that of the barriers. The truths which the masque embodied probably had at least the general assent of the audience; but in the masque they became, if not compellingly self-evident, yet beautiful—and therefore, worthy of being loved.

Chapter VII · Virtue and Fame

There are very few standards by which any legitimate line of demarcation can be drawn between "Middle Ages" and "Renaissance"; the attitudes toward fame and glory might provide one of them. Medieval theology tended to look upon mundane glorification as a species of false pride, and it is probably no accident that the few portraits which have descended to us from that period normally represent the portrayed in a subordinate act of reverence toward the Christ or saint who forms the real subject of the picture—a kind of votive candle, perpetuating a prayer, and not an attempt to catch a characteristic independence in the manner of Titian or Holbein. The great buildings of the Middle Ages were dedicated to the glory of God and his saints in an attitude quite foreign to the advice given by the gentlemen of Gray's Inn to their queen in 1594:

in one Point my Lords [the previous speakers] have well agreed; that they both, according to their several Intentions, counselled your Excellency to win Fame, and to eternize your Name; . . . But the plain and approved Way that is safe, and yet proportionable to the Greatness of a Monarch, to present himself to Posterity . . . is the Magnificence of goodly and Royal Buildings and Foundations.[1]

How many medieval analogues could be found to that ubiquitous and ultimately hackneyed promise of Renaissance poets to eternize the fame of their subjects in their verses? Certainly Churchyard's praise of Spillman in 1588, that he "seems, as yet, to care for naught but fame,"[2] would have counted as pure libel three hundred years previously.

I.

The "serious" literature of glory in the Middle Ages was hagiographic, by and large, although existing side by side with the romances which dealt in another variety of glory. Neither species died in the Renaissance, as Foxe and Spenser eloquently show; but romances came under heavy attack from Renaissance humanists for their unedifying pre-Spenserian characteristics, and the miracle-strewn hagiography of the *Golden Legend* was more useful for devotion than for the development of a way of life. This made a difference to the serious thinkers of the Renaissance, for fame and glory have two edges and it is pertinent to distinguish them. Alexander's lament that there was no one to sing Homer to his Achilles was for the sake of his own reputation, which was to him an adequate end in itself: no one could lose but he if that reputation were neglected. But, as Ben Jonson could read in his copy of Rosinus' *Roman Antiquities,* the Roman Senate some time later exiled Fulvius for the offense of rejecting the honor of a triumph which the Senate offered him. This penalty was inflicted, according to Rosinus, for the sake of those who, by Fulvius' refusal, would be cheated out of an inspiring example which could inflame them with a desire for virtue, a desire to imitate the excellencies honored triumphantly in the person of Fulvius.[3] Fame can be a sop to vanity, but it can also be an ethical instrument. This latter view of fame was transformed in the Middle Ages, not obliterated: the glory of the saints was to inspire the pious to a burning desire for grace and the approval of God. Such an independent figure as Pico della Mirandola still found the "wytnes of martyrs and example of saintes" (in the words of Thomas More's translation)[4] to be one of the "twelve weapons of spiritual battle" for the man of the Renaissance. This Christian transfiguration of the ancient attitude toward glory remained alive; but the Renaissance also resurrected as its complement a more authentic version of the attitude of the ancients, and thus found a legitimate glory in the achievement of more exclusively human and mundane perfections.

In the Christian heart of the Renaissance, these two versions of glory were in harmony: antiquity reveals the perfection of man in himself, while the Christian dispensation reveals the possibility of the full completion of that perfection in a higher order. When Sir Thomas Elyot wrote for his sister a treatise on *The Education or bringinge vp of children* (ca. 1535), he did it by translating advice from Plutarch, and Diogenes Laertius served him for the major part of his *Of the knowledg whiche maketh a wise man* (1533), because in the ancients he found the clearest formulation of that doctrine of self-knowledge and virtue which forms the most stable and satisfactory foundation for the perfect Christian life. "This is the course of most absolute wisedom," says Vives in Richard Morisine's early sixteenth-century translation of the *Introduction to Wisedome,* "whereof the first steppe is, to knowe thy self, and the last of all to know God";[5] in the precepts of the ancients we learn to know ourselves and to perfect ourselves in the accomplishments of the first step of true virtue, for one of the chief fruits of the study of the ancient writers is the discovery, as Morisine says, of "thinges of great weight, thinges very necessarie for the quiet and honest leading of mans life, things worthy to be of all men imbraced: worthy to be set, fixed, and engrafted in all mens hertes."[6] The end of wisdom is "rooting the loue & desire of vertue in your hert," and the study of the ancients is an excellent way toward this goal; but there is nothing, not even study, which is quite so effective as good example for making men desire these perfections, as Fulvius' judges knew: and therefore, "Trew glorie, is to be well spoken of for vertues sake."[7]

Religion was often taken for granted by Renaissance writers, and their attention to pagan authors and to virtue rather than grace usually assumes that the reader will realize that he is not being offered an alternative to Christianity but rather a foundation of human excellence and perfection on which their religion might build. This foundation was of an importance second only to religion itself, and in some ways its construction was a more difficult task than the establishment of piety; and thus it needed, in order to be realized, attention, study, and inspiring exemplars. The first two were the task of the revolution in education; the last was the job of a new—and ancient—approach to fame and glory.

The worst of psychologists through the ages have not been fooled about the importance of good example for ethical development, and the notorious pronouncements by Plato on the subject of gods' reputations in the writings of poets echo a typical concern in antiquity for the right kind of fame. Good example works only when it is distinguishable in value from bad example, and fame does not automatically make that distinction, because it does not consistently reflect responsible standards of worth. To be sure, this is a more sophisticated version of fame and worthiness than the Greeks found in their first tutor, Homer, in whose heroic world *areté* or virtue is not always distinguishable from reputation itself. But by Plato's day, it was well understood that the two are separable, and that it was desirable to be careful about the kinds of exemplars whose imitation fame would encourage. Socrates and Plato tried to establish a reasoned approach whereby good repute would be based upon the subject's knowledgeable virtue, but theirs was a losing battle: reason carried a lesser impact than great deeds greatly told, and it was not Plato but Homer that Alexander had always with him —and it was Homer, not Plato, whose version of fame Alexander coveted.

Alexander had his way. It is for his Achillean qualities that he is remembered today, not for his Socratic ones. But if this is taken for granted now, it was not so in the Renaissance. While the Medieval *de casibus* version of history lingered on in the sixteenth century there grew alongside it a less tendentious historical attitude—or at least a more flexible one—which helped re-create a concern for the classical problem of fame: for if we study history for its political applicability, our analysis of it must sort out the good and pertinent precedents from the harmful ones, and we may not further with impunity the renown of heroes whose example would be unfortunate to follow. Sir Thomas Blundeville, in *The true order and Methode of wryting and reading Hystories* (1574), recommends that all persons who are fit examples of virtue and vice should be chronicled, and that in order to keep the lines clear, the writer of history should compromise his scholarly completeness to the extent of reporting not *all* the actions of worthy men but only *worthy* actions, for one of the three reasons for history is to encourage virtue and discourage vice.[8] Under such scrutiny as this, Alexander's standing often suffered setbacks. The compendious ethical allegory by Bartolommeo Delbene, *Civitas Veri*, discovers the great conqueror not in a place of honor but befogged in one of the valleys of vice, and the Dutch humanist Marcile, in a commentary, agrees that this is the most fitting place for such a man as he.[9] The same thing was happening in England. Thomas Rogers asserts in 1576 that "all ambitious *Alexanders* . . . are more to bee abhorred for their poisoned behauior, then any viper,"[10] and in *Fennes Fruites,* published in 1590, Lady Fame repudiates Alexander as an example of "the vnsatiable appetite of aspiring minds."[11]

It is quite significant that they even bothered with a readjustment of Alexander's reputation. A great man whose error in the direction of audacity and ambition disqualifies him as an exemplar—this is the verdict of Delbene and Marcile and Rogers and Fenne on Alexander the Great, who paid too much attention to his Homer and too little to his tutor, Aristotle. Fame is a matter for serious concern.

Renaissance humanism regarded fame as a definite value, and was at pains to insure that it was neither bestowed upon the unworthy nor neglected in the worthy. Obviously, unworthy people continued to become and to remain famous, but the idea of fame as a function of true worth became well established: Churchyard's "seems, as yet, to care for naught but fame" is clearly shorthand for "seems to care for naught but to deserve fame," a shorthand made possible by the intervention of humanistic revaluation of fame, which in turn depends upon the humanistic attention to the more complete and more satisfactory mirrors for human self-knowledge which they found in the writings of the ancients and which they hoped would make full human perfection more universally attainable. Fame and perfection, reputation and worthiness, were to remain problematic to the Renaissance, never to be solved or resolved. Churchyard's shorthand is made intelligible by the humanists, but not justifiable, since there were always too many ways of obtaining fame without deserving it. Spillman himself, Churchyard's hero, was being celebrated for founding a paper mill.

Renaissance writers never tired of pointing out that the Temple of Fame in ancient Rome was accessible only through the adjacent Temple of Virtue. One of the tasks, doomed from the outset, of the Renaissance propagandist and didacticist was to convince people that the fame which is built upon virtue is the true fame, that no other fame is worthy of the name, and that it was a laudable and excellent thing to be desirous of it. Spenser is one splendid example, with his devoted concentration upon glory in the *Faerie Queene,* standing at once for an ideal earthly renown and its mirror image in heavenly glory. A second example of the poet's serious attention to this matter is the masques of Ben Jonson.

It is hardly necessary at this point to demonstrate that the subject of virtue appears with reliable regularity in Jonson's masques: commendations of virtue seem there to be almost as much *de rigueur* as in dedications of Renaissance books. Throughout the masques can be found dozens of examples of the familiar pattern in which the King (or Queen or Prince) is held up as a paragon of virtue, fit for all men's imitation, a pattern usually emphasized by some allegorical turn of action in the masque itself. This in itself is plainly a species of fame, although its most ephemeral form. Jonson was, of course, well aware of this, and supplied by publication of the masques not only a remedy for their ephemerality but an enhancement of their possibilities as conductors of fame. In the preface to his first masque, the *Masque of Blackness,* he wrote:

The honor, and splendor of these *spectacles* was such in the performance, as could those houres haue lasted, this of mine, now, had been a most vnprofitable worke. But (when it is the fate, euen of the greatest, and most absolute births, to need, and borrow a life of posteritie) little had beene done to the studie of *magnificence* in these, if presently with the rage of the people, who (as a part of greatnesse) are priuiledged by custome, to deface their *carkasses,* the *spirits* had also perished. In dutie, therefore, to that *Maiestie,* who gaue them their authoritie and grace; and, no lesse then the most royall of predecessors, deserues eminent celebration for these solemnities: I adde this later hand, to redeeme them as well from Ignorance, as Enuie, two common euills, the one of *censure,* the other of *obliuion.*[12]

By publication, Jonson gives to the present and to posterity a monument to the Queen's magnificence, as well as a memorial to her "grace." It must be remembered that the publication of a masque was a fairly new thing, and that Jonson is perhaps the first in England to claim any serious value for such transitory entertainments. The claim he makes in his preface for the transmission to posterity of the Queen's excellence through the publication of masques, is a bold claim under the circumstances. And his argument for publishing is that her virtue deserves to be famous, and therefore this emblem of it merits preservation.

Jonson would never have claimed that she needed his help to be famous, and could never have applied to the King or Queen or Prince the general formula proclaimed in the late masque *Chloridia:* "Vertue it selfe by *Fame* is oft protected, / And dies despised ... Where the *Fame's* neglected."[13] But the reason that this formula is awkward to apply to royalty is that it is tactless, not that it is irrelevant. Fame can be considered simply as the enlargement and perpetuation of the memory of someone, and in that sense the fame of the royal family was rather well assured. But the obviously more important sense of the term has to do with the *way* in which one is remembered; and from this point of view it is important for the promotion of virtue not only to perpetuate the memories of the right people, but also to have them remembered for the right reasons. In the conception of the role of fame which Jonson shared with other men of the Renaissance, fame itself was not a worthy thing, unless it was fame based upon virtue. And that applied to kings as well.

Jonson's ideas on fame and virtue are fortunately gathered into his masque on that subject, the *Masque of Queens,* and it is there that they become most clear, although as I shall show presently they appear in nearly all the masques.

Jonson tells us in the preface to the *Masque of Queens,* that when he cast about for a subject worthy of the performers, "I chose the Argument, to be, *A Celebration of honorable, & true Fame, bred out of Vertue:* obseruing that rule of the best *Artist,* to suffer no obiect of delight to passe w'hout his mixture of profit, & example."[14] At the Queen's request, he devised the action so that a "false-*Masque*" would precede the main action, and integrated the two parts by inventing what was to be a standard feature of subsequent masques: the antimasque, in this case a grotesquerie of twelve hags, "sustayning the persons of *Ignorance, Suspicion, Credulity,* &c. the opposites to good *Fame.*"[15] It is against this foil that the masquers were to appear, and against the grotesque gestures and "hollow and infernall musique" of the antimasque that the grace and harmony of the main-masque were to have their setting—an obvious application of the principle that virtue is, as Jonson says elsewhere, "more seene, more knowne, when Vice stands by."[16] Again, the encumbrance of the Queen's whim is turned to profitable account.

The *Masque of Queens* begins with the hags gathered for an orgy of Anti-Fame rites, hoping to drown *"Fame, & Glory"* in their envy: "Let not these bright Nights / Of Honor blaze, thus, to offend oᴿ eyes," pleads one of the witches,

> I hate to see these fruicts of a soft peace,
> And curse the piety giues it such increase.
> Let vs disturbe it, then; and blast the light;
> Mixe Hell, wᵗh Heauen; and make *Nature* fight
> Wᵗhin her selfe; loose the whole henge of Things;
> And cause the Endes runne back into theyᴿ Springs.[17]

Notice the implications of this last speech: the "bright night of honor" which the masque is to present is the fruit of peace and piety, and is linked with light, with nature's order, with heaven. The enemies of fame are the enemies of all these blessings.

Fittingly, it is by a blast of music that the witches are driven from the scene—a music figuring "FAMES loud sound"—while a "glorious and magnificent Building" (the House of Fame) appears, revealing the masquers on a throne "circled w^{t}h all store of light."[18] Heroic Virtue then delivers a long speech, saying that at the sight of virtue and the sound of fame the enemies of light are overwhelmed; that Fame is the daughter of Heroic Virtue, who is her "Strength" as well as her parent; and that, conversely, Heroic Virtue remains as strong as ever through the ages as long as he preserves his Fame.

With a paean of praise for the virtues of the Queen (who is to lead the masque of Famed Women as the most notable of them) and another on the King's excellence, Heroic Virtue concludes by asserting that by means of Fame, the good of these ladies is communicated to all times and places, "And euery Age, the Benefit endures."[19] Fame then appears, thanks "*Virtue,* my Father, and my Honor"[20] for making her both good and great, and directs the masque in a triumph of the Queens over the vanquished hags of Anti-Fame.

It is appropriate that Jonson should use the triumph form for a masque expressing the relationship between virtue and fame. The deep seriousness with which the Romans regarded triumphs, and which cost Fulvius so dearly, was well known in the Renaissance, even on the popular level; Alain Chartier's sweeping catechism of general knowledge includes the brief exchange "Why did they prepare Arkes and Pageantes of triumphs at Rome? To sturre men to vertue."[21] On a more elevated level of society, Francis Bacon concurred. He saw little purpose in masques, but felt that "the Triumph, amongst the *Romans,* was not Pageants or Gauderie, but one of the Wisest and Noblest Institutions, that euer was," and that it was "able to enflame all Mens Courages."[22] Since Jonson thought that masques too were wise and noble, he took advantage of the ethical overtones that clung to the triumph, and frequently used it as a form of the masque. Bacon, far more historian than poet, perhaps could not appreciate the value of a symbolic triumph as much as a literal one. But Jonson could, and his symbolic triumph of Queens over witches was not far distant in purpose from the more martial varieties to which Bacon admiringly turned.

"Sing then *good Fame,* that's out of *Vertue* borne, / For, Who doth fame neglect, doth vertue scorne."[23] After riding about the scene in state to the accompaniment of this song, the Queens perform their dances, triumph once more about the stage, and are celebrated in a last song:

> Who, *Virtue,* can thy power forget,
> That sees these liue, and triumph yet?
> Th' *Assyrian* pompe, the *Persian* pride,
> *Greekes* glory, and the *Romanes* dy'de:
>   And who yet imitate
> They[r] noyses, tary the same fate.
>   Force Greatnesse, all the glorious wayes
>   You can, it soone decayes;
>   But so *good Fame* shall, neuer:
> Her triumphs, as they[r] Causes, are for euer.[24]

I quote this last song in full because it helps remove a possible misunderstanding about the *Masque of Queens.* The women celebrated in Jonson's House of Fame are, for the most part, warriors, and are partakers of Heroic Virtue in its military form. The concentration upon this type to the exclusion of such candidates as Alcestis or Catherine of Alexandria or Lucrece might be taken to imply a particular glorification of battle-minded women. Such an intention on Jonson's part would certainly be somewhat odd; he is, after all, writing a masque around a queen who is hardly an Amazon, and presenting it before a king who takes great pride in his pacific nature.[25] This last song vindicates one's suspicions by its direct rejection of the military motif: "who yet imitate / They[r] noyses, tary the same fate." The point that the song seems to be making is that the military aspect of the fame of these women is accidental rather than substantial: it is for their virtue that they are rightly famous and it is of little importance that this virtue found its expression in fighting rather than something else. Anne is said to possess all the various virtues found in the rest of these queens taken together; this is said as prelude to a dance, not a barriers. It is certainly true that if Jonson's primary intention had been to demilitarize the renown of militant heroines, he might have done better to mix some nonmilitary figures in with the others and thereby more easily establish the common denominator as virtue while de-emphasizing the Amazonian particulars. The probability is that Anne asked for a masque of Amazons as she had requested a masque of blackamoors four years earlier,[26] and that Jonson had to make the best of it from there. In any case, the final song of the masque deliberately steps away from the possible militaristic implications while pointing to the heart of the matter: virtue, independent of the "forced greatness" of military deeds. Viewed in this light, these conquering queens can confer, through fame, their highest benefits even upon the peaceable kingdom of James, inspiring virtue by the light with which fame makes them splendid.

II.

There is one further important link in the humanistic restitution of fame as the daughter of virtue. It is implied in every reconsideration of the subject: fame needs its supervisors and custodians. Obviously, they must be men of understanding and men of persuasive power, and it is equally obvious what sort of men Jonson would have in mind to fill this serious office. The speech of Heroic Virtue in the *Masque of Queens* calls the particular attention of the audience to one element of the scenery: the columns upon which the House of Fame is supported are

> Men-making *Poets,* and those well made *Men,*
> Whose strife it was, to haue the happiest pen
> Renowme them to an after-life, and not
> W^{t}h pride to scorne the Muse, & dye, forgot.[27]

Jones's design has the lower columns as statutes of poets, holding up the upper columns, which are in the form of heroes.

The poets, Jonson observes in his description, are thus "the substantiall supporters of *Fame*."[28]

Fame exists as a value through those who are famous, and their particular fames derive from the poets who have caused them to be remembered, and to be remembered for the right reasons. Jonson rarely missed an opportunity to make this point in his masques. In the *Masque of Blackness,* he observes parenthetically that in England "raigne those beauties, that with so much fame / The sacred MVSES sonnes haue honored,"[29] and he shows in both the scene and the spoken text of the *Masque of Beauty* the poets singing hymns in celebration of the worth of the beauties in the scene.[30] In the *Haddington Masque,* he pays a generous compliment to James by comparing him to Aeneas, carefully adding "and what name, / MARO, the golden trumpet of his fame, / Gaue him."[31] The Lady of the Lake is chided in *Prince Henry's Barriers* for having suppressed "The learned MERLIN":

> when thou shutst him there,
> Thou buriedst valure too, for letters reare
> The deeds of honor high, and make them liue.[32]

The poets are again brought to the support of the King's fame in the *Masque of Augurs,*[33] and Poesy is shown as one of the chief supporters of fame and virtue in *Chloridia.*[34] In *Time Vindicated,* Jonson takes the further step of bringing in Lady Fame to repudiate the cheap interests of popular taste and to share Jonson's contempt for the poet who appeals to them—authentic fame is far more noble and requires the kind of poetry which "is not borne wᵗh euery man; Nor euery day."[35] There are several other instances of this theme, but nowhere more clear and concise than in *The Golden Age Restored:* in order to bring long-dead exemplars of virtue back to earth, Pallas instructs her servants the poets to wake them.

In this last allegory, both of the major parts are important. It is notable, in the first place, that the poets have their special relationship to Pallas: "Our best of fire," they sing, "Is that which PALLAS doth inspire."[36] This is a theme recurrent in Jonson's works and scarcely atypical of the Renaissance in general. The poet must be a man of learning and of wisdom. Jonson's repeated insistence in his masques, in opposition to his detractors, that such displays must be "grounded vpon *antiquitie,* and solide *learnings*"[37] goes along with his frequent elaborate documentation of his sources as the proof of a point: a concern for the solid ground of learning qualifies him as one of the highest kind of humanistic poets, fit for the most serious tasks of poetry. Jonson professed, and perhaps believed, the noble Socratic doctrine that there is (in the words of his note in *Love Freed From Ignorance*) "no folly but is borne of ignorance."[38] When the foolish and vicious courtiers of *Cynthia's Revels* are to be cured, Jonson sends them not to the Mount of Penitence but to the Spring of Helicon. It is part of a great complex of Renaissance thought, part of the hope that attention to the wisdom of the ancients would beget in itself the fundamental virtue of the moderns. Knowledge is the spring of virtue, and also the instrument by which true virtue may be recognized and celebrated by the poets who possess it. Jonson wrote to Prince Henry in the dedication to him of the *Masque of Queens* that

Yo[r] fauor to letters, and these gentler studies, that goe vnder the title of Humanitye, is not the least honor of yo[r] wreath. For, if once the worthy Professors of these learnings shall come (as heretofore they were) to be the care of Princes, the Crownes they[r] *Soueraignes* weare will not more adorne they[r] Temples; nor they[r] stamps liue longer in they[r] *Medalls,* than in such Subiects labors. *Poetry,* my Lord, is not borne wth euery man; Nor euery day. . . .[39]

Jonson plainly counts himself one of "the worthy Professors of these learnings" and thus associates himself with that humanistic complex devoted to the furtherance of knowledge, virtue—and fame. As a knowledgeable man, he is capable of assessing and castigating folly and of pointing the way to the springs of Helicon. As a poet, he is capable of perpetuating the memory of worthy exemplars and, more important, causing their fame to be founded upon the ideal reasons.

The other half of the allegory in *The Golden Age Restored* is that of the poets waking the virtuous to re-establish the Golden Age. The image can work in two ways, and was very likely intended to do so: the more literal version shows the poet waking the memories of the dead whose virtue merits fame; this in itself suggests the other reading—the poet wakens sleeping virtue in living men.

"As the seale leaueth the impression of his forme in wax," runs one of the aphorisms in *Politeuphuia: Wits Common-wealth* (1597), "so the learned Poet, engraueth his passions so perfectly in mens harts, that the hearer almost is transformed into the Author."[40] Jonson was decidedly of the same opinion: "We doe not require in him [the poet] meere *Elocution;* or an excellent faculty in verse; but the exact knowledge of all vertues, and their Contraries; with ability to render the one lov'd, the other hated, by his proper embattaling them."[41] Here is at once the heart of the case for the *learned* poet, servant of Pallas, and for the *effective* poet, who stirs sleeping virtue into wakefulness. Fame is an instrument to which the poet may profitably turn in both capacities. In the first place, through the celebration of a virtuous fame, he can inspire in others an imitation of the virtues which fame rewards; and, in the second place, he can even enlarge and specify the fame of the living in such a way as to inspire them to live up to the image of virtue presented by the poet's praise.

This latter principle may appear somewhat fanciful, but it can be defended on psychological grounds and, more pertinently for the investigation of Jonson's purpose, had a firm place in Renaissance thinking. Erasmus speaks of it in his *Institutio Principis Christiani,*[42] and Bacon enunciates it as a principle in his essay "Of Prayse": "Some *Praises* come of good Wishes, and

Respects, which is a Forme due in Ciuilitie to Kings, and Great Persons, *Laudando praecipere;* When by telling Men, what they are, they represent to them, what they should be."[43] Compliment too can be a means of teaching and moving, and when dealing with kings, this is the most prudent and decorous method of instruction. One may suspect that Ben Jonson was thinking of a particular king when he confessed to Selden that he had "prais'd some names too much, / But 'twas with purpose to haue made them such."[44] The poet does not necessarily suspend his higher purposes even when he flatters.

There is another motive as well for which the poet may turn his attention to fame: mere ambition. Jonson's repeated hints concerning the poet's ability to confer special glory upon the subjects of his poems are certainly, whatever else they may be, attempts to feather his own nest.

The *Name* of BEL-ANNA . . . is kept by mee, in all my *Poemes,* wherin I mention her *Maiesty* w^{t}h, any shadow, or *figure.* Of w^{c}h, some may come forth w^{t}h a longer *desteny,* then this *Age,* commonly, giues the best Births, if but helpd to light, by her gratious, and ripening fauor.[45]

If he played to the vanity of his potential patrons he is, to be sure, in the company of nearly everyone who wrote a dedication in the Tudor and Stuart reigns. We are obliged to be more severe with Jonson, however, since he claims to take fame more seriously than the common hack. It can hardly be doubted that he often sinned against sincerity, in the modern sense of the word. But it must be remembered that hyperbole was as well established in the Renaissance as litotes under the Saxon kings, and this makes a significant difference. Taken literally, many of the paeans to Elizabeth would have been blasphemous, and many of the dedications of Renaissance books would have been cold lies. But, Jonson's friend Owen Feltham reminds us, "for *Flatterie,* no man will take *Poetrie literall:* since in *commendations,* it rather shewes what men *should bee,* then what they *are.*[46] In a word, the language of dedications and of poems of praise was recognized as a department of rhetoric: our criteria of sincerity are largely irrelevant. To a lesser but still established extent, they were departments of didacticism, teaching the object to deserve such commendation and teaching others to admire in him the virtues already present: *laudando praecipere.* Even if the poet plays on vanity, he must be given the benefit of the doubt, for the humanists had rehabilitated the constructive possibilities of vanity and saved it from absolute classification under the category of false pride. "And if they obiect," wrote George Pettie of his possible detractors, "that that seeking of immortalitie, is a signe of vaine glorie: to answere them plainelie and humanelie, I am flat of this minde, that they which passe not of praise, will neuer doe anie thing worthie of praise."[47] The poet's activity of praising and giving fame may still, even when the praise is hyperbolical, be part of "that which PALLAS doth inspire." The same is true even when it is profitable.

King, Queen, and Prince are often so idealized in Jonson's masques as to be almost unrecognizable historically. But the accuracy of historical correspondence is essentially irrelevant. Their ideal images, charged by the poet with an inspiring glory, are worthy of imitation, by themselves as well as others. The specific character of these images tends to attach to the persons upon whom they are built, thus communicating to them particular forms of ideal fame that both reinforce the royal primacy and further the cause of virtue by the institution of living exemplars brightened by an efficaciously tendentious fame. When the real is idealized, some of the idealization rubs off on it—this is a psychological fact of which the iconoclastic Reformation was well aware.

Blundeville's historian is allowed—even advised—to suppress unworthy actions of otherwise worthy persons, for the sake of virtue; Jonson's poet is allowed—even obliged—to hyperbolize to the same end. The masque-image is to the King as Spenser's Gloriana is to the Queen. The poet's task is to render fame a vehicle of virtue while magnifying it; if the object of that fame comes off better than he deserves, that is to his advantage, but it may also be to the advantage of all. Like all fame, that which Jonson created for those he celebrated was almost necessarily productive of either envy or admiration, and to the extent that it begot admiration it established them as efficacious examples for their own time and forever: "And euery Age, the Benefit endures."[48] It was almost inevitably admiration, not envy, which was excited by the masques' frequent praise of James as the King of Peace; and almost inevitably admiration which was stirred by the masques themselves, "the donatiues, of great Princes, to their people,"[49] true signs of the primary kingly virtue of magnificence. A respectable portion of fame belonged to Jonson's subjects by right; the rest, if literally inappropriate, was theirs by virtue of a higher end. For fame escapes the leveling and oblivion to which events and persons are pulled by objective scrutiny and by the passage of time—that is fame's purpose and its strength. It is by nature a distorter, as is poetry, and may thereby serve virtue better. Jonson was concerned not with mere objective history, but with poetry, with fame, and with virtue.

Chapter VIII · Order and the King

There can be few patterns of thought in which we are more decidedly the children of the Greeks than in those ideas of world order and world harmony to which repeated references have been made in previous chapters. Perhaps the past tense would be more accurate: for modern thought has, to use an awkward but largely accurate generalization, discovered with surprise that such ideas are indeed inheritances and not inevitable postulates, and for the first time in over two thousand years there is widespread philosophical dissent from the pictures of harmonious order that were constantly revised but always cherished throughout the history of Western thought. Whether we look back with nostalgia or contempt upon our ancestral *harmonia mundi,* it is certainly impossible to understand the past without grasping something of this central doctrine.

Universal order was, in the time of the English Renaissance, not only a popular idea: it was an official one. It is given formal expression in the tenth of the official homilies appointed in 1547 for universal publication through the churches—and as such was preached and published not only throughout the succeeding Tudor reigns, but was "thought fit to bee reprinted by Authority from the KINGS most excellent Maiestie" in 1623. Its importance justifies the quotation of a long excerpt:

Almightie God hath created & appointed al thynges, in heauen, yearth, and waters in a most excellent and perfect ordre. In heauen he hath appointed distinct ordres and states of Archangelles and Angels. In yearth he hath assigned kynges, princes, with other gouernors vnder them, all in good & necessary ordre. The water aboue is kept and raineth doune in due time and ceason. The sunne, moone, sterres, rainbow, thuder, lightnyng, cloudes, and al birdes of the aire, do keep their ordre. The yearth, trees, seedes, plantes, herbes, corne, grasse, and al maner of beastes, kepe them in their ordre. All the partes of whole yere, as winter, somer, monthes, nightes & daies, continue in their ordre. All kindes of fishes in the sea, riuers and waters, with all fountaines, sprynges, yea, the seas themselfes, kepe their comely course and ordre. And man himself also, hath al his partes, both within & without, as soule, harte, mynd, memory, vnderstandyng, reason, speache, withall and synguler corporall membres of his body, in a profitable, necessary and pleasaunt ordre. Euery degre of people, in their vocacion, callyng, & office, hath appoynted to them, their duetie and ordre. Some are in high degre, some in lowe, some kynges & princes, some inferiors and subiectes, priestes and laimen, masters and seruauntes, fathers and children, husbandes & wifes, rich and poore, and euery one haue nede of other, so that in al thinges, is to be lauded & praised ye goodly ordre of God, without ye whiche, no house, no cite no common-wealth, can continue & endure.[1]

Everything has its place. Elizabethan theories of government, of natural law, of astronomy, of medicine continually and consistently reflect the *a priori* postulate of this world order. "Everie one in his ranke according to naturall order and degree" is a principle that could be applied on every level from the cosmic to the most minute—this particular quotation is, in fact, from a description of how to use the fingers in playing the lute.[2]

Everything is consigned to its proper place. This property of the Medieval-Renaissance theory of order is the one most emphasized by the homily, but it is not, of course, the only important property. Another one, given a more emphatic place in the discussions of other Renaissance writers, appears in the quotation from the homily in a shadowy form, in the rough parallels implied between the groups of ordered beings who compose heaven, the commonwealth, the natural world, and man. These orders were commonly seen as variations on the ultimate pattern of God, in whose image heaven, earth, and man are created (or from whom they are emanations). Each of these orders is therefore the perfect reproduction of the others, according to the natures of their particular spheres. This theory of harmonious correspondence has consequences which do not obtain in a universe which is merely organized according to an ordained system. The most obvious of these is that every truth has extendable validity in other orders; man, for instance, can learn what he is and what he ought to be through contemplation of the world. Thus Leone Ebreo asserts that the sun and moon were "made to be the patterns of the intellect and the soul,"[3] and accordingly discourses about the moon in order to learn about the soul. The validity of truths analogously applied is to him one of the real properties of the universe.

The ordained patterns of order harmoniously repeat on earth

as well as between earth and heaven, making every phenomenon in nature a source of instruction for the lives of men. As Edward Forsett explains,

the incomprehensible wisdome of God, in the composing & ordering of his works in nature, hath so dignified them with all perfection, as that they be left vnto vs as eminent and exemplary patterns, as well for the consoladating, as for the beautifying of that wee worke by arte or policie; as well for conioyning of all discordances into firmnesse, as also for the applyablenesse of particulars in their many seruices, for the vse and benifit of the whole.[4]

This attitude was habitually applied by Renaissance writers. Du Plessis Mornay follows a disquisition on physiology with the gratuitous but, for his time, relevant observation that "Heerein truly nature gaue vs the lawe & example of communicating our graces, gyfts, and perfections, from one to another."[5] The full title of Forsett's book suggests the strength of the popular convictions about these harmonies to which he could appeal—*A Comparative Discourse of the Bodies Natural and Politique: Wherein out of the principles of Nature, is set forth the true forme of a Commonweale.* The notion of sermons in stones and books in the running brooks is not merely a piece of sentimentality: it is a pious acceptance of the universal harmony designed by God, for "Surely *God* made so many *varieties* in his *Creatures* as well for the *inward soule,* as the *outward senses,*" writes Owen Feltham in 1628, citing with approval a monk who insisted that he could do without books because "The *Nature* of the *Creatures* was his *Library:* wherein, when hee pleased, hee could muse vpon *Gods deepe Oracles.*"[6]

It was usually in terms of such harmonic predispositions that Renaissance writers wrote about that immensely important subject, the nature of the political and social order. Arguments based on the principle of harmonious correspondence were virtually self-verifying, since they indicated the pattern which was ordained by God to be paridigmatic for human societies.

There was a large supply of parallel patterns to which writers could appeal in proof of the divine ordination of the traditional government and society.

Recent commentators have often pointed out that the works of Shakespeare are full of pointed allusions and comparisons of this kind: the commonwealth is like a human body, a musical instrument, the heavens, and so on. Such analogies can be found cropping up whenever a Renaissance writer touched on the subject of the commonwealth. Each was thought to be valid and illuminating, and each appealed to a standard ideal pattern which recognized that the commonwealth is composed of a diversity of related elements designed by nature (and therefore by God) to operate in particular orderly ways, under the primacy of the king. The particular ways are dictated partly by hierarchical stability, which forbids the born plowman access to the Privy Council and the Privy Councillor's son to the plow, and partly by the will of the superiors of the commonwealth; the homily which begins with a sermon on order, quoted at the beginning of this chapter, is on the subject of Obedience.

It is well known that the official answer to the question of obedience, obviously a key issue in the order of the commonwealth, was not always passively assented to in the days of Ben Jonson. Elizabeth had a little trouble in the early days of her reign, but the most notable deviation, the "bloody syllogism" of John Knox, was on the more convenient side of the fence and touched the Queen of Scots rather than her; however, the same tune sung by Jesuit mouths in her later years was a more uncomfortable phenomenon. James was her heir in this, too, and faced in addition a growing discontent among the antiepiscopal religious reformers. Both camps challenged the doctrine of unconditional obedience on religious grounds. It is small wonder that official theories of kingship, which were the only reliable foundation and defense for theories of obedience, tended under James to reach new heights in claiming a divine origin and a divine significance for the office of a king:

The State of MONARCHIE is the supremest thing vpon earth: For Kings are not onely GODS Lieutenants vpon earth, and sit vpon GODS throne, but euen by GOD himself they are called Gods.... In the Scriptures Kings are called Gods, and so their power after a certaine relation compared to the Diuine power.[7]

Thus King James, speaking to Parliament in 1609, and going on to expand the latter point: the king, like God, has power to raise and lower the fortunes of men, can judge, has power over life and death.[8] It is a bolder stand than Elizabeth took on the subject of kingship, and it was taken in the face of a more serious challenge to royal supremacy than the beloved Queen had to face. The tactics are the usual ones: analogical description based upon the best reasons for the *status quo*. Such was the standard formula for political propaganda of this sort.

Propaganda was assuredly common enough in Elizabeth's reign as well, although she had less need than James to promulgate it herself. It is Elizabeth, not James, who comes to mind when we think of literature extravagantly devoted to the glory of a monarch. But that was largely the tribute of love, unasked and really not needed. James was in a less favorable position; and it was he, not Elizabeth, who demanded "the mysticall reuerence, that belongs vnto them that sit in the Throne of God."[9] If James was to have obedience on his terms, if his version of the way in which the kingdom must regard the king was to become established, he needed the aid of propaganda in a way that Elizabeth never did. He was realistic enough to be aware of this, as a production like Mocket's *God and the King,* printed by the King's command in 1615, bears witness. In the following year was published Ben Jonson's first folio edition of his works; in that year King James granted him a pension.

James's own ideas bore in themselves the stamp of that very interpenetration of orders which is so consistently portrayed in Jonson's masques: the king is a man, yet a man with a special relationship to God and with powers, granted him from heaven, similar to the power of God. Official doctrine, but made to order for Jonson's poetry.

The masques do not relate James explicitly to God, of course, but rather implicitly, through the grammar of powers and antique deities already formed to the purposes of poetry. Consider, for instance, Astraea's final song in *The Golden Age Restored*:

> Of all there seemes a second birth,
> It is become a heau'n on earth,
>   And *Ioue* is present here,
> I feele the Godhead: nor will doubt
> But he can fill the place throughout,
>   Whose power is euery where.[10]

There can be no doubt about who is designated as Jove. The whole idea of this stanza is an elevation to a quasi-divine level of a commonplace about the king: "As the soule in the body, doth giue to all the members, moouing and life: So the prouidence of a godly king, is present to eurie part of his kingdome, stirring vp his whole commonwealth, to vertue and godliness."[11] The analogical translation of *king* to *Jove* has the obvious implication of aligning the King intimately with the transcendent powers, that is, it is also a translation of the analogy drawn by James between the power of the king and the power of God. In *Pan's Anniversary* the same point is somewhat daringly made in speaking of James as Pan, using the language applied by St. Paul to God: "*PAN* is our All, by him we breath, wee live, / Wee move / we are."[12] Such is "the mysticall reuerence, that belongs vnto them that sit in the Throne of God."

The portrayal of the king as Jove or as Pan brings home the supernatural character of his office and also demonstrates the participation of the ideal commonwealth in the harmony of the heavens. The Arcadians in *Pan's Anniversary* are called out to their dances in just such terms:

> And come you prime Arcadians forth, that taught
> By PAN the rites of true societie,
> From his loud Musicke, all your manners wraught,
> And made your Common-wealth a harmonie,[13]

and the fact that these "Arcadians" are courtiers of James's court renders the scene a parable of particular point.

The allegory here condenses several related ideas. On the lowest level, in which Pan is the leader of the shepherds, one can see the simple principle of obedience, the subjects conforming to the will of the King. There is also the more complimentary implication that the harmony comes not merely from their willingness to obey but from the rightness of his rule. Pan is, in addition to being the leader of the shepherds, Nature and God; and the Arcadians, who have wrought their manners from his music, have therefore perfected themselves within the natural order and conformed themselves to the will of God, achieving thereby that perfectly harmonious commonwealth possible only when virtuous men form their society in accordance with the ideal pattern that imitates God and the order of Nature— the music of Pan is the universal harmony in which we live and move and are. Ideally, both man and the state are perfected in the image of "the *worlds soule,* true *harmony.*"[14]

The note which Jonson appended to the line I have just quoted reminds us that the harmonious world-soul is above all "The Platonicks opinion."[15] I have noted frequently in earlier chapters the many ways in which Jonson took advantage of the Neoplatonic notions that were fashionably, if somewhat vaguely, popular in the court which formed his audience. Like Beaujoyeulx, Jonson knew that those who were instructed in the Platonic discipline were in a position to respond readily to his Platonized uses of music and dance, his references to that true beauty that is founded on order, his presentation of the unifying force of love, and his continual allusions to and symbolic representations of that great frame of universal harmony in which all things have their being and are perfected. Universal harmony was by no means exclusively a Neoplatonic principle, but it was pre-eminently so, and Jonson found that the harmonic ideas of Renaissance Platonism made an appropriate and effective instrument for the poetry of the masques.

An instrument, not a subject. For in their deep involvement with ideas of harmony, Jonson's masques move not toward metaphysics but toward ethics; with Sidney, Spenser, and the vast majority of serious writers of the English Renaissance, Jonson found upon the summit of Parnassus not the motion of the spheres but the shrine of virtue. As he remarked in the preface to *Love's Triumph,* court masques "ought to be the mirrors of mans life," and should not fail to carry "profit."[16] The resemblance of these profitable microcosms to the macrocosm, through the poetically invoked universal harmony, is above all the poetic proof of their importance, excellence, and truth. It may be nothing more.

It is indeed impossible to say how much interest Jonson had in the masques' image of universal harmony apart from its ethical implication for the obvious reason that the two are never completely separated. The essential element of the masque is the masquers themselves, and in them Jonson epitomizes an interpenetration of the transcendent and the earthly: in their glorified state, the masquers embody a perfection that is not always particularized, but which always carries implications of the transfiguration of man by virtue. The masques, after all, deal with profitable doctrine—the nature of true love, true beauty, true fame, the ideal commonwealth—and the glorified masquers stand somewhere between earth and heaven, between man and the gods, linking the two extremes. We are made aware of the presence of the upper extreme in the masquers by the way in which they are always related to some higher celestial power; we know the presence of the other extreme not simply because we know that these masquers are, under their roles, people, but because they are the Countess of Arundel, Lady Anne Winter, the Earl of Newport, and Sir Robert Stanley. The audiences at Jonson's masques saw not merely abstract powers and glories but particular members of their court idealized by being portrayed in a harmonious relationship with powers of a higher harmony, in a world from which all discord has been amputated or suppressed. Such a pattern may be made to imply many things; but in that time and place, it could not fail to be apprehended as symbolic of virtue, whatever else it may be at the same time.

Above these glorified courtiers in Jonson's masques stands their still more glorious King, who takes his place among the gods. The harmony of the masquers' relationship with the gods therefore frequently carries with it the implications which are made explicit in *Pan's Anniversary:* that the commonwealth too is an imitation of the great perfecting harmony, and that the courtiers' conformity to the music of Pan as Nature and Pan as the King will insure their achievement of the ideal social and political order. I pointed out earlier that the court's harmony with Pan taken as Nature (and God) also implies virtue as well as civil order: this is in fact even one of the implications of Pan taken as King James. The idealized King is portrayed not only as a politically wise leader but as an example whose "loud Musicke" can be admired and profitably imitated by those who aspire to virtue. The moral order is thus invoked along with the political and social order within the King's sphere of proper influence.

> Seeke you maiestie, to strike?
>   Bid the world produce his like.
> Seeke you glorie, to amaze?
>   Here, let all eyes stand at gaze.
> Seeke you wisedome, to inspire?
>   Touch, then, at no others fire.
> Seeke you knowledge, to direct?
>   Trust to his, without suspect.
> Seeke you pietie, to lead?
>   In his foot-steps, only, tread.
> Euery vertue of a king,
> And of all, in him, we sing.[17]

The extension of the office of the ideal king into the moral order may seem a gratuitous addition on Jonson's part. In fact, it is not. It was part of the commonplaces of kingship. "As God hath placed in heauen the sun, to be a most noble and excellent pattern of his beautie: so hath he placed in the common wealth a wise, iust, and liberall Prince, to bee a representer of his ver- tues";[18] "Euen as a brooke doth follow the nature of the foun- taine, from whence it commeth: So people do follow the disposition of their prince."[19] "It would be a disorder in Nature, to see bad subiects vnder a good Prince . . . All the greatnesse, and happinesse of a Prince, is, to make in his Vertues, a visible image of inuisible Diuinity; then to imprint the same on his subiects, as the Sun doth his brightnesse on the Rainbow."[20] The king of the masques would be lacking unless he fulfilled this function of the ideal monarch as well, unless he could be said to "cherish euery great Example / Contracted in yo[r] selfe,"[21] unless

> *vertues* hang on him, as on theire working cause.
> His handmaid *Iustice* is,
> *Wisdome* his wife,
> His Mistresse *Mercie,*
> *Temperance* his life,
>
> .   .   .   .
> And all that followes him, *felicitie.*[22]

It is in the image of the king as the moral unmoved mover of his kingdom that the complex of human order is fulfilled and made intelligible. In the *Masque of Augurs,* the chorus intro- duces the main dance with these words, "More is behind, which these doe long to show, / And what the Gods to so great vertue owe."[23] After the dance, another song clarifies this curious notion of the gods' debt to James: it is, of course, that James has done the work of the gods in promoting order in terms of peace, concord, piety. The keener members of the audience probably did not need this explication, for the introductory couplet promises that it will be shown in the dance, in which members of the court move in harmonious order before the king: in the dance is a metaphor of the participation of earth in the harmonious order of heaven through the mediation of the divinely ordained king.

The lessons on order which Jonson's masques hold out to the spectator are applicable to the king as well. While the subjects are shown the intrinsic majesty of the kingly office in order to awaken their awe and reverence, and the seal of transcendent harmony on love, virtue, peace, and civil concord in order to inspire in them a longing for these ideal qualities, so the ideal mirror is held up to the king in order that he might see how well he is carrying out the sacred duties of his office. Here again the crucial issue is *virtue:* on this depend the worthiness of the king and the excellence of his subjects who look to him for inspiring example. James was most assuredly not the paragon of virtues delineated in the masques, but neither was Lady Cranborne a warrior queen of antiquity. James played a role in the masques. They did not break through to him in order to pay him homage, but rather incorporated him into the framework, and that should be evident enough from the frequent practice of giving him a name or function designed to operate in terms of the masque, by which he becomes Jove or Pan or the Sun or Hesperus or the institutor of the Golden Age. With a form of decorum, Jonson saw to it that the masquers, who were known to be particular courtiers in roles of a more-than-human order, remained subordinate to the king, who was therefore made a particular king in a role of more-than-kingly significance. Even the scene gave support, for when the masques refer to the king as sun or star, when they speak of his grandeur or of the power of his brightness, they speak of the man who, during the performance, sat high in the lighted chair of state:

> Now looke and see in yonder throne,
> How all those beames are cast from one.
>   This is that Orbe so bright,
> Has kept your wonder so awake;
> Whence you as from a mirrour take
>   The Suns reflected light.

> Read him as you would doe the booke
> Of all perfection, and but looke
>   What his proportions be;
> No measure that is thence contriv'd,
> Of any motion thence deriv'd,
>   But is pure harmonie.[24]

Reflecting the light of the divine Sun, the king becomes a source-book for harmony—the harmony of the state, knit together in peace and love under the king, and the harmony of the self, ordered in virtue and in wisdom under reason and understanding. Alas, it was wishful thinking. But yet it was something more. We, and *a fortiori* the original audiences of the masques, see the difference between the Jacobean reality and the perfection of order toward which the masques point. That is the way Jonson wanted it. If the beauty and desirability and excellence of the latter are at all moving to us who have only the poetry without the supporting spectacle, they must have been incalculably more impressive to the original viewers. That is what Jonson wanted.

Chapter IX · Epilogue

It is surprising, when we look back upon *The Vision of the Twelve Goddesses* through Jonson's achievement in the masque, to see how homely the pre-Jonsonian masque was, how casual and how loose in construction. It is astonishing, when we look at Jonson's masques through Daniel's, to see with what care and consistent skill Jonson unified the constituents of the masque —costume, music, dance, poetry, lighting—into a single whole, and it is remarkable to see with what unity of purpose he selected from the array of established possibilities the elements of which his masques are composed, and with what artistry he compelled each of them to make the fullest possible contribution to his design. And the essence of that design was, first and last, the old ideal of Sidney and Spenser: to show the splendor of a golden world and to move men to love and desire the virtuous life by which their brazen world may be alchemized to gold.

Jonson was no dreamer of lovely dreams; that would be an abdication from his poetic role, which to him was one of the most serious and most realistic callings possible to man. It was Daniel who said that a masque was but a frivolous dream, while Jonson insisted that it was immeasurably more: each of them wrote accordingly. Jonson, after a struggle, left many of his contemporaries convinced that his plays were serious undertakings; but he never succeeded in disabusing them of the Danielian conception of the masque, and when he left the scene in defeat the masque settled back comfortably into the playful extravagance in which it died. Out of the Italian equivalents of the Stuart masque sprang opera, and out of the French equivalents, ballet; from the Stuart masques themselves grew—nothing.

They died of an overdose of spectacle—that much is clear enough. Jonson spent the latter part of his masque-writing career struggling with Inigo Jones over the very issues that determine the rise and fall of the Stuart masques. Jones wanted display, scene-changes, elaborate and varied spectacle; Jonson wanted "nourishing and sound meats" in which every other aspect of the masque was subordinate to the poetic "soul." The court sided with Jones. Jonson had traveled a long way between the *Masque of Beauty,* in which he simply acknowledges that the scenic work was done by "the *Kings* Master Carpenter,"[1] and *Chloridia* (whose eight antimasques already spell the defeat of his principles), over which he had his conclusive falling-out with Jones concerning the order of their two names on the title page. As Professor Gordon has shown,[2] Jones defended his claim by asserting the status of architecture as one of the liberal arts; but that he should exalt his contribution of a body to the masque over the poet's provision of a soul was intolerable to Jonson, who knew that his whole purpose was doomed under such an arrangement. Thereafter, supported by the encouragement of the court and by the assistance of other poets who provided him with a text to aid his scenic manipulations, Inigo Jones had his way; and the Stuart masque, a unique phenomenon with no parallel in English history before or since, died without issue.

Yet, in a touch of ironic justice, Jonson had his way with posterity. The inevitable loss of the spectacle that formed an integral part of Jonson's masques makes it difficult to appreciate the extent to which Jonson's poetic truths were immediately enhanced and their impact strengthened by the harmonized and subordinate contributions of his composers, choreographers, and designers, and the loss is regrettable; but it does leave us with the literary text foremost, so that there is no chance of our failing to realize, as Jonson's audiences seemed to have done at least toward the end of his life, that the masque is in the last analysis a species of poetry.

And in the hands of Jonson it inevitably was a poetry of the most responsible sort. Jonson's all-embracing conception of the poet, a particularly distinguished product of Renaissance humanism, would allow nothing of lesser dignity:

I could never thinke the study of *Wisdome* confin'd only to the Philosopher: or of *Piety* to the *Divine:* or of *State* to the *Politicke*. But that he which can faine a *Common-wealth* (which is the *Poet*) can governe it with *Counsels,* strengthen it with *Lawes,* correct it with *Iudgements,* informe it with *Religion,* and *Morals;* is all these. Wee doe not require in him meere *Elocution;* or an excellent faculty in verse; but the exact knowledge of all vertues, and their Contraries; with ability to render the one lov'd, the other hated, by his proper embattaling them.[3]

The last clause is obviously pertinent to Jonson's handling of antimasques and masques, and it involves the rest of the quotation as well. *All* virtues: this includes piety and political prudence, and all the other excellences which contribute to the perfection of a man and the right order of the state. These the true poet must represent in order to teach, and render desirable in order to perfect. This is the issue at the ethical heart of that world harmony dealt with in the last chapter. True order, the order of perfection, is something to be *achieved,* not merely discovered: it broods over us in a bright potential world which breaks through to us and beckons, but it is won only with difficulty. In Jonson's world as in Spenser's, there are many beasts to be slain and it is always the hour of decision and action. The poet confronts the world of becoming with the world of being, in order that our image in that mirror may stir us to awe and to perfection; and he points the way toward the achievement of that perfection. Such is Sidney's image of the ideal poet. Between Spenser and Jonson, the outlines of this ideal are very nearly realized.

But it was too late. Things had changed since Sidney—even since Spenser—and even in Sidney's day the battle for his kind of poetry was uphill. English poetry (ironically, with the assistance of Spenser and Sidney) had, in its achievement of a genuine elegance, begun to move away from the humanistic ideal that forms part of the greatness of the *Faerie Queene* and of Jonson's plays. Delight, toward the end of the sixteenth century, was emerging as an independent end of poetry. It was happening all over Europe, and is not to be lamented in England: it not only gave us *Venus and Adonis* and liberated us from George Whetstone, but also made possible *The Alchemist* and the *Masque of Beauty*. Ascham and Elyot would probably have been enraptured by Jonson's masques, but the nature of accumulating tradition is such that their work had to ripen for longer than their lifetimes before the masques were conceivable; and by the time the masques could be written, their basic seriousness already seemed a bit pedantic and old-fashioned.

Every rhetoric invalidates itself by creating a new vocabulary. The process is unending and continually uncovers those two most interesting groups of every age, the conservatives and the revolutionaries. Most sturdy and reasonably long-lived people are both at one time or another—Jonson's masques revolutionized the form and were ultimately overrun by the Jonesian revolution which they had made possible—but they usually end as conservatives, if only because the process of change is irreversable. Jonson was no exception. Like most minds that are excellent but short of greatness, his seems to have been extremely sensitive to the dangers of innovation. He appears to have been a sturdy defender of royal absolutism, even in his Roman Catholic days, out of a desire for the most stable form of civil order and the form most conducive to the leading of the good life; had he lived to see the civil war, he would undoubtedly have thought that it proved him right. Hence, the image of monarchy and of civil order which is projected in his masques: he believed that a truly virtuous court, under a virtuous and enlightened king who knows what virtue is and how it can be encouraged in his subjects, can reintroduce a golden age in the kingdom. Indeed, that lovely formula was always hard to doubt; the Philosopher King has his defenders even today, although the evidence of history and psychology show the inevitable reluctance of his subjects to respond to his example and encouragement. Jonson did not forget this entirely. In *Cynthia's Revels* he places the simpler argument in the mouth of Cynthia,

> Princes that would their people should do well
> Must at themselves begin, as at the head;
> For men, by their example, pattern out
> Their imitations, and regard of laws:
> A virtuous court, a world to virtue draws;[4]

but this is simply a statement of the first principle. Cynthia is carrying out the second, hinted at in the final line of the quotation, by punishing the offenders in the court and rewarding Crites, the judge and poet who obviously stands for Jonson himself, for having uncovered them. The play is primarily a

satire on the shallow and vapid frivolity that pretends to be
sophistication among courtiers, and the intention of the satire
is made abundantly plain in the dedication:

To the speciall fovntain of manners: The Court.

Thou are a bountifull, and braue spring: and waterest all the noble
plants of this *Iland*. In thee, the whole Kingdome dresseth it self, and
is ambitious to vse thee as her glasse. Beware, then, thou render mens
figures truly, and teach them no lesse to hate their deformities then
to loue their formes: For, to grace, there should come reuerence: and
no man can call that louely, which is not also venerable. It is not
pould'ring, perfuming, and euery day smelling of the taylor, that con-
uerteth to a beautiful obiect: but a mind, shining through any sute,
which needes no false light either of riches, or honors to help it. Such
shalt thou find some here . . . Now, vnder thy PHOEBUS, it will be
thy prouince to make more.[5]

The intention is, in a general way, worthy enough. It is certainly
true that powder, perfume, and tailors are not the producers of
authentic excellence and that the kingdom would have been in
much better stead if all the courtiers were profoundly concerned
with the acquisition of true virtue; but, after all, the courtiers
did not think that good scent and virtue were synonymous and
they were not all concerned very deeply about the latter. *Cynthia's Revels* asks them to stop and think it over and to identify
themselves at least a little bit with the foolish courtiers of the
play, for their own edification; but it remained optional, and
it is not likely that very many were reformed by contemplating
the moral totalitarianism in which the play is resolved. Something of the righteous frustration of Jonson as would-be poetic
reformer comes through in one of Crites' speeches to Mercury:

All power is iust: Nought that delights is sinne.
And, yet the zeale of euery knowing man,
(Opprest with hills of tyrannie, cast on vertue
By the light phant'sies of fooles, thus transported)
Cannot but vent the *Ætna* of his fires,
T'enflame best bosomes, with much worthier loue

Then these of outward, and effeminate shades:
That, these vaine ioyes, in which their wills consume
Such powers of wit, and soule, and are of force
To raise their beings to aeternitie,
May be conuerted on workes, fitting men.
And, for the practice of a forced looke,
An antique gesture, or a fustian phrase,
Studie the natiue frame of a true heart,
An inward comelinesse of bountie, knowledge,
   And spirit, that may conforme them, actually,
    To *Gods* high figures, which they haue in power.[6]

In the masques, Jonson tries this other side of the coin, and shows the courtiers their shapes conformed to *"Gods* high figures," teaching them the effects and the beauty of that "much worthier loue." The masquers are images no less didactic than the foolish courtiers of *Cynthia's Revels*—or the antimasquers—but the identification is dramatically much more complete, since the masquers actually *are* the courtiers, and more likely to take hold, since the image is a complimentary one.

But there is one other way in which the masque has an advantage over *Cynthia's Revels:* it beards the lion of frivolity in its own den. A masque was a framework for a ball—it was so before Jonson's introduction to the form and he almost certainly would not have been able to change it even if he had desired to —and thus was an occasion *par excellence* for the display of the works of powderers, perfumers, and tailors, and every form of vapid sophistication. Jonson, making a virtue of necessity in an extremely clever way, sets a tone of holy seriousness into the joyful grace of the masque itself and then gives the revels a similar blessing when their time comes, thus drawing them into the serious masque's sphere of influence. The revels become an extension of the masque; the entire audience dances under the aegis of the powers of the masques, extending and preserving the images of order and harmony. This trick of setting the revels in perspective with the rest of the masque can be found in virtually every one of Jonson's masques. It is most overt in *Pleasure Reconciled to Virtue,* in which the masquers are the Virtuous Princes who act out the reconciliation by enjoying the pleasures of the revels with the blessing of Virtue, who has granted them this respite from their toils with her in the hill of knowledge; they are given graceful instruction on how to comport themselves with the ladies in the revels, and afterwards they are returned to their hill with a reminder that they are Virtue's princes and are "to walk w'h Pleasure, not to dwell."[7] Even the very frivolity of the court is given a meaning and a place; it is allowed, even within a didactic scheme, to be fun— indeed, its fun is enhanced by the graceful make-believe which Jonson deliberately exports to the revels from the masque—but the fun is not left alien to the masque's more serious posture: it is tamed and incorporated. A pleasurable recreation is thus made gently and gracefully reminiscent of the lineaments of true virtue. The purposes of *Cynthia's Revels* were perhaps much better served in James's, under Jonson's direction.

But frivolous sophistication was too firmly entrenched; it had its own poses and its own language, and was not going to reassess its position on the basis of what Jonson taught it about the true nature of love, beauty, renown, order, and holy virtue. Sophistication had its own traditions to conserve. Lady Frances Howard, despite *Hymenaei,* had her own ideas about the nature and place of marriage in the scheme of things. Jonson's was not the only indignation; the court paid dearly for its sins before the century was half over.

Not that the Stuart court was so much worse than the Tudor —that would be a rather hard thesis to defend. Jonson would probably have been thwarted just as completely a hundred years earlier, in the first blooming of the English Renaissance when More and Fisher were sent to the block. The failure of Jonson's masques, from his own point of view, was that they were appreciated for the wrong reasons. He was not a neglected poet—on the contrary, he was popular among the courtiers for

whom he was writing and was financially rather successful—
but on his own terms he did not succeed. It was not his fault,
as he would have insisted. His failure is simply a specific example
of the general failure of humanism in the Renaissance. Steering
between Savanarola and Lorenzo, between Calvin and Catherine
de'Medici, between Knox and the Queen of Scots, Renaissance
humanism was essentially a private movement. It was not only
caviare to the general, but often brown bread to the courtier
and froth to the religious reformer. To the extent that humanists
hoped to achieve a universal revolution toward humanism they
were not only wrong but silly. Most of them knew that their
movement was private, and none insists on this more than
Jonson. As Mercury says to his persona, Crites,

> Then let the truth of these things strengthen thee,
> In thy exempt, and only man-like course:
> Like it the more, the less it is respected;
> Though men faile, vertue is by gods protected.[8]

Upon the title page of the 1616 folio stands the motto: *neque
me vt miretur turba laboro: Contentus paucis lectoribus.*

If that were all there was to it, Jonson and humanism succeeded, *paucis lectoribus,* and the rest of the world may be left
to wander in darkness while the few "plac'd high on the top of
all vertue, look'd downe on the Stage of the world, and con-
temned the Play of *Fortune.*"[9] But humanism helped to make
its own periphery vaguely fashionable, and fashionable at the
expense of the real thing. Armed with tags of Latin poetry and
a little secondary scholarship, a courtier could set up shop as a
critic and accuse a more learned mind of pedantry. It was against
this corruption of humanism that Jonson fought. His insistence
that masques ought to be "grounded vpon *antiquitie,* and solide
learnings"[10] led him to an elaborate—and pedantic—documentation of his sources, by which he attempted to vindicate
humanism in the face of its abuse by giving examples of its
proper use in the service of a vision of the good life, a vision

which he believed was the fruit only of study and knowledge.[11]

It is as a humanistic poet that we must finally view Jonson the masque-writer. Humanism at its best has always been an expression of the serious concern of generous intelligence for authentic knowledge, in the service of wisdom and the good life. It is in this spirit that the humanistic poet approaches his poetry, mirroring in it the beauty of the humanistic ideal and making all things good. For him the task of perfection is arduous and urgent; for him the stones and the stars, even the loves and sports and frivolities of the court, join in pointing the way to the holy road of virtue and sing of the splendor of the palaces to which it leads. The masques of Ben Jonson are essentially faithful to this vision. They did not succeed in imparting it. But it may be that if we are to be fair to them, we must say of them, as of the humanists of the Renaissance, that they did not fail: they were failed.

NOTES

Notes to Preface

1. C. V. Wedgwood, *Poetry and Politics Under the Stuarts,* Cambridge (Eng.), 1960, p. 15.

2. After the initial stimulus of the publication of the masques in Herford and Simpson's *Ben Jonson,* Vol. VII, Oxford, 1941, the turning point was perhaps Professor D. J. Gordon's article, "The Imagery of Ben Jonson's *The Masque of Blacknesse* and *The Masque of Beautie," Journal of the Warburg and Courtauld Institutes,* VI (1943), 122–41, followed by his other important articles in the same journal, "*Hymenaei:* Ben Jonson's Masque of Union," VIII (1945), 107–45, and "Poet and Architect: The Intellectual Setting of the Quarrel between Ben Jonson and Inigo Jones," XII (1949), 152–78, and by his study of "Ben Jonson's 'Haddington Masque'" in *Modern Language Review,* XLII (1947), 180–87. Professor Allan H. Gilbert's highly suggestive article "The Function of the Masques in *Cynthia's Revels*" appeared in *Philological Quarterly,* XXII (1943), 211–30, and revealed the serious purposefulness of those masques. Three years later was published the first important general reappraisal of Jonson's masques, Professor Ernest William Talbert's "The Interpretation of Jonson's Courtly Spectacles," *PMLA,* LXI (1946), 454–73. Professor Gilbert's indispensable *The Symbolic Persons in the Masques of Ben Jonson* appeared in 1948. Since that time some of the best contributions in the re-evaluation of Jonson's masques have been Delora Cunningham's general essay, "The Jonsonian Masque as a Literary Form," *ELH,* XXII (1955), 108–24; the detailed explications of several of Jonson's masques in DeWitt T. Starnes and Ernest William Talbert, *Classical Myth and Legend in Renaissance Dictionaries,* Chapel Hill, 1955; incisive remarks on the masques in the brilliant study of the Banqueting House at Whitehall, Per Palme's *Triumph of Peace,* London, 1957; the excellent monograph by W. Todd Furniss, "Ben Jonson's

Masques," published in *Three Studies in the Renaissance,* New Haven, 1958, pp. 89–179; and the fullest study to date, Stephen K. Orgel's *The Jonsonian Masque,* Cambridge (Mass.), 1965.

Notes to Chapter I

1. Preface to the *Masque of Blackness,* in *Ben Jonson,* ed. C. H. Herford, and Percy and Evelyn Simpson, Vol. VII, Oxford, 1941, p. 169. All quotations from Jonson's masques will be from this volume of this edition, by page number.

2. *The Shepheardes Calender,* "January," line 24. It is perhaps a touch of ironic justice that Elizabeth's wardrobe was pillaged to provide sufficiently splendid costumes for the new Queen's first masque in 1604 (reported in a letter from Arabella Stuart to Lord Shrewsbury, December 18, 1603, and quoted in *The Vision of the Twelve Goddesses,* ed. Ernest Law, London, 1880, p. 9).

3. See Albert Feuillerat, *Documents Relating to the Office of the Revels in the Time of Queen Elizabeth,* Louvain, 1908, *passim;* or consult the abstract tables, pp. xiii–xvii.

4. *The Pain of Pleasure,* sig. H3-3v.

5. The Spanish Ambassador, De Silva, wrote on July 10, 1564, about his entertainment at court five days previously: "The comedy ended, and then there was a masque of certain gentlemen who entered dressed in black and white, which the Queen told me were her colours, and after dancing awhile one of them approached and handed the Queen a sonnet in English, praising her. She told me what it said and I expressed my pleasure at it." *Calendar of Letters and State Papers (Spanish) 1558–1567,* London, 1892, p. 368.

6. *George Gascoigne: The Posies,* ed. John W. Cunliffe, Cambridge (Eng.), 1907, pp. 75–86. Benvolio argues at the beginning of *Romeo and Juliet,* I, iv, that Romeo's prepared introduction should be omitted from their masque: "The date is out of such prolixity."

7. For an account of the former, see E. K. Chambers, *The Elizabethan Stage,* Vol. I, Oxford, 1923, p. 159; Throgmorton's letter describing his intentions for the latter is quoted from the Hatfield MSS. in the same volume, p. 168.

8. *Faerie Queene,* III, xii, 26.

9. For an account of Goldingham's masque, see John Nichols, *The Progresses...of Queen Elizabeth,* Vol. II, London, 1788, under the date 1578. This form was by no means entirely novel; it has much in common with the fifteenth-century Eltham mumming found in *The Minor Poems of John Lydgate,* ed. Henry Noble MacCracken (EETS), Part II, London, 1934, pp. 672–74.

10. Published in the Malone Society's *Collections: Part II,* ed. W. W. Greg, Oxford, 1908, pp. 144–48.

11. For more detailed surveys of the history of the masque, see Herbert Arthur Evans, *English Masques,* London, 1897; Rudolf Brotanek, *Die Englishen Maskenspiele,* Leipzig, 1902; Paul Reyher, *Les Masques Anglais,* Paris, 1909; Percy Simpson, "The Masque," *Shakespeare's England,* Vol. II, Oxford, 1916,

pp. 311–33; Chambers, "The Mask," *The Elizabethan Stage*, Vol. I, pp. 149–212; Enid Welsford, *The Court Masque*, Cambridge (Eng.), 1927; Cornelia Emilia Baehrens, *The Origin of the Masque*, Groningen, 1929; and Glynne Wickham, *Early English Stages*, London, 1959, pp. 191–228.

12. There are two versions of this masque, both published in the Malone Society's *Gesta Grayorum*, ed. W. W. Greg, Oxford, 1915 (for 1914). The more authentic of the two, from MS. Harley 541, is printed on pp. xii–xxi; another version, published originally in 1688 with a slightly inferior text but more ample description and commentary, is reprinted on pp. 57–68 of Greg's edition. My quotations of text are from the former, and of parentheticals and commentary from the latter. There was another masque performed during the same set of festivities, with a text that has not survived—a brief contemporary description can be found in Greg's edition on pp. 43–44.

13. It was used at least as early as 1511 for a masque of ladies. See Hall's *The Vnion of the two noble and illustre famelies of Lancastre & Yorke*, under Henry VIII, sig. B3: "a pageaunt deuised lyke a mountayne ... was with vices brought vp towardes the kyng, and out of the same came a ladye, appareiled in cloth of golde, and the children of honour called the Henchemen, whiche were freshly disguysed, and daunced a Morice before the kyng. And that done, re-entred the mountayne, and then it was drawen backe. . . ."

14. This summary makes the entry of the pigmy torchbearers appear rather incongruous, but in the masque itself they are carefully anticipated in the Squire's expository speech and their entry dramatically justified.

15. Feuillerat, *Documents*, p. 270.

16. Greg, *Gesta Grayorum*, p. 57.

17. Samuel Daniel, *The Vision of the 12 Goddesses, presented in a Maske the 8. of Ianuary, at Hampton Court.* London, 1604.

18. *Ibid.*, sig. A7.

19. *Ibid.*, sig. A3v.

20. *Ibid.*, sig. A3v.

21. *Ibid.*, sig. B2-2v.

22. *Ibid.*, sig. B3.

23. The two turns around the hall are not mentioned in the published masque, but reported by Dudley Carleton in a letter to John Chamberlain, dated January 15, 1604 (*State Papers, Domestic, James I*, Vol. VI, no. 21) quoted by Law in his edition of *The Vision*, p. 46.

24. Daniel, *The Vision*, sig. B7-7v.

25. The title of the pirated edition is *The True Discription of a Royall Masque.* Worcester's purchase is recorded in a letter from him to Lord Shrewsbury, quoted in John Nichols, *Progresses . . . of King James the First*, Vol. I, London, 1788, p. 317.

26. Quoted in Law's edition of *The Vision*, p. 46: "The songes and speaches that were there used I send you here inclosed."

27. Daniel, *The Vision*, sig. A7v.

28. *Ibid.*, sig. A4. That Daniel was sensitive to the "misticall interpretations"

when he composed the masque, and not merely when he sprang to its defense, is indicated by Iris' apologetic remarks about the goddesses, in whom antiquity "hath giuen mortall shapes to the gifts & effects of an eternall power, for that those beautiful Caracters of sense were easier to be read then their mysticall *Ideas,* dispersed in that wide, and incomprehensible volume of Nature" (sig. B3). But Daniel was not entirely faithful to this conception of his goddesses and apparently decided that his best defense lay in pretending that he had never taken it seriously.

29. *Ibid.,* sig. A7v, A8v.

30. *Ibid.,* sig. B1.

31. *Tethys Festival,* printed as an appendix to *The Order and Solemnitie of the Creation of the High and mightie Prince Henrie,* London, 1610, sig. E2.

32. *The Essayes,* London, 1625, sig. Ff4 (p. 223).

33. Daniel, *The Vision,* sig. A3v.

34. *Ben Jonson,* Vol. VII, p. 249.

35. *Ibid., Masque of Queens,* p. 282.

36. *The Essayes,* sig. Ff4 (p. 223).

37. *Ben Jonson,* Vol. VII, preface to *Hymenaei* (1606), p. 209.

38. *Ibid.,* pp. 209–10.

39. Daniel, *The Vision,* sig. A8v.

40. *Balet Comique de la Royne, faict au nopces de Monsieur le Duc de Ioyeuse & mademoyselle de Vaudemont, sa soeur,* Paris, 1582.

41. *Ben Jonson,* Vol. VII, preface to *Love's Triumph,* p. 735.

42. *Balet Comique,* sig. A2.

43. *Ibid.,* sig. I2v.

44. *Ibid.,* sig. L1.

45. *Ibid.,* sig. O3.

46. *Ibid.,* sig. a2v.

47. *Ibid.,* sig. a2v.

48. *Ibid.,* sig. a2v.

49. *Ibid.,* sig. a3.

50. *Ibid.,* sig. a3.

51. *Ibid.,* sig. a3-3v.

52. Yates, *The French Academies of the Sixteenth Century,* London, 1947, p. 240.

53. *Balet Comique,* sig. e2v.

54. *Ibid.,* sig. M4.

55. *Ibid.,* sig. G2.

56. *Ibid.,* sig. M3v.

57. *Ibid.,* sig. T2.

58. The best treatment of Gordon is by Dorothy Mackay Quynn, "The Career of John Gordon, Dean of Salisbury 1603–1619," *The Historian* (Autumn, 1943), pp. 3–23. This article amplifies and corrects the *DNB* article on Gordon. Neither noticed his connection with the *Balet Comique.*

59. *Balet Comique,* sig. T3.

60. *Ibid.*, sig. T3v.

61. See, for instance, Mercury's speech on sig. F3: "I taught men to obey the law; the arts and sciences and cities are my doing," and so forth. The commentary explicitly notes that Mercury "was got up just as the poets describe him."

62. *Ben Jonson,* Vol. VII, preface to *Hymenaei,* p. 209.

Notes to Chapter II

1. "We come not now (in a Pageant)," writes Dekker, "to Play a Maiesters prize. For *Nunc ego ventosae Plebis suffragia venor.* The multitude is now to be our Audience, whose heads would miserably runne a wooll-gathering, if we doo but offer to breake them with hard words" (*The Magnificent Entertainment,* London, 1604, sig. A4v). Dekker appears, however, to agree with Jonson on the position of the poet in these devices: "The Soule that should giue life, & a tongue to this *Entertainment,* being to breathe out of Writers Pens" (sig. B2v).

2. *Ben Jonson,* ed. C. H. Herford, and Percy and Evelyn Simpson, Vol. VII, Oxford, 1941, p. 91.

3. *Ibid.,* pp. 84–89.

4. *Ibid.,* p. 91.

5. *Ibid.,* p. 90.

6. *Ibid.,* pp. 90–91.

7. *Ibid.,* p. 106.

8. Samuel Daniel, *The Vision of the 12. Goddesses,* London, 1604, sig. A3v.

9. *A Letter: Whearin, part of the entertainment vntoo the Queenz Maiesty, at Killingwoorth Castl . . . iz signified,* N.P., N.D., sig. E8.

10. William Vaughan, *The Golden-groue,* London, 1600, sig. H2.

11. *The Political Works of James I,* ed. Charles Howard McIlwain, Cambridge (Mass.), 1918, p. 319.

12. *Nicomachean Ethics,* IV, ii.

13. *Ben Jonson,* Vol. VII, preface to *Love's Triumph* (1631), p. 735.

14. *Ibid.,* preface to *Hymenaei,* p. 210; preface to *Masque of Queens,* p. 282.

15. Bernard Weinberg, *A History of Literary Criticism in the Italian Renaissance,* Vol. II, Chicago, 1961, p. 801.

16. *Discoveries,* in *Ben Jonson,* Vol. VIII, p. 636.

17. *Ibid.,* p. 619.

18. *An Apologie for Poetry,* in *Elizabethan Critical Essays,* ed. G. Gregory Smith, Vol. I, Oxford, 1904, p. 158.

19. See Francis Meres, *Palladis Tamia,* London, 1598, sig. A2 ff.

20. *Discoveries,* p. 640.

21. See pages on the poet in *ibid.,* pp. 595, 620, and the corresponding notes in *Ben Jonson,* Vol. XI, pp. 246, 265.

22. *Apologie,* p. 159.

23. *Ibid.,* p. 179.

24. Henry Crosse, *Vertues Common-wealth,* London, 1603, sig. O1-1v.

25. *Discoveries,* pp. 587–88. This passage, incidentally, is also adapted from Quintilian on oratory.

26. *Ibid.*, p. 636.

27. *Ben Jonson*, Vol. VII, pp. 287, 367.

28. *Ibid.*, pp. 209-10, 249, 281.

29. *De gl'Heroici Furori*, ed. Francesco Flora, Turino, 1928, p. 99.

30. William Camden, *Remains Concerning Britain*, London, 1674, pp. 447–48.

31. That such a device was probably common in lost Elizabethan masques is suggested by Jonson's note in the *Masque of Blackness* explaining his reasons for using expressive hieroglyphics rather than *imprese:* he is apparently justifying his variation of a standard practice.

32. *The Fountaine*, sig. A3v.

33. See, for example, the remarks in *Natalis Comitis Mythologiae sive explicationis Libri Decem*, Patavia, 1637, sig. A1–iv; and George Sabinus, *Fabularum Ovidii Interpretatio*, Cambridge (Eng.), 1584, sig. 4–4v.

34. *The Alchemist, Ben Jonson*, Vol. V, pp. 327–28.

35. *The Poems of George Chapman*, ed. Phyllis Brooks Bartlett, New York, 1941, p. 327.

36. Franck L. Schoell, "Les Mythologistes Italiens de la Renaissance et la poésie élisabéthaine," *Revue de Littérature Comparée*, IV (1924), 7, 15. For further details on the rise of Renaissance mythography, see E. H. Gombrich, "Icones Symbolicae," *Journal of the Warburg and Courtauld Institutes*, XI (1948), 163–192; Jean Seznec, *The Survival of the Pagan Gods*, New York, 1953; and the very good introduction in Charles W. Lemmi, *The Classic Deities in Bacon*, Baltimore, 1933. For a treatment of the minor handbooks, see the first two chapters of DeWitt T. Starnes and Ernest William Talbert, *Classical Myth and Legend in Renaissance Dictionaries*, Chapel Hill, 1955.

37. *The Countesse of Pembrokes Emanuel*, London, 1591, sig. B2v.

38. *The Third Part of the Countess of Pembrokes Yuychurch*, London, 1592, sig. B1v–2.

39. *Apollo Christian*, p. 41.

40. See especially Allan H. Gilbert, *The Symbolic Persons in the Masques of Ben Jonson*, Durham, N.C., 1948; and DeWitt T. Starnes and Ernest W. Talbert, *Classical Myth and Legend in Renaissance Dictionaries*, Chapel Hill, 1956, Chapter 6.

41. "Speeches Delivered to Her Majesty . . . at Bissam . . . 1592," in John Nichols, *The Progresses . . . of Queen Elizabeth*, Vol. II, London, 1788, p. 2.

42. *Ben Jonson*, Vol. VII, *Pan's Anniversary*, p. 535; *Natalis Comes Mythologiae Libri Decem*, Book V, Chapter 6. Jonson's *Oberon* obliquely characterizes James as Pan in the same manner: "He doth shine, and quickens euery thing / Like a new nature: so, that true to call / Him, by his title, is to say, Hee's all" (p. 353).

43. First published in Rome in 1593; Jonson used the revised and augmented edition of 1603.

44. *Ben Jonson*, Vol. VII, *Masque of Queens*, p. 283.

45. *Ibid.*, p. 287.

46. "An Expostulation with Inigo Jones," *Ben Jonson*, Vol. VIII, p. 404.

47. Signifying her enmity for Hercules. Jonson's note runs "So was she

figur'd at *Argos*, as a *Step-mother* insulting on the spoyles of her two *Priuigni*, *Bacchus* and *Hercules*" (*Hymenaei*, p. 217).

48. *Le Imagini dei Dei degli Antichi*, Padua, 1603, sig. C7v.

49. *Natalis Comitis Mythologiae Siue Explicationis Fabularum Libri Decem*, Patavii, 1637, sig. M8; on M4 and M5 are pictures of Apollo with the lyre.

50. *The Third Part of the Countess of Pembrokes Yuychurch*, London, 1592, sig. I3v.

51. Ben Jonson, Vol. VII, *Neptune's Triumph*, p. 692; *The Fortunate Isles*, p. 723.

52. *Ibid.*, *Hymenaei*, pp. 217–18.

53. *Ibid.*, p. 192.

54. *Ibid.*, preface to *Masque of Queens*, p. 282. Although he applies it retrospectively to the *Haddington Masque*, Jonson had not used the term "antimasque" before.

55. Cf. *ibid.*, *The Golden Age Restored*, pp. 422–23; *Pleasure Reconciled to Virtue*, pp. 482–85.

56. Presented by the gentlemen of Gray's Inn as part of the festivities for the wedding of Somerset and Lady Frances Howard, and published the same year (1614). It is reprinted in John Nichols' *The Progresses . . . of King James the First*, Vol. II, London, 1788, pp. 735–45.

57. Ben Jonson, Vol. VII, p. 688.

58. See, for instance, the letters about *Pleasure Reconciled to Virtue* (1618), quoted in *Ben Jonson*, Vol. X, pp. 576–77. The consensus of the court seems to have been that the masque was dull and disappointing, needing more antimasques and more scenic changes. Jonson parodies this critical attitude in the *Masque of Augurs* (1621) under the figures of Notch and Vangoose, who complain about the dryness of wit which the King's Poet and his Architect have recently displayed in their masques. But Notch eventually had his way— the growing demand for variety in antimasques and in scenic changes ultimately ruled the masque.

59. *Ben Jonson*, Vol. VII, p. 633.

60. *Ibid.*, p. 638.

61. *Ibid.*, p. 664.

62. *Ibid.*, *Pleasure Reconciled to Virtue*, p. 491.

63. *Ibid.*, *Oberon*, p. 352.

64. *Ibid.*, *Mercury Vindicated*, pp. 414–15.

65. *Ibid.*, *Pan's Anniversary*, p. 534.

Notes to Chapter III

1. Leo Spitzer, *Classical and Christian Ideas of World Harmony*, Baltimore, 1963, p. 8. I am deeply indebted to this excellent study, and refer the reader to it in general for supporting evidence; I have not felt the need to reproduce any more than the barest outline of his findings, since anyone interested can turn to him for completeness.

2. *The Deipnosophists,* XIV, 632, trans. Charles Burton Gulick (Loeb Classical Library), Vol. VI, Cambridge (Mass.), p. 411.

3. *Timaeus,* 47D; *Plato,* ed. and trans. R. G. Bury (Loeb Classical Library), Vol. VII, Cambridge (Mass.), pp. 108–109.

4. Spitzer, *op. cit.,* p. 13. See also Edward A. Lippman, "The Sources and Development of the Ethical View of Music in Ancient Greece," *Musical Quarterly,* XLIX (1963), 188–209.

5. *Laws,* 673A; *Plato,* Vol. IX, pp. 156–57.

6. *Phaedo,* 85E ff.; *Plato,* Vol. I, pp. 296 ff.

7. John Dowland, preface to *Second Book of Ayres,* London, 1600; Robert Burton, *The Anatomy of Melancholy,* Part I, sec. 2, mem. 6, subs. 3.

8. Albert D. Menut, "Castiglione and the Nicomachean Ethics," *PMLA,* LVIII (1943), 309–21.

9. Spitzer, *op. cit.,* pp. 17–19.

10. The Christian liturgy could, and did, turn for precedent to the psalmist as well as to the already ancient tradition of world harmony musically understood. Spitzer (pp. 19 ff.) has a brief but excellent section showing the alignment between grace and music in the thought of the early hymnodists. The two are available to a purely intuitive association, in my opinion, and it is actually not necessary to claim a continuous tradition from, say, Ambrose to William Lawes before one is justified in pointing to the fairly obvious association of music and grace in their privative relationship to the character of Shylock.

11. Gretchen L. Finney, "A World of Instruments," *ELH,* XX (1953), 87. Mrs. Finney has published this article in a revised form, along with other of her excellent studies, in her book *Musical Backgrounds for English Literature: 1580–1650,* New Brunswick, N.J., 1962.

12. James Hutton, "Some English Poems in Praise of Music," *English Miscellany,* II, ed. Mario Praz, 1951, pp. 1–63.

13. *Ben Jonson,* ed. C. H. Herford, and Percy and Evelyn Simpson, Vol. VIII, Oxford, 1941, p. 82.

14. *Merchant of Venice,* V, i; *Troilus and Cressida,* I, iii.

15. Thomas Lodge's reply to Gosson, ca. 1579, sig. B5 (no copy of the title page has survived).

16. *Religio Medici,* II, 9, ed. Jean-Jacques Denonain, Cambridge (Eng.), 1953, pp. 106–107.

17. For an indication of the extent and the extremes to which the musical analogies were carried, in both figurative and literal thinking, see Chapter 2, "Music: A Book of Knowledge," in Finney, *Musical Backgrounds.*

18. *Lodge, op. cit.,* sig. B8, B5.

19. Richard Hooker, *Of the Lawes of Ecclesiasticall Politie,* London, 1611, Book V, Chapter 38 (sig. Dd3v–4).

20. *Religio Medici,* II, 9, p. 107.

21. Baltasar Beaujoyeulx, *Balet Comique de la Royne,* Paris, 1582, sig. Biv.

22. *Ibid.,* sig. L4v.

23. To the Cook's query about the lateness of the show, the Poet replies that "It was not time, / To mixe this Musick with the vulgars chime" (p. 686).

24. Sir Thomas Browne, *Religio Medici,* p. 107.

25. Beaujoyeulx, *Balet Comique,* sig. Bɪv.

26. Browne, *loc. cit.*

27. John Playford, *An Introduction to the Skill of Musick,* London, 1674, sig. A4.

28. Claude LeJeune, *Le Printemps,* ed. M. Henry Expert, Paris, 1901, p. 3.

29. Gretchen L. Finney, " 'Organical Musick' and Ecstasy," *JHI,* VIII (1947), 273.

30. D. P. Walker, "Musical Humanism in the 16th and Early 17th Centuries," *The Music Review,* II (1941), 12. Dr. Walker has probably published more sound and carefully documented studies of Renaissance musical humanism than anyone else, and this article is to be particularly recommended to anyone interested in the subject.

31. "Musical Harmony . . . is a most powerful imaginer of all things, which whilst it follows opportunely the Celestial bodies, doth wonderfully allure the Celestial influence, and doth change the affections, intentions, gestures, motions, actions, and dispositions of all the hearers, and doth quietly allure them to its own properties, as to gladness, lamentation, to boldness, or rest, and the like." *Three Books of Occult Philosophy, written by Henry Cornelius Agrippa,* trans. J. F., London, 1651, p. 255.

32. *Ibid.,* p. 257. For a further discussion of the theory and practice surrounding Ficino's musical ideas, see D. P. Walker, *Spiritual and Demonic Magic from Ficino to Campanella,* London, 1958, Chapter 1, and his "Le Chant Orphique de Marcile Ficin," *Musique et Poésie au XVIᵉ Siècle* (Paris, 1954), 17–28.

33. *Balet Comique,* sig. e3v.

34. *Ben Jonson,* Vol. VII, p. 185.

35. *Politics,* VIII, vii, ed. H. Rackham (Loeb Classical Library), Cambridge (Mass.), 1950, pp. 666 ff. Aristotle apologizes briefly for the obscurity of "katharsis": "the term purgation we use for the present without explanation, but we will return to discuss the meaning that we give to it more explicitly in our treatise on poetry" (p. 671). For a discussion of the comparison of this passage with the *Poetics* among the Italian musical humanists, and the resulting impetus toward humanistic music, see Marvin Orville Thompson, "Uses of Music and Reflections of Current Theories of the Psychology of Music in the Plays of Shakespeare, Jonson, and Beaumont and Fletcher," unpublished Ph.D. thesis, University of Minnesota, 1956, pp. 117 ff.

36. Preface to *Le Nuove Musiche* (1602), in *Le Origine del Melodramma,* ed. Angelo Solerti, Torino, 1903, p. 56. The translation was made under consultation with that in Oliver Strunk, *Source Readings in Music History,* New York, 1950, p. 378.

37. Walker, "Musical Humanism," *op. cit.,* p. 306. Monody was not a negation of harmony to the Greeks; see Edward A. Lippman, "Hellenic Conceptions of Harmony," *Journal of the American Musicological Society,* XVI (1963), 3–35.

38. For a linking of the English "Ayres" with the Caccini experiments described in the next quotation, see Bruce Pattison, "Literature and Music," *The*

English Renaissance, ed. V. de Sola Pinto, London, 1938, pp. 132–34; and C. Hubert H. Parry, *The Music of the Seventeenth Century* (The Oxford History of Music, Vol. III), 2nd ed., London, 1938, pp. 193–94. Parry singles out Ferrabosco as being the most declamatory (and thus, closest to the Italians) of those he discusses. For the "Ayre" in general, see Peter Warlock, *The English Ayre,* London, 1926, and Bruce Pattison, *Music and Poetry of the English Renaissance,* pp. 113–40, esp. 128 ff.

39. Solerti, ed., *Le Origine del Melodramma,* p. 145; cf. Strunk, *Source Readings,* p. 364.

40. *Le Origine,* p. 50; cf. Strunk, *op. cit.,* p. 371.

41. Walker, "Musical Humanism," *op. cit.,* p. 291.

42. *L'Euridice,* Florence, 1600, sig. A2; also in Solerti, ed., *Le Origine,* p. 40; cf. Strunk, pp. 367–68.

43. *L'Euridice,* sig. A2v *(Le Origine,* pp. 40–41). For Bardi's reminiscence, see his letter to Doni, *Le Origine,* p. 146.

44. *Le Origine,* pp. 45–46; cf. Strunk, *op. cit.,* p. 374.

45. D. P. Walker, "The Aims of Baïf's *Académie de Poésie et de Musique,*" *Journal of Renaissance and Baroque Music,* I (1946), 92. See also Frances A. Yates, *The French Academies of the Sixteenth Century,* London, 1947, pp. 19–76.

46. Walker, "Musical Humanism," *op. cit.,* pp. 3, 9.

47. Yates, *The French Academies,* p. 49. Cf. Raymond Lebeque, "Ronsard et la Musique," *Musique et Poésie au XVIe Siècle* (Paris, 1954), 105–14.

48. Walker, "The Aims of Baïf's *Académie,*" *op. cit.,* p. 91.

49. D. P. Walker and Francois Lesure, "Claude Le Jeune and *Musique Mesurée,*" *Musica Disciplina,* III (1949), 167.

50. *Le Printemps,* ed. Expert, Paris, 1901, p. 3.

51. *Philostrate,* Paris, 1611, Vol. I, p. 282; quoted in Frances A. Yates, "Poésie et Musique dans les 'Magnificences' au Mariage du Duc de Joyeuse," *Musique et Poésie au XVIe Siècle* (Paris, 1954), 243.

52. Walker, "The Aims of Baïf's *Académie,*" *op. cit.,* p. 97.

53. Yates, *The French Academies,* p. 237.

54. *Balet Comique,* sig. e3v.

55. *Ibid.,* sig. e1v. The poem quoted is by Auguste Costé.

56. Edward J. Dent, *Foundations of English Opera,* Cambridge (Eng.), 1928, pp. 16–17.

57. See Bruce Pattison, *Music and Poetry of the English Renaissance,* London, 1948, pp. 62–65, 128–36.

58. Walker, "The Aims of Baïf's *Académie,*" *op. cit.,* p. 91.

59. C. Hubert H. Parry, *The Music of the Seventeenth Century,* Oxford, p. 196.

60. *Dictionary of National Biography,* s.v. "Alphonso Ferrabosco."

61. W. Barclay Squire, in *DNB,* s.v. "John Coperario."

62. Jonson remarks in *Lovers Made Men* that "the whole Maske was sung (after the Italian manner) *Stylo recitativo,* by Master *Nicholas Lanier;* who ordered and made both the Scene, and the Musicke" (p. 454). This note, how-

ever, was not printed in the quarto of 1617 but only in the folio of 1640, and it has recently been cogently argued that Lanier's music (which has not survived) was in the style of the declamatory ayre rather than real *stile recitativo*, and that Jonson called it *recitativo* only in mistaken (or dishonest) retrospect after the authenitc sort had really been introduced at some later time. (McD. Emslie, "Nicholas Lanier's Innovations in English Song," *Music and Letters*, XLI [1960], 111–26.)

63. Pattison, *Music and Poetry*, pp. 136–37.

64. Little can be inferred from Jonson's silences, but I think it is at least safe to say that he did not share the illusion of some of the Italian and French writers that he was reviving the ancient form of drama. But it is impossible to believe that he would not have noticed some of the resemblances between what he was doing in the masques and what the ancients had done in the achievement of their famously effective dramatic forms: the poet who disclaimed classical authenticity in *Cataline* with a remark about the difficulty of handling a chorus would certainly have realized that the masques brought him closer to ancient drama in this regard.

65. *Ben Jonson*, Vol. VIII, p. 82.

66. John Playford, *An Introduction to the Skill of Musick* (1674), sig. E4. Playford here quotes, without acknowledgement, Caccini's preface to *Le Nuove Musiche* (1602).

Notes to Chapter IV

1. Athenaeus, *The Deipnosophists*, XIV, 628, trans. Charles Burton Gulick (Loeb Classical Library), Vol. VI, Cambridge (Mass.), p. 389.

2. The Greek respect for the dance was not shared by the Romans, whose attitude seems in general to have been closer to Cicero's "Nemo enim fere saltat sobrius, nisi forte insanit, neque in solitudine neque in convivio moderato atque honesto." *(Pro Murena*, VI, 13). It was therefore to the Greeks that the Renaissance writers turned for support of the dance.

3. *Des ballets anciens et modernes selon les regles du théatre*, Paris, 1682, pp. 35–36. The reference to Plato is an allusion to *Laws*, 657. Cf. Peter Martyr's tract on the dance, published in English in the late sixteenth century under the title, *A brief Treatise, concerning the vse and abuse of Dauncing*.

4. *Lodovici Caelii Rhodigini Lectionum Antiquarum Libri XXX*, Lyons, 1560, sig. v6v (Book V, Chapter 3). The ultimate source of this passage, which will be quoted further on, is Lucian, *Peri Orcheseos*.

5. "Convivialium" (or "Symposium"), IX, 15.

6. *Des ballets*, p. 36. Cf. Macrobius, *In Somno Scipionis*, II, 3: "per stropham rectus orbis stelliferi motus, per antistropham diuersus vagarum regressus praedicaretur. Ex quibus duobus motibus primus in natura hymnus dicandus deo sumpsit exordium."

7. *Lodovici Caelii Rhodigini*, sig. v4. Cf. Jonson's note in *Masque of Augurs:* "Saltationes in rebus sacris adhibebantur apud omnes paene gentes" (p. 641).

8. *Des ballets*, p. 26.

9. Euripides, *The Bacchae,* trans. William Arrowsmith; *The Complete Greek Tragedies,* Vol. IV, Chicago, 1960, p. 546.

10. *Des ballets,* pp. 28–29. See Basil, *Epist. I ad Greg.* Sacred dancing was a rarity in the Christian era (but see E. Louis Backman, *Religious Dances,* London, 1952; and G. R. S. Mead, "The Sacred Dance of Jesus," *The Quest* (October, 1910), pp. 45–67); with a few exceptions, the weight of ecclesiastical opinion was suspicious of dancing altogether, and frequent pronouncements against dancing were made by Councils (for examples see Fritz Aeppli, *Die Wichtigsten Ausdrücke für das Tanzen in den Romanischen Sprachen,* Halle, 1925, pp. 44–45). The tradition of disapproval was continued in the Renaissance by the religious reformers: see H. P. Clive, "The Calvinists and the Question of Dancing in the 16th Century," *Bibliothèque d'Humanisme et Renaissance,* XXIII (1961), 296–323. Elizabeth's masque of the wise and foolish virgins in 1561 might be considered a kind of sacred dancing—it was so taken by Noverre's anonymous translator two centuries later *(The Works of Monsieur Noverre,* Vol. I, London, 1783, pp. xvi–xvii). But even beyond such dubious interpretations, there remain a few bits of evidence for religious dances in the Renaissance, one of particular interest being a strange set of verses reported by Jeffrey Mark from an old MS. describing the "Old Measures" of the Inner Temple in the early seventeenth century: "Holy Sister, please you to dance / With a Holy Brother for recreation. / Not as the wicked do—nor as / Hemini and Gemini in the wilderness. / But leading on to virtue and back from vice retireing / Not on this side, nor on that side, / Nor profanely turning round, / But as the Spirit mooves us" *(Music and Letters* 3 [1922], p. 369). Nicholas Caussin's oblique remark in *The Christian Diurnal* (1632) about "those, who would spiritualize dauncing" (p. 349) might refer to such a practice as this.

11. Pindar, 1st Pythian Ode. The *Ion* derives the dance from the inspiration of the muses.

12. *The Apocryphal New Testament,* trans. Montague Rhodes James, Oxford, 1953, p. 253.

13. *Enneads,* VI, ix, 8. Dante extends the same metaphor in the dance of the blessed in *Paridiso,* VII, 1–9; XII, 1–27; XXIV, 10–18.

14. "The Dance" *(Peri Orcheseos),* VII; in *Lucian,* ed. A. M. Harmon (Loeb Classical Library), Vol. V, Cambridge (Mass.), p. 221. Renaissance writers do not appear to have entertained the modern suspicion that this dialogue is ironic. An ironic reading would not at any rate disqualify Lucian's dialogue as a source of Greek ideas about the dance: sympathetically nor not, it attests to their presence. The dance-form with which Lucian primarily deals was pantomimic, but Renaissance writers applied his statements nonetheless to their quite different dance forms. Some do not appear to have realized the difference; others apparently felt that it was unimportant, and that the modern unpantomimic dance could be as expressive as the ancient forms in most of the ways Lucian describes.

15. Trans. Cyril W. Beaumont, London, 1925, pp. 162–63.

16. *Witts New Dyall,* London, 1604, sig. K1.

17. The bracketed numbers indicate the stanzas; all quotations from *Orchestra* are taken from the facsimile edition of *The Poems of Sir John Davies*, ed. Clare Howard, New York, 1941.

18. Jonson was clearly familiar with Davies' *Orchestra*, and quoted it twice in his conversations with Drummond (*Ben Jonson*, ed. C. H. Herford and Percy Simpson, Vol. I, Oxford, 1925, pp. 143, 147).

19. *Works*, Vol. VII, 1941, p. 189: "This *Throne* . . . had a circular motion of it [sic] owne, imitating that which wee call *Motum mundi*, from the *East* to the *West* . . . The steps, whereon the *Cupids* sate, had a motion contrary, with *Analogy, ad motum Planetarum*, from the *West* to the *East*."

20. *Ibid.*, p. 191. Jonson's marginal gloss reads: "As, in the creation, he is said, by the *ancients*, to haue done" (cf. Lucian and Davies).

21. *Ibid.*, p. 385.

22. *Ibid.*, p. 415.

23. *Ibid.*, p. 470.

24. *Ibid.*, pp. 217–18.

25. *Ibid.*, pp. 257–58.

26. *Ibid.*, p. 486.

27. *Ibid.*, pp. 522–24.

28. *Ibid.*, p. 213.

29. *Idem.*

30. *Ibid.*, p. 384.

31. *Ibid.*, p. 426.

32. *Ibid.*, p. 385.

33. *Ibid.*, p. 736.

34. *Ibid.*, pp. 739–40.

35. Davies, *Orchestra*, stanza 56.

36. *Des Ballets*, pp. 33, 31.

37. *Timaeus*, 47e; and especially, *Laws*, 653e ff.

38. John Locke, *Some Thoughts Concerning Education*, London, 1693, p. 67. Mulcaster's *Positions* (1581) is still somewhat defensive about asserting the dignity and worth of dancing; but by 1607, John Cleland can recommend it with breezy confidence and a sweeping catalogue of its pedigrees (ΗΡΩ-ΠΑΙΔΕΙΑ, *or the Institution of a Young Noble Man*, sig. Ff 1).

39. *Lodovici Caelii Rhodigini*, sig. v5v.

40. *Des ballets*, p. 38.

41. *Ibid.*, pp. 37–38.

42. *Ibid.*, p. 41.

43. *Ibid.*, p. 26.

44. Lucian, *op cit.*, pp. 218–19.

45. *Ibid.*, p. 215.

46. *Ibid.*, pp. 239, 277.

47. *The Boke Named The Gouernour*, ed. Henry Herbert Stephen Croft, Vol. I, London, 1880, pp. 204–205, 232.

48. See Frances A. Yates, *The French Academies of the Sixteenth Century*,

London, 1947, pp. 60-62; D. P. Walker, "The Aims of Baïf's *Académie de Poésie et de Musique*," *Journal of Renaissance and Baroque Music*, I (1946), 91–100.

49. *Il Ballerino di M. Fabritio Caroso da Sermoneta, Diuiso in due Trattati*, Venice, 1581, sig. A4v–B1.

50. *Ibid.*, sig. B2v. Cf. Vincenzio Mucci's poem to Caroso as "Novello Orfeo," sig. B3.

51. The dances included in *Il Ballarino* are in honor of particular Italian noblewomen. Caroso's change of title is therefore a movement from the dances themselves to their significance—which may in itself suggest a greater confidence in the dignity and metaphorically expressive powers of the dance.

52. *Nobiltà di Dame*, Venice, 1600, sig. A1v. Cf. sig. H4–4v, where Caroso insists that perfection is achieved "con vera Regola, e con perfetta Theorica, & non per prattica."

53. *Ibid.*, sig. Ff4.

54. *Ibid.*, sig. Ss2v.

55. *Ibid.*, sig. S2.

56. *Ibid.*, sig. Hh2.

57. *Ibid.*, sig. H3.

58. *Balet Comique de la royne, faict au nopces de Monsieur le Duc de Ioyeuse & mademoyselle de Vaudemont, sa soeur*, Paris, 1582. Ben Jonson's copy of this work is now in the New York Public Library.

59. Yates, *The French Academies*, p. 268.

60. *Balet Comique*, sig. e3v.

61. By Billard; *ibid.*, sig. e1.

62. By Costé; *ibid.*, sig. e1v.

63. By Volusian; *ibid.*, sig. e2v–3.

64. *Ibid.*, sig. e3v.

65. *Ibid.*, sig. O3v–O4.

66. The quotations are from *Masque of Beauty, Ben Jonson*, ed. C. H. Herford and Percy and Evelyn Simpson, Vol. VII, Oxford, 1941, p. 191. Jonson never describes his dances quite as directly as does Samuel Daniel in *The Vision of the 12. Goddesses*, London, 1604, where the dance is defined as "consisting of diuers strains, fram'd vnto motions circular, square, triangular, with other proportions exceeding rare and full of variety" (sig. A8). But with the exception of letter-dances, the disposition of figures in the dances of Jonson's masques is usually described in terms of geometrical figures: Order, who leads the dances in *Hymenaei*, wears a garment "painted full of *Arithmeticall*, and *Geometricall* Figures" and holds "a *Geometricall Staffe*" (*Ben Jonson*, Vol. VII, p. 219). It is probably to geometrical figures that Jonson refers in the song-instruction to the dancers in *Mercury Vindicated*: "Moue, moue againe in formes as heretofore. / 'Tis forme allures" (*Ibid.*, p. 416).

67. Paul Lacroix, *Ballets et mascarades de cour*, Geneva, 1868, I, pp. 237–69.

68. *Ibid.*, p. 244.

69. *Ibid.*, p. 256.

70. E.g., in *Hymenaei* (1606) and the *Masque of Queens* (1610), *Ben Jonson*,

Vol. VII. The letter-dance had been uesd in earlier French ballets; examples
from 1585 and 1603 can be found cited in Roy C. Strong, "Festivals for the
Garter Embassy at the Court of Henri III," *Journal of the Warburg and
Courtauld Institutes*, XXII (1959), pp. 68–69.

71. Lacroix, *Ballets*, I, pp. 264–65.

72. *Ibid.*, pp. 265–68.

73. *Ibid.*, pp. xxiii–xxiiii.

74. The druids enjoyed a rather high reputation as philosophers and masters
of the secrets of nature; they "instructed youth, disputed of the immortalitie
of the soule, of the mouings of the firmament, of the greatnesse of ye world,
and of the nature of things, and so lead the estate of their life in vertuous occupations and works, not letting one minute of the time to slip without bearing
some profite to the common weale" (*Theatrum Mundi, The Theatre or rule of
the world . . . by Peter Boaystuau, and translated into English by Iohn Alday*,
London, n.d., sig. I3). The druidic alphabet would have been understood to
possess the same kind of contemplative efficacy as the hieroglyphics, for which
see Liselotte Dieckmann, "Renaissance Hieroglyphics," *Comparative Literature*,
IX (1957), 308–21, and E. H. Gombrich, "Icones Symbolicae," *Journal of the
Warburg and Courtauld Institutes*, XI (1948), 163–92. Proponents of the validity of the esoteric tradition, of which there were not few in the Renaissance,
as these articles demonstrate, would support the validity of such a contemplative exercise as the consideration of the moral expressiveness of the druidic
symbol portrayed in dance. The same goes, of course, for any hypothetical
hieroglyphics which Jonsonian dances might have employed; I make no claims.

75. Robert Laneham, *A Letter*, sig. B1-1v.

76. Elyot, *op. cit.*, p. 218.

77. *Ibid.*, pp. 229–31.

78. *Il Ballarino*, sig. A4v.

79. *Ibid.*, sig. A2v. Cf. Cesare Negri, *Nuove Inventioni di Balli*, Milan, 1904,
sig. A1v. For an earlier expression of the same notions, see Guglielmo Ebreo's
tract on the dance, published in 1873 from a fifteenth-century MS., under the
title *Tratto Dell'Arte del Ballo*, pp. 6–7.

80. Elyot, *op. cit.*, pp. 235–36.

81. *Ibid.*, p. 238.

82. *Idem.*, p. 238.

83. Caroso, *Trattato Secondo del Ballarino*, Venice, 1581, sig. g2–3v, oo2v–3,
hh2v–3, aa4v–Bbl, e1–e2v, ff2v–3v, r1–2.

84. *Ben Jonson*, Vol. VII, p. 736.

85. Elyot, *op. cit.*, p. 239.

86. London, 1651, sig. A2v.

87. Elyot, *op. cit.*, p. 240–41.

88. Davies, *Orchestra*, ed. cit., stanzas 125 and 122.

89. Richard Mulcaster, *Positions*, London, 1581, sig. Klv.

90. Elyot, *op. cit.*, p. 285.

91. *Ben Jonson*, Vol. IV, pp. 158–59.

92. *Ibid.*, Vol. VII, p. 353.

93. *Ibid.*, p. 489.

94. *Ibid.*, *Love Freed*, p. 370; *Mercury Vindicated*, p. 416; *Pleasure Reconciled to Virtue*, p. 489.

95. *Ibid.*, p. 384.

96. *Ibid.*, p. 224. The dances with which Shakespeare concludes *Much Ado About Nothing* and *As You Like It* exemplify the same visual metaphor.

97. *Ben Jonson*, Vol. VII, p. 213.

98. *Ibid.*, p. 740.

99. It is certain that the guests were provided with souvenir copies in some of Jonson's masques; Herford and Simpson (*Ben Jonson*, Vol. X, p. 567) thus explain the bibliographical peculiarities of *Lovers Made Men*, *Neptune's Triumph*, *The Fortunate Isles*, and the *Masque of Augurs*—to which list should probably be added the *Haddington Masque*. The provision of copies of entertainments and speeches was fairly common in Elizabeth's day, and seems to have been not unusual in Jacobean masques as well. Ford (*Lover's Melancholy*, III, iii) and Shirley (*The Constant Maid*, IV, iii) both dramatize masques the programs for which are provided in advance. And it will be recalled that the action of Jonson's *Neptune's Triumph* begins with "The POET entring on the STAGE, to disperse the Argument" (*Ben Jonson*, Vol. VII, p. 682). The provision of an argument or libretto of some sort was, as I have pointed out, the practice in French entertainments as well. It has an obvious relevance to this study, since programs would make all the poetic intricacies of Jonson's masques easier to follow, including the role of the dance.

100. *Ben Jonson*, Vol. VII, pp. 641–44.

101. *Ibid.*, p. 488.

102. *Ibid.*, *Pleasure Reconciled to Virtue*, p. 489.

Notes to Chapter V

1. *Ben Jonson*, ed. C. H. Herford, and Percy and Evelyn Simpson, Vol. VII, Oxford, 1941, *Love Freed*, p. 369.

2. *Ibid.*, *Love's Triumph*, p. 740.

3. *Ibid.*, *Hymenaei*, p. 214.

4. *Ibid.*, *Prince Henry's Barriers*, p. 324.

5. *Ibid.*, *Masque of Queens*, p. 288; *News from the New World*, p. 524.

6. *Ibid.*, *Hymenaei*, p. 226.

7. *Ibid.*, *Pleasure Reconciled to Virtue*, p. 491.

8. *Ibid.*, *Hymenaei*, pp. 217–18.

9. *Ibid.*, p. 172.

10. *Ibid.*, p. 173.

11. *Ibid.*, pp. 174–75.

12. *Ibid.*, p. 177.

13. *Ibid.*, pp. 177, 180.

14. *Ibid.*, p. 173.

15. *The Courtiers Academie*, London, n.d., sig. E2v.

16. *Ben Jonson*, Vol. VII, *Masque of Blackness*, p. 177.

17. *Ibid.*, p. 251.

18. *Ibid.*, p. 254.

19. *Ibid.*, p. 255.

20. *Ibid.*, p. 255.

21. *Ibid.*, pp. 257–59.

22. *Ibid.*, p. 261.

23. *Ibid.*, p. 257.

24. This allegorical reading, for which Jonson left ample clues, is treated at length in Professor D. J. Gordon's fine article "Ben Jonson's 'Haddington Masque'"; *MLR*, XLII (1947), pp. 180–87.

25. *Ben Jonson*, Vol. VII, p. 233.

26. *Ibid.*, p. 240.

27. *Ibid.*, pp. 288 ff.

28. *Ibid.*, pp. 324–25, 335.

29. *Ibid.*, p. 368.

30. Patrick Scot, *The Tillage of Light*, London, 1623, sig. B2–2v.

31. Forsett, *A Comparative Discourse of the Bodies Natural and Politique*, London, 1606, sig. E4v–F1. For the historical background of Forsett's distinction, see the brilliant study by Ernest H. Kantorowicz, *The King's Two Bodies*, Princeton, 1957.

32. *Ben Jonson*, Vol. VII, p. 214.

33. *Ibid.*, p. 176.

34. The quotation is from the *Haddington Masque, ibid.*, p. 251.

35. It is so described at her entrance, see *ibid.*, p. 250.

36. Marginal note in *ibid.*, p. 325.

37. *Ibid.*, pp. 239–40.

38. *Ibid.*, p. 241.

39. That is, in addition to the torchbearers, who probably accompanied the masquers in all of Jonson's masques. Jonson's descriptions unfortunately do not provide enough information about the torchbearers to permit the identification of allusions to them in the text. When the information is adequate—e.g., in the descriptions of the *Masque of Beauty*—Jonson's exploitation of their light can be demonstrated, but the cases are too few. He probably made independent use of the torchbearers only on infrequent occasions, and the rest of the time treated their torches as functions of the two other features which I am here about to describe.

40. *Ben Jonson*, Vol. VII, p. 288.

41. *Ibid.*, p. 323.

42. *Ibid.*, p. 369.

43. *Ibid.*, p. 429.

44. *Ibid., Mercury Vindicated*, p. 415.

45. *Ibid., Masque of Beauty*, p. 182.

46. *Ibid.*, p. 737.

47. *Ibid.*, p. 382.

48. *Ibid.*, p. 354.

49. *Ibid.*, p. 522.

50. *Ibid.*, p. 425. A scene of this sort was used in the masque of the Duke of Lennox on New Year's Night, 1604. Dudley Carleton's description runs ". . . and thereupon a travers was drawne and the maskers seene sitting in a vaulty place with theyr torchbearers and other lights which was no unpleasing spectacle" (Letter to John Chamberlain, *Cal. State Papers James I,* Vol. VI, no. 21; quoted here from Ernest Law, ed. *The Vision of the Twelve Goddesses,* London, 1880, p. 34).

51. *Calendar of State Papers: Venetian,* Vol. XI, p. 86.

52. *Ben Jonson,* Vol. VII, p. 171.

53. *Ibid.*, p. 189.

54. *Ibid.*, p. 257.

55. *Ibid.*, p. 302.

56. *Ibid.*, p. 346.

57. *Ibid.*, p. 415.

58. The decrees of the Council of Trent clearly played a part: see Émile Mâle, *L'Art Religieux,* Paris, 1951.

59. *Ben Jonson,* Vol. VII, p. 425.

60. *Ibid.*, p. 185.

61. *Ibid.*, p. 190.

62. *Ibid.*, p. 217.

63. *Ibid.*, p. 302.

64. *Ibid.*, p. 665.

65. *Ibid.*, p. 693.

66. *Ibid.*, pp. 383–84.

67. *Ibid.*, p. 534.

68. *Ibid.*, p. 522.

69. E.g., *The Golden Age Restored* in *ibid.*, p. 428; *Lovers Made Men,* p. 458.

70. E.g., *Love Restored* in *ibid.*, p. 385; *Time Vindicated,* p. 670.

71. E.g., *Masque of Beauty* in *ibid.*, p. 185; *Fortunate Isles,* p. 728.

72. *Ibid., Lovers Made Men,* p. 458.

73. *Ben Jonson,* Vol. VIII, p. 597.

74. *Ibid., Discoveries,* p. 607.

Notes to Chapter VI

1. Thus Nicholas Caussin, summarizing the doctrine of "The Platonists" in *The Holy Court: Fourth Tome,* n.p., 1638, sig. A4–4v.

2. The quotation is from the title page of *The Courtyer,* 1561.

3. Most of the Renaissance Neoplatonic love-theory derives primarily from Ficino and Leone—for a discussion of the whole movement from Petrarch through the *trattati,* see Nesca A. Robb, *Neoplatonism of the Italian Renaissance,* London, 1935; and, for a more specialized treatment of two main streams of Italian love-theory, John Charles Nelson, *Renaissance Theory of Love,* New York, 1958. To my knowledge, there was no native English treatise on love. Anyone who was not satisfied with what he could learn from general discussion could turn to *The Courtyer* (which went through at least nine editions in

England before 1604) or to the *Fowre Hymes*, or to the Italian treatises, or to
a few other translations (e.g., Geoffrey Fenton's *Monophylo*, 1572; Annibale
Romei's *The Courtiers Academie* [1598]; Thomas Buoni's *Problems of Beautie*,
1606). None of these latter books goes nearly as far in systematizing Neoplatonic
love as some of the Italian treatises do, but any one of them would be sufficient
to generate Neoplatonizing attitudes in a receptive courtier, and the characteristics of the movement in England suggest that such general attitudes were
enough to satisfy the fashion. Differences between the apparent doctrine of two
writers is much less significant in England than in Italy; the English tended
to overlook the finer systematic distinctions.

4. Leone Ebreo, *The Philosophy of Love* [*Dialoghi d'Amore*], trans. Fried-
berg-Seeley and Barnes, London, 1939, pp. 307 ff.; *Marsilio Ficino's Commentary on Plato's Symposium*, ed. and trans. Sears Reynolds Jayne, Columbia,
Missouri, 1944, pp. 140 ff.; and Pico della Mirandola's commentary on Beni-
vieni, trans. Thomas Stanley in 1651 and ed. Edmund G. Gardner as *Pico: A
Platonick Discourse upon Love*, London, 1914, pp. 17 ff. Further references to
these and to other Renaissance love theorists are merely intended to locate
ideas among the Neoplatonists generally, not to imply direct borrowings from
the books cited.

5. *Ben Jonson*, ed. C. H. Herford, and Percy and Evelyn Simpson, Vol. VII,
Oxford, 1941, p. 190.

6. Leone, *The Philosophy of Love*, pp. 389 ff.; Ficino, *Commentary*, pp.
125–26; Pico, *Platonick Discourse*, p. 27.

7. *Ben Jonson*, Vol. VII, p. 191.

8. *Ibid., Masque of Beauty*, p. 193.

9. *Ibid.*, p. 240.

10. *Ibid., Masque of Queens*, p. 280: "I haue . . . calld to mind that doctrine
of some great Inquisitors in *Nature*, who hold euery royall and *Heroique*-forme
to pertake, and draw much to it of the heauenly vertue. For, whether it be y^t a
diuine soule, being to come into a body, first chooseth a Palace fit for it selfe;
or, being come, doth make it so; or that *Nature* be ambitious to haue her worke
aequall; I know not. . . ."

11. "An Hymne in Honour of Beautie," line 139.

12. *The Courtyer*, 1561, sig. Tt4v.

13. *Ben Jonson*, Vol. VII, p. 370.

14. Ficino, *Commentary*, p. 130. Cf. Castiglione, *The Courtyer*, sig. Zz2v,
and Romei, *Courtiers Academie*, sig. F3.

15. *The Courtyer*, sig. Vv2.

16. Du Plessis Mornay, *The True knowledge of a mans owne selfe*, London,
1602, sig. A5v–6; the same story appears in Buoni, *Problems of Beautie* (1606),
sig. E3–3v, and Thomas Floyd, *The Picture of a perfit Common wealth* (1600),
sig. F8v–9.

17. *The True knowledge*, sig. A6.

18. Sir Thomas Elyot, *Of the knowledg whiche maketh a wise man*, London,
1533, sig. B8.

19. *Ben Jonson*, Vol. VII, p. 737.

20. *Ibid.*, p. 192.
21. *Ibid.*, p. 192.
22. Ficino, *Commentary*, p. 165.
23. *Ben Jonson*, Vol. VIII, p. 74.
24. *Ben Jonson*, Vol. VII, *Masque of Beauty*, p. 185.
25. *Ibid.*, p. 249.
26. *Ibid.*, p. 192.
27. *Ibid.*, p. 737.
28. *Ibid.*, p. 736.
29. *Ibid.*, p. 453.
30. *Ibid.*, p. 455.
31. *Ibid.*, p. 458.
32. *Ibid.*, p. 458.
33. *Ibid.*, p. 459.
34. *Ibid.*, p. 460.
35. *Ibid.*, p. 250.
36. *Ibid.*, p. 250.
37. *Ibid.*, p. 253.
38. *Ibid.*, p. 255.
39. *Ibid.*, p. 259.
40. *Ibid.*, p. 257.
41. *Ibid.*, p. 258.
42. *Ibid.*, p. 257.
43. *Ibid.*, p. 258.
44. *Ibid.*, p. 260.
45. *Ibid.*, p. 261.
46. *Ibid.*, p. 382.
47. Cf. Natalis Comes' treatment of the myths of Cupid, *Mythologia*, IV, 14.
48. *Ben Jonson*, Vol. VII, p. 384.
49. *Ibid.*, p. 384.
50. *Ibid.*, p. 382.
51. *Ben Jonson*, Vol. VIII, p. 594.
52. *Ben Jonson*, Vol. VII, p. 362.
53. *Ibid.*, p. 367.
54. *Ibid.*, p. 367.
55. *Ibid.*, *Love's Triumph*, p. 737.
56. *Ibid.*, p. 368.
57. A well-documented survey of this traditional *topos* can be found in the excellent Yale Ph.D. dissertation by W. Todd Furniss, "Ben Jonson's Masques and Entertainments," published in abbreviated form in *Three Studies in the Renaissance*, New Haven, 1958, pp. 89–179.
58. "*Hymenaei:* Ben Jonson's Masque of Union," *Journal of the Warburg and Courtauld Institutes*, VIII (1945), pp. 107–45.
59. *Ben Jonson*, Vol. VII, see Jonson's note, p. 210.
60. *Ibid*, p. 217.
61. *Ibid.*, p. 212.
62. *Ibid.*, p. 213.

63. *Ibid.*, p. 221.
64. *Ibid.*, p. 213.
65. *Ibid.*, pp. 224–25.
66. *Ibid.*, p. 236.

Notes to Chapter VII

1. *Gesta Grayorum,* ed., W. W. Greg, Oxford, 1915, p. 36.

2. In John Nichols, *The Progresses . . . of Queen Elizabeth,* Vol. II, London, 1788, under the date 1588, p. 52.

3. Joannes Rosinus, *Antiquitates Romanae,* Amsterdam, 1685, pp. 756–57: "Eum, qui *triumphi* honorem sibi a Senatu ob res gestas decretum spreverat, & repudiaverat, fuisse exilio mulctatum. Causa huius decreti fuit, quod indicarunt insolentiam, quae gradus publicorum honorum superbe contemneret, apectare ad virtutis perniciem, dum scilicet, quae multos ad studium eius accendere solent, ita projicerentur." Jonson used the edition of 1583.

4. *Giovanni Pico della Mirandola: His Life,* trans. More, ed. J. M. Rigg, London, 1890, p. 63.

5. *Introduction,* London, n.d., sig. N6v.

6. Morisine's preface to *Introduction to Wisedome,* sig. A4.

7. *Ibid.,* sig. A5v, B4.

8. *The true order,* sig. C2ff.

9. *Civitas Veri sive Morum,* Paris, 1609, sig. G2v–3, H1v. Dante puts Alexander in Hell, but that is exceptional not only for the Middle Ages in general but for Dante himself, who eulogizes Alexander in both the *Convivio* and the *De Monarchia.*

10. *A philosophical discourse, Entituled, The Anatomie of the minde,* London, 1576, sig. A2v.

11. Thomas Fenne, *Fennes Frutes,* London, 1590, sig. B2. The Renaissance response to Alexander was by no means universally negative; but, interestingly, his encomia frequently avoid his martial prowess and commend him for chastity or for temperance.

12. *Ben Jonson,* ed. C. H. Herford, and Percy and Evelyn Simpson, Vol. VII, Oxford, 1941, p. 169.

13. *Ibid.,* p. 759.

14. *Ibid.,* p. 282.

15. *Ibid.,* p. 282.

16. *Ibid., Pleasure Reconciled to Virtue,* p. 491.

17. *Ibid.,* pp. 288–89.

18. *Ibid.,* pp. 301–302.

19. *Ibid.,* p. 304.

20. *Ibid.,* p. 305.

21. *Delectable demaundes and pleasaunt Questions, with their seuerall Aunswers,* London, 1566, sig. Aa2.

22. "Of the true Greatnesse of Kingdomes and Estates," *The Essayes,* London, 1625, sig. Aa4v-Bb1.

23. *Ben Jonson,* Vol. VII, *Masque of Queens,* p. 315.

24. *Ibid.*, p. 316.

25. The *Masque of Queens* specifically alludes to this in having the figure of Heroic Virtue tell the King that Fame cannot increase his renown "Not, though her loudest Trumpet blaze yor peace" (see *ibid.*, p. 304).

26. See Jonson's introduction to the *Masque of Blackness* in *ibid.*, p. 169. There were Elizabethan precedents for masques of both Moors and Amazons.

27. *Ibid.*, pp. 302–303.

28. *Ibid.*, p. 313.

29. *Ibid.*, p. 177.

30. *Ibid.*, p. 185.

31. *Ibid.*, p. 256.

32. *Ibid.*, p. 326.

33. *Ibid.*, pp. 639 ff.

34. *Ibid.*, pp. 759–60.

35. The quotation is from Jonson's preface to the MS copy of the *Masque of Queens*, see *ibid.*, and is addressed to Prince Henry.

36. *Ibid.*, p. 425.

37. *Ibid.*, p. 209.

38. *Ibid.*, p. 367. Cf. the allegorical procession of witches in the *Masque of Queens*, designed to show that "the opposition to all *vertue* begins out of *Ignorance*" (p. 287).

39. *Ibid.*, p. 281.

40. *Politeuphuia*, sig. H4v.

41. *Discoveries*, in *Ben Jonson*, Vol. VIII, p. 595.

42. See *The Education of a Christian Prince*, trans. Lester K. Born, New York, 1936, p. 199: Erasmus warns the Prince to judge himself when he is praised, and "if he is not yet such an one as his praises proclaim him, let him take that as advice and give his attention to making his acts correspond to his praises."

43. *The Essayes*, 1625, sig. Rr1-1v.

44. "An Epistle to Master John Selden," from *The Underwood*, in *Ben Jonson*, Vol. VIII, p. 159. Professor Allan H. Gilbert shows another of Jonson's uses of this tradition in his excellent article "The Function of the Masques in *Cynthia's Revels*," *PQ* 22 (1943), pp. 211–30.

45. *Ben Jonson*, Vol. VII, *Masque of Queens*, pp. 312–13.

46. *Resolves*, London, 1628, sig. V5.

47. Introduction to *The ciuile Conuersation of M. Stephen Guazzo*, London, 1586, sig. A6v.

48. *Ben Jonson*, Vol. VII, *Masque of Queens*, p. 304.

49. *Ibid.*, *Love's Triumph*, p. 735.

Notes to Chapter VIII

1. *CERTAYNE Sermons, or homilies, appoynted by the kynges Maiestie, to bee declared and redde, by all persones, Vicars, or Curates, euery Sondaye in their churches, where thei haue cure.* Anno. 1547, sig. K1-K1v. The quotation from the 1623 edition is from the title page. The latter edition differs from the

former, in the above quotation, only in spelling and an occasional unimportant word.

2. William Barley, *A new Booke of Tabliture,* London, 1596, sig. C1v.

3. *The Philosophy of Love,* London, 1939, p. 207.

4. *A Comparative Discourse,* London, 1606, sig. #3v.

5. *The True Knowledge of a mans owne selfe,* London, 1602, sig. B6v.

6. *Resolves,* sig. K5.

7. *The Political Works of James I,* ed. Charles Howard McIlwain, Cambridge (Mass.), 1918, p. 307.

8. *Ibid.,* p. 308.

9. James to the Star Chamber, 1616, in *ibid.,* p. 333.

10. *Ben Jonson,* ed. C. H. Herford, and Percy and Evelyn Simpson, Vol. VII, Oxford, 1941, p. 429.

11. Anthonie Fletcher, *Certaine Very Proper, and Most Profitable Similes,* London, 1595, sig. B1v.

12. *Ben Jonson,* Vol. VII, p. 535.

13. *Ibid.,* p. 534.

14. *Ibid., Masque of Beauty,* p. 193.

15. *Ibid.,* p. 193.

16. *Ibid.,* p. 735.

17. *Ibid., Pan's Anniversary,* pp. 353–54.

18. *Palladis Tamia,* London, 1598, sig. Ff6v.

19. Fletcher, *Certaine Very Proper . . . ,* sig. B3.

20. Nicholas Caussin, *The Holy Court,* Paris, 1626, sig. *3–4.

21. *Ben Jonson,* Vol. VII, *Masque of Queens,* p. 304.

22. *Ibid., Masque of Gypsies,* p. 614.

23. *Ibid.,* p. 643.

24. *Ibid., News From the New World,* pp. 523–24.

Notes to Chapter IX

1. *Ben Jonson,* ed. C. H. Herford, and Percy and Evelyn Simpson, Vol. VII, Oxford, 1941, p. 190.

2. D. J. Gordon, "Poet and Architect: The Intellectual Setting of the Quarrel between Ben Jonson and Inigo Jones," *Journal of the Warburg and Courtauld Institutes,* XII (1949), 152–78.

3. *Discoveries,* in *Ben Jonson,* Vol. VIII, p. 595.

4. See *Ben Jonson,* Vol. IV, p. 180. Also, a striking statement of this principle can be found in Nicholas Caussin's *The Holy Court* (1626) in an address to the nobility: "Blame none but your selues, if you make not a new world, that you banish not vice from the earth, and make a golden age return agayne. God hath placed you vpon the highest steps of greatnesse, and causeth you, first of all to see the storme, and calme. God hath planted you with his hand, as starres in this goodly firmament of honour; vpon your influences depend all the course of this inferior world. If they be good, they bring health, sollace, and life into the whole world" (sig. M3v).

5. *Ben Jonson*, Vol. IV, p. 33.

6. *Ibid.*, pp. 157–58.

7. *Ben Jonson*, Vol. VII, p. 491.

8. *Ben Jonson*, Vol. IV, p. 158.

9. *Discoveries*, in *ibid.*, Vol. VIII, p. 597.

10. *Ibid.*, Vol. VII, p. 209.

11. It is true that some of Jonson's own scholarship was misleadingly culled—without credit—from secondary sources (see especially Ernest W. Talbert, "Current Scholarly Works and the 'Erudition' of Jonson's *Masque of Augurs*," *SP*, XLIV (1947), 605–24). But Jonson's learning is nevertheless beyond question, and his occasional use of unacknowledged short-cuts is hardly dishonest or necessarily inconsistent with his general ideas about humanism and poetry.

INDEX